Coming Home to Earth

Coming Home to Earth

Mark Brocker

CASCADE *Books* · Eugene, Oregon

COMING HOME TO EARTH

Cascade Books
An Imprint of Wipf and Stock Publishers
199 W. 8th Ave., Suite 3
Eugene, OR 97401

www.wipfandstock.com

PAPERBACK ISBN: 978-1-4982-2173-3
HARDCOVER ISBN: 978-1-4982-2175-7
EBOOK ISBN: 978-1-4982-2174-0

Cataloging-in-Publication data:

Names: Brocker, Mark S., author.

Title: Coming home to earth / Mark Brocker.

Description: Eugene, OR : Cascade Books, 2016 | Includes bibliographical references and index(es).

Identifiers: ISBN 978-1-4982-2173-3 (paperback) | 978-1-4982-2175-7 (harcover) | 978-1-4982-2174-0 (ebook)

Subjects: LCSH: Human ecology—Religious aspects—Christianity | Environmentalism—Religious aspects—Christianity | Ecology—Religious aspects—Christianity | Kingdom of God.

Classification: BT695.5 .B66 2016 (print) | BT695.5 (ebook)

Manufactured in the U.S.A.   SEPTEMBER 9, 2016

Contents

1

Introduction

Getting to Heaven Anxiety

As a young teenager in rural Wisconsin I lay awake one night worrying whether I believed in Jesus enough to get to heaven. It was unusual for me not to fall asleep right away. During the day I tended to be preoccupied with school and sports. But at least on this one night, concern for my personal salvation kept me awake longer than usual.

My Norwegian Lutheran forbears were not strong proponents of rapture theology. I do not remember hearing talk about being "left behind." Nonetheless, we tended to be afflicted with "getting to heaven anxiety," a milder version of "left behind" thinking, reflecting an excessive focus on individual salvation and a loss of concern for the well-being of Earth. We had prematurely written off our Earth home.

My forbears have not been alone in being afflicted with this milder "left behind" thinking. Wendell Berry observes that for many in the church "the life of the spirit is reduced to a dull preoccupation with getting to Heaven."[1] This dull preoccupation can lead to contempt for the body, and contempt for the body manifests itself "in contempt for other bodies—the bodies of slaves, laborers, women, animals, plants, the earth itself. Relationships with all other creatures become competitive and exploitive rather than collaborative and convivial. The world is seen and dealt with, not as an ecological community, but as a stock exchange, the ethics of which are based on the

1. *The Unsettling of America*, 108.

tragically misnamed 'law of the jungle.'"[2] In "A Theology for Earth" Joseph Sittler stresses that "the earth is not merely a negative illustration of the desirability of heaven."[3] Sittler refers to God as an "undeviating materialist." Why would God not be a materialist? After all, God created material.[4]

Too often Christians have talked as if Earth is a place we are passing through on our way to a better place.[5] It is common to hear at funerals and memorial services that at least the one who has died is now in a better place. People who are passing through Earth are less likely to be motivated to care for it. Given the serious ecological challenges we face, Wangari Maathai, winner of the 2004 Nobel Peace Prize and founder of the Green Belt Movement, expresses her hope "that every preacher, imam, rabbi, guru, sensei, and priest would balance making sure we gain some surety over what happens after we die with an equal insistence on the preservation of the earth and our particular accountability for the survival of the planet's ecosystems." Maathai insists that we are not just "passing through."[6]

My primary intention in *Coming Home to Earth* is not to cast stones at my Norwegian Lutheran heritage or my Christian tradition for its loss of love for Earth. I deeply appreciate the focus on faith in Jesus that my forbears bequeathed to me. But a faith that leaves Earth behind is misguided. I intend to show that faith in Jesus can open us up to a more holistic concept of salvation and to a deeper concern for the well-being of Earth. People of faith have an ecological responsibility to bequeath a healthy planet to our children and grandchildren. As Rachel Carson so eloquently states in the foreword to *Under the Sea Wind*, "to stand at the edge of the sea, to sense the ebb and the flow of the tides, to feel the breath of a mist moving over a great salt marsh, to watch the flight of shore birds that have swept up and down the surf lines of the continents for untold thousands of years, to see the running of the old eels and the young shad to the sea, is to have

2. Ibid., 105.

3. "A Theology for Earth," in *Evocations of Grace*, 30.

4. Ibid., 29.

5. In *A Sand County Almanac*, Aldo Leopold compares relegating happiness to heaven to relegating grizzlies to Alaska. The problem in both cases is that "one may never get there" (199). He was critical of the assumption, prevalent in his time, that since there were plenty of grizzlies in Canada and Alaska they did not need to be protected in other states.

6. *Replenishing the Earth,* 147. The Green Belt Movement has planted more than fifty million trees in Maathai's native land of Kenya and inspired tree planting all over the world. She died in 2011.

knowledge of things that are as nearly eternal as any earthly life can be."[7] What a blessing to pass such eternal knowledge on to our children and grandchildren!

The Seeds of Love for Earth

Reflecting on my early teen years, I realize that since that time I have been on a journey to come home to Earth. The truth is that the tradition that afflicted me with getting-to-heaven anxiety and an excessive focus on individual salvation is the same tradition in which the seeds of appreciation and concern for creation were first sown in me. My dad was one of the leaders in the Norwegian Lutheran tradition who helped begin sowing the seeds of love for Earth in me. He was ordained in the American Lutheran Church in 1962, the same year Rachel Carson published *Silent Spring*. He became the director of Luther Park Bible Camp in Chetek, Wisconsin, in 1965. Early in his ministry he became a proponent of what he calls creation theology, and he incorporated stewardship of creation themes and practices into summer Bible camp programs.[8] As a boy, I loved to hang around camp, and camp counselors were some of my first heroes. I especially enjoyed camping with the big kids (high school youth) at Outpost, a 320-acre farm near Birchwood, Wisconsin, that had been donated to Luther Park. Surely I was influenced by my father's emphasis on stewardship of creation, and I developed an affection for spending time outdoors.[9] Nonetheless, despite

---

7. Carson, *Under the Sea Wind*, 3.

8. After I delivered the Fifth Annual Knutson Lecture at Pacific Lutheran University in the fall of 2010 on the theme "No Salvation Apart from the Earth," my dad dug out his notes for a workshop on creation theology he had led in the early 1970s. That would have been about the time I lay awake worrying about getting to heaven. I was pleasantly surprised to discover the insightful content a Bible camp director had included in the early 1970s in a presentation on our relationship to creation. See outline of his notes for this workshop in the Appendix.

9. In *Last Child in the Woods* Richard Louv laments the startling shift in our relationship to the natural world even in summer camp settings that, one would assume, are devoted to nature. Louv observes, "Not that long ago, summer camp was a place where you camped, hiked in the woods, learned about plants and animals, or told firelight stories about ghosts or mountain lions. As likely as not today, 'summer camp' is a weight-loss camp, or a computer camp. For a new generation, nature is more abstraction than reality. Increasingly, nature is something to watch, to consume, to wear—to ignore" (2). Louv is a strong advocate of a camp revival, one based not on "nostalgia for s'mores and campfires" but on the "restorative power of nature" (231).

this influence, when it came to matters of salvation, I remained subject to the prevailing mindset in my faith tradition with its focus on believing in Jesus to get to heaven.

For the Love of Oregon

In October 1970, shortly after my night of getting-to-heaven anxiety, my family moved to Portland, Oregon. My dad had been called to serve half-time as Director of Lutheran Outdoor Ministries of Oregon and half-time as Pastor of Mt. Carmel Lutheran Church in Southwest Portland. Camp Colton, the main Bible camp, was about forty miles away, so I did not hang around camp as much as I had in Wisconsin. But living in a family engaged in outdoor ministry continued to influence my relationship to Earth and all its creatures.

When we moved, I had just begun eighth grade. I do not remember ecology being a major emphasis at my new school, Capitol Hill in Southwest Portland, or at Jackson High School in subsequent years; but it was not ignored either. I will never forget my eighth-grade fruit fly experiment. Each of us was provided with a female and male fruit fly in a glass jar. The first thing we did in class each day was examine our glass jar and report any changes. It was exciting to arrive one morning and see that the fruit fly population had multiplied. Initially it was easy to count how many new fruit flies had been born. But as time went on, it became impossible to count them all. I recall one day being amazed by the number of fruit flies—the jar was teeming with them. When I arrived the next day, they were all dead. They had died in their own waste. It was an early lesson for me in the consequences of ecological degradation. Our science teacher had taught us a simple lesson in what can happen when we ignore life's limits.

The most decisive influence in raising my ecological awareness during my teenage years in Oregon was Republican Governor Tom McCall. He was in the middle of his tenure as governor—he served from 1967 to 1975—when we moved to Oregon. McCall was known around the country and even the world for his leadership on environmental issues. In the fall of 1973, as a junior in high school, I attended the annual Oregon Youth Legislature event at the state capitol in Salem. It was a tradition for the governor to visit a session of the Youth Legislature. When Governor McCall and our Youth Governor walked into the House chamber, I could feel the electricity in the room. It is hard to imagine a governor having such an impact on a group of high school students today. In *Fire at Eden's Gate* Brent Walth refers to Governor McCall's efforts to protect the environment as the "Oregon Story." Governor McCall and the Oregon Story inspired in many young Oregonians, including me, a lifelong concern for environmental issues.

In Governor McCall's inaugural address in January 1967 he stressed the importance of the environment to the well-being of the state: "Health, economic strength, recreation—in fact, the entire outlook and image of the state—are tied inseparably to environment. Water, air, land and scenic pollution threaten these and other values in Oregon—a state pictured in Oregon's first inaugural address in [1859] as 'one of the most attractive portions of the North American continent' . . . The overriding challenge—the umbrella issue—of the campaign and the decade is quality—quality of life in Oregon."[10]

As governor, McCall went right to work cleaning up the Willamette River. Cleanup had already begun, but McCall was determined to accelerate the process. As a news reporter at KGW-TV in Portland, McCall had produced a documentary in 1962 entitled *Pollution in Paradise* that exposed the polluted condition of the Willamette River. The Willamette never caught fire as the Cuyahoga River in Ohio did on June 22, 1969, but the environmental degradation of such a prominent river as the Willamette was an embarrassment for McCall and Oregon. In March 1967, two months into office, he appeared before the State Senate Air and Water Quality Committee and called on the legislature to work with him in drawing a line against pollution. McCall insisted that Oregon must enforce "an 11th commandment: Thou shall not pollute."[11] After the chair of the Oregon State Sanitary Authority died in April, McCall took the unprecedented step of appointing himself as chair. In effect, he became the leader of the Willamette River cleanup.

McCall's next major environmental initiative focused on preserving and securing public access to the beach on the Oregon coast. Like many Oregonians, I enjoy retreating to the Oregon coast, one of my favorite places to visit. A walk along the beach with the mighty waves of the Pacific Ocean rolling in has a way of putting life in perspective. It is a calming and humbling experience, reminding me of who I am in relationship to the Creator and the universe. Oregonians take for granted public access to the coastal beaches. But public access to Oregon's beaches was not permanently

10. McCall, "Inaugural Message, 1967."
11. Walth, *Fire at Eden's Gate*, 182.

secured by law until the passage of the Beach Bill in 1967. Almost from the beginning of statehood, Oregon had a tradition of publicly owned beaches along the coast. In 1913 Governor Oswald West led the charge to put that tradition into law by drafting "a simple short bill declaring the seashore from the Washington line to the California line a public highway."[12] This bill was a stroke of genius. The public and the legislature supported it. In 1947 legislators changed the designation of the Oregon beach from "highway" to "recreation area." But a loophole remained in West's original bill—public ownership applied only to the wet sands. In 1966 William Hay, an owner of the Surfsand Motel in Cannon Beach, built a fence in the dry sands so that motel guests would have more privacy. At high tide this fence blocked people from walking along the beach. The Oregon Highway Department, with McCall's full support, proposed the Beach Bill to fix this problem, to close the loophole in West's bill, and to ensure that the public would have full access to the wet and dry sands of the coastal beaches. When McCall's fellow Republican legislators sought to block the Beach Bill, McCall took the case to the press and the public. In short order, the Beach Bill sailed through the Oregon House and Senate. As Walth notes, "The Beach Bill has stood for decades as a landmark of conservation and typified the McCall doctrine: Preservation over development, aesthetics over commercialism."[13]

Oregon developed a reputation during the McCall years as an innovator in addressing environmental issues. A key step in establishing that reputation was the passage of the Bottle Bill in 1971, which outlawed non-returnables and placed a five-cent deposit on all soft drink and beer bottles and cans. The true father of the Bottle Bill was Richard Chambers, by trade a logging equipment salesman. He shunned publicity, fame, and money; but he was zealous in his effort to clean up litter along Oregon trails, beaches, and roadsides. He viewed the Bottle Bill as crucial to this effort. The Bottle Bill was introduced in the 1969 legislative session but was not approved until the 1971 session, after McCall threw his support behind it. Beverage and container companies fought hard against the Bottle Bill, but they were no match for McCall, Chambers, and other passionate supporters of this creative piece of legislation. In January 1970 McCall had expressed his commitment to a Salem civic club "to put a price on the head of every beer and pop can and bottle in the United States."[14] The passage of the Bottle Bill

12. Ibid., 186.
13. Ibid., 191.
14. Ibid., 317.

was critical in changing the attitude and behavior of Oregonians toward the environment. As an eighth-grade boy, having just moved to Oregon, I was initially most interested in the spending money I could earn from returning a pop can or bottle for a refund. I learned quickly to be on the lookout for cans and bottles to return. Over time I became more aware of the beneficial environmental impact of the Bottle Bill. For many people today, five cents is not an adequate incentive for returning bottles and cans. But Oregonians tend to be passionate about recycling—and Oregon's trails, beaches, and roadsides are relatively free of litter.

Shortly before McCall's second term as governor began, in an interview with CBS News reporter Terry Drinkwater, McCall uttered what became the unofficial slogan for the state of Oregon: "Come visit us again and again. This is a state of excitement. But for heaven's sake, don't come here to live." The short form was, "Visit, but don't stay." This statement reflected McCall's intention to project an image of Oregon as a state in which livability was a top priority. Overpopulation was a threat to the qualities that made Oregon a special place to live. We Oregonians joined in McCall's unofficial campaign to limit Oregon's population with a number of humorous sayings poking fun at how much it rains in Oregon. I can still recite two of my favorites: "In Oregon we don't tan, we rust"; and "We don't pedal our bikes in Oregon, we paddle them." At the time I conveniently chose to overlook that my family and I had recently come to Oregon to live.

In the summer of 1972, at the age of fifteen, I was hired to pump gasoline at an Exxon station in Southwest Portland. Gasoline shortages hit in the winter of 1973–74. From October 1973 to March 1974 OPEC placed an embargo on oil to the United States. This embargo along with oil companies holding back reserves led to severe shortages. Major oil companies used the occasion to squeeze out independent gas stations. Because Oregon had a large number of independent gas dealers, the shortages were particularly acute. Many stations in Oregon began closing on weekends due to low supply. The station I worked at was able to stay open at least for several hours on Saturdays and Sundays. I remember working by myself one Sunday afternoon from one to five. For four solid hours I was pumping gas at every pump. To prevent panic buying and long lines, McCall instituted the "odd-even" gasoline rationing plan. Cars with odd-numbered license plates were allowed to purchase gasoline on odd-numbered days, and cars with even-numbered license plates on even-numbered days. Lines soon vanished and panic buying ceased. Shortly thereafter a number of other states followed Oregon's example.

In 1973 Oregon also faced an electricity shortage due to low water levels behind the great dams of the Columbia River Basin. For years McCall had been warning about American overconsumption of energy. Rather than join the chorus of political leaders demanding more energy sources, McCall stressed the need for Americans to learn how to conserve. Faced with the electricity shortage of 1973, McCall asked Oregonians to reduce their driving speed to fifty-five miles per hour, to turn down the thermostats in their homes, and to stagger work schedules. Later that year he issued an energy emergency for the state, imposing sixteen conservation measures on state government, which included banning air conditioners and exterior lighting on state buildings, turning off water heaters, closing state buildings by 6:00 p.m., and ordering state vehicles to be driven at fifty-five miles per hour or less and with no fewer than two people in them.[15] He hoped businesses and other government entities in the state would follow suit. Not long after, he issued an executive order banning commercial lighting after hours.

Cleaning up the Willamette River, the Beach Bill, the Bottle Bill, "Visit, but don't stay," the odd-even rationing plan, and energy conservation measures were significant contributions to Oregon's environmental legacy. But McCall's signature environmental initiative was statewide land-use planning. In his view the root of most environmental degradation was poor planning for growth, and the best way to control growth was to protect the land.[16] Walth summarizes McCall's land-use doctrine in these terms: "Growth only for growth's sake was foolhardy and irresponsible; development had its place, but under strict control and guidance."[17] This level of intentional land-use planning was unprecedented in the United States. McCall insisted that he was not advocating a "no growth" policy but a "wise growth" policy.[18] He had little time for developers who were not on board with this wise growth policy. He ridiculed developers who sold land in central and eastern Oregon that lacked basic services to unsuspecting buyers, referring to these developers as "sagebrush saboteurs."[19] In the 1969 state legislative session Senate Bill 10 passed, requiring local governments to

15. Ibd., 378.
16. Ibid., 242.
17. Ibid., 243.
18. Ibid., 246.
19. Ibid., 244.

draw up zoning plans within two years. In those two years the population of Oregon grew at a rate of nearly 5 percent, but few local governments completed their zoning plans, let alone enforced them.

As the 1973 legislative session approached, the final session during McCall's tenure as governor, he realized that decisive action was needed to establish and enforce effective land-use planning. In a forceful speech to the 1973 legislature he warned,

> But there is a shameless threat to our environment and to the whole quality of life—unfettered despoiling of the land. Sagebrush subdivisions, coastal "condomania," and the ravenous rampage of suburbia in the Willamette Valley all threaten to mock Oregon's status as the environmental model for the Nation.
>
> We are dismayed that we have not stopped mis-use of the land, our most valuable finite natural resource.
>
> Umbrage at blatant disrespect for sound planning is not taken only at Salem. Less than a month ago the Jefferson County commissioners appealed to me for a moratorium on subdivision because the speculators had outrun local capacity for rational control.
>
> We are in dire need of a state land-use policy, new subdivision laws, and new standards for planning and zoning by cities and counties. The interests of Oregon for today and in the future must be protected from grasping wastrels of the land. We must respect another truism: That unlimited and unregulated growth leads inexorably to a lowered quality of life.[20]

The Oregon Legislature responded by passing Senate Bill 100, which established statewide, coordinated land-use planning and created the Land Conservation and Development Commission and the Department of Land Conservation and Development. Authority was given to each county to develop a comprehensive land-use plan.[21] As Walth explains, "Statewide land-use planning became the cornerstone of Oregon's environmental work."[22]

The "grasping wastrels of the land" immediately went to work to overturn statewide land-use planning. McCall labored almost until the day he died to thwart their efforts. His final battle was to stop passage of Ballot Measure 6, which would have repealed Senate Bill 100, in November 1982.

20. McCall, "Legislative Message, 1973."

21. Oregon Department of Land Conservation and Development, "40th Anniversary of Senate Bill 100."

22. Walth, *Fire at Eden's Gate*, 361.

Suffering from terminal cancer, McCall made several public appearances in the campaign that were crucial to turning public opinion against Measure 6. In September a poll taken by opponents of Measure 6 had given it a twenty-six-point lead.[23] Two months later it went down to defeat. McCall died in January 1983. In the fall of 1975 I left Oregon to attend college and then seminary. I did not return to live in Oregon until I was called to serve as the pastor of Trinity Lutheran Church in McMinnville in 1992. While I was away from Oregon, I remained somewhat aware of my home state's politics. But until I read Walth's biography of Tom McCall when it first was published, I had no idea how hard McCall had to fight to preserve Oregon's land-use planning laws.

Ironically, while I was serving at Trinity, Oregon land-use planning law blocked our efforts to purchase ten acres of land on the west side of McMinnville. We had outgrown our church facility, which was located on less than two acres. A family had offered to sell us ten acres on the west side of Hill Road for $200,000—a real bargain. Hill Road was the urban growth boundary on the west side of McMinnville. This ten acres, therefore, was just outside the urban growth boundary. We went before the city council and argued that Oregon's land-use plan supports east and west growth rather than north and south growth in the Willamette Valley. The plan for McMinnville was to encourage growth to the west into the foothills of the Coast Mountains. Our ten-acre plot was right in the path of the plan for growth. The council was sympathetic but would not budge. It would be at least eight to ten years before the urban growth boundary would be extended. I left Trinity in 2000. Not long after that Trinity ended up yoking with the United Methodist Church to form McMinnville Cooperative Ministries and sharing a facility in downtown McMinnville. A beautiful fellowship hall has been added that serves a variety of needs for the congregations and the community. Even though we were disappointed by the decision of the city council, one could argue that the urban growth boundary did its job.

I am grateful for the impact Tom McCall and the "Oregon Story" had on me during my high school years. McCall's deep love of Oregon is a prototype of the deep love of Earth we need to recover. Yet this impact did not keep me from an act of ecological degradation just after high school graduation that haunts me to this day. To celebrate graduation three classmates and I went on a backpack fishing trip. We hiked seven miles up the Eagle Creek Trail and made a base camp. Eagle Creek is a beautiful mountain

23. Ibid., 460.

stream with glorious waterfalls. For several days we fished for trout and went on short day hikes. We had great success catching trout. We followed all the fishing rules. But we could only eat so many fish, and we were not prepared to preserve them and carry them out. A lot of fish went to waste. The only consolation was that other animals probably ate what we left behind. A few years later I returned to Eagle Creek and fished the same stretch with far less success. As one who inherited the McCall legacy and came of age during the decisive years of the Oregon environmental story, I am ashamed that I contributed to the decimation of the trout population in that beautiful stream. The McCall years may have instilled in me a love of Oregon and a budding concern for the environment, but it was obvious I still had a long way to go in awakening to what it meant to care for Earth and all its inhabitants in a responsible way.

A Theological Breakthrough

I entered college still burdened with a concept of salvation that focused on believing in Jesus to get to heaven. During my college years I had a key breakthrough in my thinking on matters of salvation and our relationship to Earth. David Knutson introduced me to the life and writings of Dietrich Bonhoeffer in his "Modern Thought and Christian Consciousness" course at Pacific Lutheran University in the fall semester of 1978. In our study of Bonhoeffer's *Letters and Papers from Prison* Knutson emphasized a passage on the Christian hope for the resurrection. According to Bonhoeffer, redemption myths focus "on redemption from cares, distress, fears, and longings, from sin and death, in a better world beyond the grave." The Christian hope of the resurrection, however, sends us back to "life on earth in a wholly new way." Christians, unlike those devoted to redemption myths, have "no last line of escape available from earthly tasks and difficulties into the eternal." Like Christ himself Christians "must drink the earthly cup to the dregs," and only in doing so is the crucified and risen Lord with them, and they with the crucified and risen Lord. "This world," insists Bonhoeffer, "must not be prematurely written off."[24]

As early as a 1932 essay titled "Thy Kingdom Come! The Prayer of the Church-Community for God's Kingdom on Earth" Bonhoeffer had written, "Whoever evades the Earth finds not God but only another world, his own better, lovelier, more peaceful world. He finds a world beyond, to be sure,

24. Bonhoeffer, *Letters and Papers from Prison* (first Touchstone edition), 336–37.

but never God's world, which is dawning in this world." Then he emphasizes, "He who loves God, loves God as Lord of the Earth as it is; he who
loves the Earth, loves it as God's Earth. He who loves God's kingdom loves
it entirely as *God's* kingdom, and he loves it wholly as *God's kingdom on
Earth.*"[25] In a letter from prison to Eberhard Bethge on the Second Sunday
in Advent in 1943 Bonhoeffer insists that "only when one loves life and the
earth so much that with[out] it everything seems to be lost and at its end
may one believe in the resurrection of the dead and a new world."[26]

Bonhoeffer's insight into the Christian hope of the resurrection was
manna from heaven for a Norwegian Lutheran college student originally
from rural Wisconsin. Getting-to-heaven anxiety was a sign that we had
prematurely written off this world. If anyone had reason to write the world
off and seek a last line of escape from earthly tasks and difficulties, it would
have been a Lutheran pastor in a Nazi prison in 1944 awaiting his probable
execution. Yet Bonhoeffer affirmed a Christian hope in the resurrection
that sends us back into life on Earth in a wholly new way.

Bonhoeffer did not conceive of this new way of life in ecological
terms. In Nazi Germany he was preoccupied with how followers of Jesus
and the church as a whole are to respond to a tyrannical state. But clearly
this Christian hope in the resurrection expressed by Bonhoeffer does not
allow any notion of salvation apart from Earth. I did not emerge from this
course with a well-developed ecological theology or ethics, but the theological breakthrough triggered by Bonhoeffer's understanding of the resurrection set me on a path toward discovering a new way of life with a holistic
concept of salvation—salvation that embraces humankind and cultivates a
love of the whole Earth community.

A little over thirty years after David Knutson introduced me to Bonhoeffer's life and writings, I was invited to deliver the Fifth Annual David
and Marilyn Knutson Lecture at Pacific Lutheran University in the fall of
2010. My theme was "No Salvation Apart from the Earth." In this lecture I
made the case that an excessive focus on individual salvation in the Christian tradition has contributed in a significant way to a loss of concern for
the well-being of Earth and to the devastating ecological consequences we
are experiencing. Love of God and love of neighbor have been core values
in our Judeo-Christian tradition. Given the urgency of the ecological crisis,

25. Bonhoeffer, *Berlin: 1932–33* (DBWE 12), 288.
26. Bonhoeffer, *Letters and Papers from Prison* (DBWE 8), 213.

I proposed that we may need to consider love of creation as a third core value.

In 2013 I received a Louisville Institute Pastoral Study Project Grant to explore the theme "No Salvation Apart from the Earth" in more depth and to develop the Knutson lecture into a book. Pursuing this study project intensified my convictions that there is no salvation apart from Earth and that care of Earth is a core part of our identity and mission as followers of Jesus. In the course of this project a new title emerged: *Coming Home to Earth*. The core question guiding my study project was this: What will motivate us to make the radical changes in our way of life needed to care for Earth and thereby to participate in the salvation/healing of the wounded Earth and all of its inhabitants, both human and nonhuman? In addressing this question Bonaventure's concept of "contuition" was crucial. Contuition is a process of learning to see Earth and all of its inhabitants as God sees them. Genesis 1:31a emerged as a hinge verse, as it expresses how God sees all God has created: "God saw everything that God had made, and indeed, it was very good"—that is, God delighted in Earth and all of its inhabitants. Bonaventure viewed St. Francis of Assisi as a master of contuition. Through St. Francis's relationship with Christ he was enabled to see that all peoples and creatures are precious in God's sight.

I have become convinced that fear of impending ecological catastrophe is not adequate in itself to motivate us to make the needed radical changes in our way of life. We need to learn to see Earth and all of its inhabitants as God sees them. God's delight in and affection for all God's creatures explains why God grieves deeply with the victims, human and nonhuman, of our ecologically destructive and abusive actions. The first step in addressing the urgent ecological crisis we face is to see Earth and all of its inhabitants with delight and heartfelt grief. We share this Earth home with them. We are far more likely to make necessary sacrifices for Earth and all of its inhabitants if we share in God's delight in and affection for them and recognize them as fellow members of our Earth household.

Plan for Coming Home to Earth

The purpose of *Coming Home to Earth* is to cultivate a deep love of Earth and to bear witness to how deeply rooted that love is in our Judeo-Christian tradition. Chapter 2 focuses on our loss of love for Earth. The urgency of the ecological crisis bears witness to that loss of love. I will seek to uncover the roots of our loss of love for Earth and to highlight various aspects of the ecological crisis. I will show how that loss of love has contributed to the urgency of the ecological crisis. We have brought this crisis on ourselves; it is the inevitable result of our neglect and outright abuse of Earth. I will highlight four prophetic voices in our American environmental tradition who have alerted us to not only the ecological crisis itself but to the loss of love for our Earth home: John Muir, Aldo Leopold, Rachel Carson, and Wendell Berry.

Chapter 3, drawing on the lament tradition in the Bible, is an invitation to grieve with God for the whole Earth community. God's grief is a sign of deep love for all God has created. The truth is that all creatures are precious in God's sight. Bonaventure's concept of contuition—that is, seeing Earth and all its inhabitants as God sees them—will be explored in more depth. In grieving with God it becomes clear that nothing can separate us from God's love. In Bonhoeffer's prison writings he speaks of sharing in the sufferings of God. In a time of ecological devastation we are called to share in the sufferings of God for the whole Earth community.

Chapter 4, "The Things That Make for Peace," casts God's vision of peace (*shalom*) as an alternative vision of a transformed Earth community in which all are thriving. Followers of Jesus will pursue the things that make for peace on and with Earth and participate with God in the process of fulfilling God's vision of *shalom* for the whole Earth community. The paradigm of salvation that emerges does not allow for any salvation for human beings apart from the Earth community. Making peace on and with Earth entails both a ministry of reconciliation and an effort to establish ecological justice.

Chapter 5 issues a call for a conversion to Earth. Ecological enlightenment is not enough to motivate most people to engage in radical ecological reform. The heart as well as the mind must be moved. Our misplaced confidence in the human mind has contributed in large measure to the ecological mess we are in. The first step in the conversion process is to name our ecological sin. We need to take the ecological log out of our own eye. The call to ecological conversion involves a turning away from an excessive focus on the self and one's own kind and a turning toward God, other human beings, and creation. This call to ecological conversion is an appeal for ethical humility even as we engage in bold action to address the ecological crisis.

Chapter 6, "Taking Up Our Ecological Cross," affirms the need to sacrifice our way of life. Our willingness to sacrifice the more destructive aspects of our way of life is crucial to addressing the ecological crisis. We will have to sacrifice some things we hold dear. I will highlight three specific sacrifices: our indulgent consumptive way of life, our subjugation to chronological time, and our love affair with the automobile. Such sacrifices are the cost of ecological reformation. They are necessary to move Earth and all of its inhabitants toward *shalom*. Such sacrifices bear the hope of liberating human beings to flourish in a more sustainable way of life. In moving toward *shalom* we need to discern what political action followers of Jesus may be called to take.

Chapter 7 is an appeal to come home to Earth. We have been living in ecological exile for too long. Like that of the prodigal son, our exile is self-imposed. We have squandered our God-given Earth inheritance. It is time for the prodigal species to come home. There is no place like our Earth home. In our journey out of exile, in our coming home to Earth, it is essential that we have—and care for—a "home place." I will share how Sunriver and Beaverton have functioned as home places for our family in Oregon and have been a special part of our journey home to Earth. In this chapter I will gather together and highlight seven possible motivations for loving Earth. The church may have a number of ecological responsibilities, but the church's primary ecological responsibility in every generation is to proclaim in word and deed God's deep love for the whole Earth community and thereby cultivate a deep love of Earth.

Swimming with the Salmon

In the Pacific Northwest nothing is more iconic than the final journey of the salmon back to its place of birth. Salmon swim upstream, struggling against the current, jumping up rapids, leaping up and over falls. A salmon expends every last ounce of energy in the quest to return to its home pool. Once the salmon has laid its eggs or fertilized them, it gradually dies and floats down the river and decays on some bank or in a shallows. Even in death it provides nutrients so that life may thrive in the watershed. Some may view the death of the salmon as tragic. But all life dies and decays. Death and decay provide fertile ground for new life. The salmon returning to its home pool gives its life fully for the purpose for which God created it. Its journey home is not tragic; it is a triumph.

Coming Home to Earth focuses on the journey home we human beings must take. We need to return home to Earth, the place of our birth. It will not be an easy trip. Changing our way of life, so crucial to this journey, will be a challenge. We will have to expend every last ounce of energy we can muster, and our homing instincts are not as finely tuned as the salmon's. But make no mistake: the well-being of the whole Earth community in present and future generations depends on our making this trek. In coming home to Earth we will have given our lives fully for the purpose for which God created us.

2

Love Lost for Earth

Roots of Our Lack of Love for Earth

According to Genesis 1:26, when God made human beings, God gave us dominion over all creatures on Earth. For much of human history that dominion has been exercised in limited ecological niches. Human beings struggled to survive in their places within an ecosystem, and most ecological damage we inflicted tended to be confined within these niches. Now the tide has turned, and human beings have become the dominant threat to the survival of their own species and other species within an ecosystem as well as to the survival of entire ecosystems.[1] The results of this domination have been swift and devastating to Earth and its inhabitants; it has led to negative ecological consequences such as food and water shortages, rising coastal waters, melting glaciers and ice sheets, loss of biodiversity, soil fatigue, resource depletion, and various forms of pollution. Human beings have collaborated in the pillaging of Earth by ecological sins of commission and omission.

Christians have been fully implicated in this ecological devastation. But as Thomas Berry laments in a 1994 essay, "at the present time the protest of the pillage of Earth, compassion for Earth, and commitment to the preservation of Earth are left mainly to secular environmental organizations as though the matter were too peripheral to be of concern to

---

1. Martin-Schramm and Stivers, *Christian Environmental Ethics*, 9.

Christians."[2] Since 1994 we have seen encouraging signs of an ecological awakening among people in a wide variety of Christian communities, but we can hardly claim to have taken the lead in promoting care of Earth.[3]

The most searing critique of the Christian tradition's attitude toward Earth was published by Lynn White Jr. in 1967. In "The Historical Roots of Our Ecological Crisis" White, looking ahead to the final third of the twentieth century, took note of the growing concern for an imminent "ecological backlash." An exploitive attitude toward nature combined with the marriage of scientific knowledge and technological power in the nineteenth century had led to the rapidly intensifying ecological crisis.[4] No creature other than the human, asserts White, "has ever managed to foul its nest in such short order."[5] In his view, "Christianity bears a huge burden of guilt"[6] for the emerging ecological disaster. He traces the historical roots of this exploitive attitude toward nature back to the "striking story of creation" in Genesis. God creates all things for human benefit and rule: "No item in physical creation had any purpose save to serve [humankind's] purposes." In White's assessment Christianity, especially in its Western form, is the "most anthropocentric religion the world has seen."[7] Unless we reject the Christian axiom "that nature has no reason for existence save to serve [humankind]," the ecological crisis will continue to deepen.[8]

On the one hand, we in the Christian community can only respond to White's indictment, "Guilty as charged." To this day we who belong to the

2. T. Berry, "Women Religious: Voices of Earth," in *Christian Future*, 71.

3. Consider, for example, some signs of an ecological awakening here in Oregon and in the Pacific Northwest. Pacific Lutheran University has an intentional commitment to being a green campus. St. Andrew Lutheran Church in Beaverton, where I serve as lead pastor, has taken steps toward becoming a more ecologically responsible congregation. Our efforts to restore our wetland were cited in a June 2010 article in *The Lutheran* by Steve Lundeberg entitled "Sanctuary in the Firs." The Interfaith Network for Earth Concerns (INEC) is a ministry of Ecumenical Ministries of Oregon. INEC's signature event is the annual Earth Care Summit, which gathers hundreds of people of faith concerned with Earth care from all over Oregon and southwest Washington. Another encouraging sign has been the rise of the Evangelical Environmental Network (EEN) across the country. (For more information on EEN, see www.creationcare.org.) To address the ecological crisis we need people from all strands of the Christian tradition.

4. White, "Historical Roots of the Ecological Crisis," 17.

5. Ibid., 18.

6. Ibid., 28.

7. Ibid., 24.

8. Ibid., 30.

privileged majority within the Christian community in the West have not distinguished ourselves by adopting a more caring and less exploitive attitude toward nature. We are not eager to give up our ecologically unsustainable way of life. We bear a huge burden of guilt for the ecological mess we are in. A major ecological reformation of the church is needed to cultivate a love for Earth deep enough to respond to the ecological backlash we face.

On the other hand, we do not want to give up too quickly on the historical roots of our faith tradition. Getting back to the deepest roots of our tradition is vital in motivating and cultivating a love for Earth deep enough to transform our way of life. White himself suggests an alternative Christian view of the relationship of humankind and nature, that of St. Francis of Assisi, the "greatest radical in Christian history since Christ."[9] White highlights St. Francis's idea of the equality of all creatures, including human beings, before God. St. Francis emphasized the virtue of humility for human beings both as individuals and as a species. In the Christian tradition St. Francis exemplifies love of the whole of creation. White points out the influence of Jesus's lowly birth and humble sacrifice on the cross in St. Francis's alternative Christian view. But the roots of St. Francis's view go back even further to the very "striking story of creation"[10] that White identifies as a source of Christian domination over nature. The creation story strongly affirms the goodness of the whole of creation, an affirmation that those who exploit nature have conveniently ignored. With White we reject "the Christian axiom that nature has no reason for existence save to serve [humankind]."[11] Yet at the same time we maintain that this principle is not consistent with God's deepest intentions, and we seek an alternative defining truth that cultivates love and care for all of God's creatures and leads us toward a holistic concept of salvation.

White offers a simple assessment of St. Francis's attempt to offer an alternative Christian view of the equality of all God's creatures: namely, he failed. St. Francis's view may not have won the day, but a new day is upon us, and we need his view now more than ever. Our way of life based on human domination over nature looks more and more like a failed experiment. We need a new ecological experiment and a new way of life grounded in a deep love for Earth.

9. Ibid., 28.
10. Ibid., 24.
11. Ibid., 30.

The Urgency of the Ecological Crisis

The ecological crisis has become more urgent since White wrote his essay in 1967. We are witnessing the alarming consequences of our exploitive attitude toward nature, of our lack of love for Earth. In *The Future of Life* Edward O. Wilson asserts that we are approaching an Armageddon, "but it is not the cosmic war and fiery collapse of [humankind] foretold in sacred scripture. It is the wreckage of the planet by an exuberantly plentiful and ingenious humanity."[12] Wilson further explains, "The living world is dying; the natural economy is crumbling beneath our busy feet. We have been too self-absorbed to foresee the long-term consequences of our actions, and we will suffer a terrible loss unless we shake off our delusions and move quickly to a solution."[13]

Catastrophic Loss of Biodiversity

As a biologist Wilson views the loss of biodiversity as an ecological catastrophe. He summarizes key factors in the decline of species using the acronymn HIPPO:

- Habitat destruction
- Invasive species
- Pollution
- Population
- Overharvesting

Wilson is especially concerned about overpopulation—"too many people consuming too much of the land and sea space and the resources they contain."[14] So lethal have human beings become to other species that Wilson identifies *Homo sapiens* as "the serial killer of the biosphere."[15]

In playing our role as "planetary killer" we display extreme short-sightedness. Concerned about our immediate survival, we seem oblivious to the long-term consequences of our lethal behavior for our own species, let alone other species. We are willing to cut "the heart out of biodiversity."

12. *The Future of Life*, xxiii.
13. Ibid., xxiv.
14. Ibid., 50.
15. Ibid., 94.

Our conservation ethic "has generally come too late and too little" to save the most endangered species.[16]

The Earth Is Tired

During our morning family devotions on Earth Day 2010 our teenage daughter Hailey shared a phrase she had seen in New Orleans while attending the Evangelical Lutheran Church in America's 2009 Youth Gathering: "Tè a fatige." She had wondered what it meant. When her global studies class focused on Haiti, she learned that it means "the earth is tired."

The earthquake that hit Haiti in January 2010 was a devastating natural disaster, but Haitian farmers had already been dealing with a major agricultural disaster that had been building for centuries. Haiti has to import more than three quarters of the rice needed to feed its people. When the farmers were asked why so much rice needs to be imported, they responded, "Tè a fatige"—the earth is tired. Jangela Shumskas explains,

> Since 1492, when Columbus first set foot on the heavily forested island of Hispaniola, the mountainous nation has shed both topsoil and blood—first to the Spanish, who planted sugar, then to the French, who cut down the forests to make room for lucrative coffee, indigo, and tobacco. Even after Haitian slaves revolted in 1804 and threw off the bondage of colonialism, France collected 93 million francs in restitution from its former colony—much of it in timber. Soon after independence, upper-class speculators and planters pushed the peasant classes out of the few fertile valleys and into the steep forested, rural areas, where their shrinking, intensively cultivated plots of maize, beans, and cassava have combined with a growing fuelwood-charcoal industry to exacerbate deforestation and soil loss.[17]

No wonder the earth is tired: the short-term thinking of colonizing empires has been adopted by the Haitians themselves and over time has taken its toll on the soil. A strong tradition in Native American culture is that decisions and actions need to be considered in light of their impact on the seventh generation to come.[18] Haitians need a long-term sustainable way

---

16. Ibid., 102.

17. "Haiti's Landscape: Tè a fatige."

18. "We cannot simply think of our survival; each new generation is responsible to ensure the survival of the seventh generation" (Clarkson et al., "Our Responsibility," 3).

of caring for the soil, one that takes future generations fully into account. What has happened in Haiti is a microcosm of what is happening globally. The whole earth is growing tired, and more and more we are experiencing the consequences of failing to care for our Earth home. The whole human race needs to engage in seventh-generation thinking.

Extractive Economy Wasteland

According to Thomas Berry the natural world has been under assault from the final two decades of the nineteenth century to the present. It has been victimized by what Berry refers to as the "extractive economy." In *The Great Work* he distinguishes between an organic economy, which is ever renewing, and an extractive economy, which is terminal.[19] The commercial-industrial establishment in the form of modern global corporations is the force behind this extractive economy that has disrupted the biological integrity of the planet. In our quest to establish "wonderworld" we are producing "wasteworld." What is needed is the restoration of an ever-renewing organic economy. Only in this way can we leave wasteworld behind.[20] Berry published *The Great Work* in 1999. More than fifteen years later the assault against the natural world continues, and the commercial-industrial establishment Berry speaks of has shown only limited inclination to leave its extractive ways behind. In Berry's view the crucial political battles will no longer be fought between liberals and conservatives; they will be fought between ecologists or environmentalists and the commercial-industrial establishment that even today seems to have the upper hand.

Acute Affluenza

In Matthew 7:5 Jesus exhorts his followers to "first take the log out of your own eye, and then you will see clearly to take the speck out of your neighbor's eye." While it would be a gross understatement to describe the assault on the natural world by the commercial-industrial establishment as a speck, it would also be a gross understatement to describe our consumptive way of life as a speck. We need to take the consumptive log out of our own eye so that we can see clearly to take the log out of the eye of the

19. *The Great Work*, 138.
20. Ibid., 148.

commercial-industrial establishment. As the authors of *Affluenza* observe, our culture is addicted to the consumption of material goods. They define "affluenza" as "a painful, contagious, socially transmitted condition of over-load, debt, anxiety, and waste resulting from the dogged pursuit of more."[21] This addiction is driving our "pedal to the metal" economy, which is "based on beliefs that resource supplies are limitless and that the earth can con-tinually bounce back from abuse."[22] Thus, we as consumers are complicit in the devastating ecological consequences being fueled by the commercial-industrial establishment.

The documentary *Affluenza* was first shown on the Public Broadcast-ing Service on September 15, 1997, when the economy was humming. The second edition of the book *Affluenza* was published in 2005 at the height of the housing bubble. In 2008 the most severe economic downturn since the Depression slowed our rate of consumption, but for the majority of Ameri-cans our highly consumptive way of life continues. One of the most telling statistics cited in *Affluenza* is that the average American parent spends six hours per week shopping and only forty minutes per week playing with their children.[23] Modern technology was supposed to reduce our workload and provide us with more free time. Instead, just the opposite trend has been observed. In the early 1990s, utilizing U.S. Department of Labor sta-tistics, Juliet Schor, author of *The Overworked American*, calculated that full-time American workers were toiling 160 hours more than they did in 1969.[24] That is about one full month of work. Twenty years later we are working at least as many hours. In another study 69 percent of American workers expressed a desire "to slow down and live a more relaxed life."[25] So acute is our addiction to the pursuit of more that few of us have been able to fulfill this desire.

The human and environmental costs of this way of life continue to mount. When patients are diagnosed with high blood pressure, the first treatment doctors prescribe is a change in lifestyle. If lifestyle changes do not lower the patient's blood pressure, or if the patient does not have the will or desire to make those changes, physicians have the option of prescribing medication to control blood pressure. In the case of affluenza, there is no

---

21 De Graaf et al., *Affluenza*, 2.

22. Ibid., 170.

23. Ibid., 14.

24. Cited in ibid., 42.

25. Ibid., 43.

pill to prescribe. The only prescription is a radical change in our way of life. "Radical" refers to a decisive change, but it also implies that we need to get back to the roots of what it means to be thriving human beings in a healthy environment.

Despite the serious hazards of our American lifestyle, more and more cultures seem bent on adopting it. The commercial-industrial establishment has a vested interest in encouraging them to do so. David Korten, who wrote *When Corporations Rule the World*, was an apostle of the American way of life who urged people in developing countries to adopt consumer values.[26] To his credit Korten gradually realized how destructive his efforts were. He admitted, "I came to see that what I was promoting didn't work and couldn't work. Many people's lives were actually worse off. We were seeing the environment trashed, and we were seeing the breakdown of cultures and the social fabric."[27] Any promotion of our predominant American way of life should be required to carry a warning: "Hazardous to your health."

Runaway Greenhouse Effect

The Fourth Assessment Report of the Intergovernmental Panel on Climate Change published in 2007 concluded that "warming of the climate system is unequivocal"[28] and that, with *very high confidence* (greater than 90 percent), human activity since 1750 has cause this warming.[29] The Fifth Assessment Report of the Intergovernmental Panel on Climate Change published in 2013 reaffirmed that "warming of the climate system is unequivocal" and added that "since the 1950s, many of the observed changes are unprecedented over decades to millennia."[30] It emphasizes that the evidence for human influence has increased since the Fourth Assessment Report and that "it is *extremely likely* that human influence has been the dominant cause of the observed warming since the mid-20th century."[31] In a 2008

26. After teaching business management for a number of years at Stanford and Harvard, Korten "worked in Africa, Asia, and Central America for the Harvard Business School, the Ford Foundation, and the U.S. Agency for International Development" (ibid., 87).

27. Quoted in ibid., 87.

28. IPCC, "Summary for Policymakers," in *Climate Change 2007*, 5.

29. Ibid., 3.

30. IPCC, "Summary for Policymakers," in *Climate Change 2013*, 4.

31. Ibid., 17.

Open Atmospheric Science Journal article James Hansen, one of the most well-known climate scientists in the country, recommends, "If humanity wishes to preserve a planet similar to that on which civilization developed and to which life on Earth is adapted, paleoclimate evidence and ongoing climate change suggest that CO_2 will need to be reduced from its current 385 ppm [parts per million] to at most 350 ppm, but likely less than that."[32] Hansen offers five reasons why 350 ppm needs to be our target goal: (1) Arctic sea ice is melting faster than expected; (2) mountain glaciers are disappearing at a rapid rate; (3) Greenland and West Antarctic ice sheets are losing mass rapidly; (4) subtropical regions are expanding poleward faster than expected; and (5) coral reefs are suffering from multiple stresses.[33]

In *Storms of My Grandchildren* Hansen asserts that "human-made climate change is, indeed, the greatest threat civilization faces."[34] The monthly CO_2 average at Mauna Loa was 401.78 ppm in May 2014 and 403.94 ppm in May 2015.[35] So the urgency of addressing the climate-change issue has only intensified. Hansen draws the startling conclusion that our continued exploitation of fossil fuels has put Earth and all of its inhabitants in imminent peril.

Hansen makes a strong case that we are fast approaching "climate tipping points, beyond which climate dynamics can cause rapid changes out of humanity's control."[36] He especially fears a runaway greenhouse effect that will destroy all life on Earth. According to Hansen, the early atmosphere on Venus was filled with lots of water vapor. The sun was dimmer then, so Venus was cooler. Venus may even have had oceans. But "as the sun brightened," explains Hansen, "the surface of Venus became hotter, water evaporated, and the strong greenhouse effect of water vapor amplified the warming. Eventually a 'runaway' greenhouse effect occurred, with

32. Quoted in Martin-Schramm, *Climate Justice*, 20.

33. Hansen, *Storms of My Grandchildren*, 164–65.

34. Ibid., 70.

35. Earth System Research Laboratory, "Trends in Atmospheric Carbon Dioxide: Mauna Loa, Hawaii." The Mauna Loa Observatory (MLO) is "a premier atmospheric research facility that has been continuously monitoring and collecting data related to atmospheric change since the 1950s. The undisturbed air, remote location, and minimal influences of vegetation and human activity at MLO are ideal for monitoring constituents in the atmosphere that can cause climate change. The observatory is part of the National Oceanic and Atmospheric Administration (NOAA) - Earth System Research Laboratory (ESRL) - Global Monitoring Division (GMD)" (http://www.esrl.noaa.gov/gmd/obop/mlo/).

36. Hansen, *Storms of My Grandchildren*, ix.

the ocean boiling or evaporating into the atmosphere."[37] Hansen refers to this runaway greenhouse effect as the "Venus syndrome." He has come to the conclusion "that if we burn all reserves of oil, gas, and coal, there is a substantial chance we will initiate the runaway greenhouse." He believes that "if we also burn the tar sands and tar shale, . . . the Venus syndrome is a dead certainty."[38] Humanity has made a Faustian bargain with fossil fuels to power our way of life. Coal burning at power plants is the chief source of increasing carbon dioxide in the atmosphere.[39] That explains why Hansen's number one priority in addressing climate change is to keep coal in the ground.[40]

In Hansen's assessment humanity has reached a fork in the road: "One path has global fossil fuel emissions declining at a pace, dictated by what the science is telling us, that diffuses amplifying feedbacks and stabilizes climate. The other path is more or less business as usual, in which case amplifying feedbacks are expected to come into play and climate change will spin out of our control."[41] So far the forces of "climate change inertia" seem to be dictating the destructive path we continue to follow. Hansen expresses deep concern that the president and Congress are too beholden to fossil fuel special interests.[42] They act as if we have no obligation to our younger generations, who will inherit the mess we are leaving them.[43] They seem oblivious to how urgent the need is to address climate change aggressively. Hansen bemoans the tendency of governments to express concern about climate change without doing anything to stabilize the climate or preserve Earth.[44] The business-as-usual path will without a doubt "commit the planet to global warming of a magnitude that will lead eventually to an ice-free planet. An ice-free planet means a sea level rise of about 75 meters

37. Ibid., 225.

38. Ibid., 236.

39. Ibid., 2.

40. For Hansen's discussion of the urgency of leaving fossil fuels in the ground, see especially ibid., 173–78.

41. Ibid., 120.

42. The January 21, 2010 Supreme Court ruling *Citizens United v. Federal Election Commission* has increased the role of money in elections and the likelihood that politicians will be beholden to special interests. In Hansen's opinion the influence of money on our political leaders is "the biggest problem for democracy and for the planet" (ibid., 95).

43. Ibid., 292.

44. Ibid., x.

(almost 250 feet)."[45] Hansen is on a mission to convince our leaders and all of us that the first path—aggressively seeking to reduce carbon emissions—is the only sane and caring path to follow. We do not have time to tarry. He warns that climate change can sneak up on us. By the time we realize the major changes needed in our way of life, we may already be beyond the tipping point. It will be impossible or at least extremely difficult "to prevent catastrophic effects—such as disintegration of ice sheets or ecosystem collapse."[46] Hansen is especially motivated by his concern for the well-being of his grandchildren. My particular concern in this book is what will motivate enough of our leaders and enough of us to make the necessary changes in our way of life that lead to a stable climate and the well-being of Earth and all of its inhabitants.

American Prophetic Voices of Love for Earth

The urgency of the ecological crisis bears witness to our loss of love for Earth. We have not merely neglected Earth; we have willfully abused it. It is instructive to listen to some of the prophetic voices in our American environmental tradition who have alerted us not only to the ecological crisis itself but also to the loss of love for Earth. My "Mt. Rushmore" of American environmental prophets includes John Muir, Aldo Leopold, Rachel Carson, and Wendell Berry. As I write, only Berry remains alive; but the prophetic voices of all four continue to impact efforts to address the ecological crisis. All four share a number of characteristics crucial to their prophetic witness: a passionate love for Earth and all of its creatures; an effort to embody this love for Earth in word and deed; a desire to share their prophetic message with the American public; a pioneering spirit in calling for greater concern for the environment; a sense of kinship and interdependence with other creatures; a fearlessness in articulating the truth of the shortcomings of our way of life in relationship to our own well-being and the well-being of Earth and all its creatures. They are radical voices in the sense that they help us get back to the roots of who we are and how we are to live on Earth. Though none of them professes to speak on behalf of a community of faith, they are all influenced by faith and share some of the deepest core values of the Judaeo-Christian tradition, including love of creation.

45. Ibid., 250.
46. Ibid., 285.

John Muir: Protecting Nature for Its Own Sake

Recognized as the founder of the modern environmental movement, John Muir (1838–1914) was a passionate, articulate, and pioneering voice for wilderness protection in our country. He sought to help us recognize that human beings are part of nature and that "when we try to pick out anything by itself, we find it hitched to everything else in the universe."[47]

Muir first visited the Yosemite Valley in 1868 and was enthralled. He observed that "the Valley, comprehensively seen, looks like an immense hall or temple lighted from above." But, he exclaimed, "no temple made with hands can compare with Yosemite. Every rock in its walls seems to glow with life." He was enchanted by the way the "crystal Merced, River of Mercy" flowed through the middle of the valley, "peacefully quiet, reflecting lilies and trees and the onlooking rocks; things frail and fleeting and types of endurance meeting here and blending in countless forms, as if into this one mountain mansion Nature had gathered her choicest treasures." He marveled at the beauty and grandeur of the trees in the valley and in the magnificent forests in which the valley was embedded. Noblest of all, the king of the conifers, was the majestic Sequoia.[48]

As a child Muir was compelled by his father, an itinerant Presbyterian minister, to memorize the Bible. He memorized all of it except one-quarter of the Old Testament.[49] In the course of his wilderness experiences, he came to view nature as scripture and natural wonders as the words of God. In a September 1874 letter from the Yosemite Valley to his spiritual mentor, Jeanne Carr, he exclaimed, "Miles and miles of tree scripture along the sky, a Bible will one day be read! The beauty of its letters and sentences have burned me like fire through all these Sierra seasons."[50]

Muir's passionate campaign to protect precious wilderness areas was a vital factor in the establishment of Yosemite as a national park in 1890 and the formation of the Sierra Club, an organization committed to wilderness protection, in 1892.[51] Muir was the first president of the Sierra Club. He was

47. Muir, *My First Summer in the Sierras,* 248.

48. Muir, *Yosemite,* 615.

49. "People Who Made a Difference: John Muir (1838–1914)," para. 1.

50. *John Muir: Spiritual Writings,* 99–100.

51. In 1872 Yellowstone became the first national park in the United States. Its primary purpose was to be a "pleasuring-ground for the benefit and enjoyment of the people" (National Park Service, "History," http://www.nps.gov/aboutus/history.htm). Yosemite was established first and foremost for conservation reasons. As Terry Gifford

delighted that many had begun to venture into the wilderness: "Thousands of tired, nerve-shaken, over-civilized people are beginning to find out that going to the mountains is going home; that wilderness is a necessity; and that mountain parks and reservations are useful not only as fountains of timber and irrigating rivers, but as fountains of life."[52] Conservationists in the late nineteenth century, led by Gifford Pinchot, emphasized the "right use" of nature for human benefit. Muir and other preservationists affirmed the benefits of nature for human beings, but also argued that nature was worth preserving for its own sake.[53]

According to Muir, ventures into the wilderness helped awaken people from the "stupefying effects of the vice of over-industry and the deadly apathy of luxury."[54] In my view loss of love for Earth is one of the "stupefying effects" of our consumptive way of life. Muir also wanted people to venture into the wilderness to open their eyes to "how narrow we selfish, conceited creatures are in our sympathies! how blind to the rights of all the rest of creation!" He lamented the "dismal irreverence" with which "we speak of our fellow mortals!"[55]

Muir was intent on encouraging people to become the "lovers of wildness" they were created to be. For Muir the mountains, rivers, trees, flowers, and all things in nature "speak nature's love." We are invited to respond with affection. As Muir writes of his experiences in the wilderness, his affection shines through. In describing his venture onto the Alaskan tundra, he refrains from mentioning by name all of the plant friends he encountered; he acknowledges that few people would care to read all the names. But then he adds that everybody "would love them could they see them blooming and rejoicing at home."[56]

The struggle between preservationists, led by Muir, and conservationists, led by Pinchot, came to a head in the process of deciding whether to dam the Toulumne River in Yosemite National Park. The proposal was to put a dam at the head of the Hetch Hetchy Valley, which would form a

---

emphasizes, Muir developed a "national park philosophy" and is properly regarded as the "founder of the National Park movement." Gifford, "Introduction," 15.

52. Muir, *Our National Parks*, 459.

53. Kline, *First Along the River*, 65. For an analysis of the "Continuum of Attitudes toward Nature," see Martin-Schramm and Stivers, *Christian Environmental Ethics*, 23–30.

54. Muir, *Our National Parks*, 459.

55. Muir, *Thousand Mile Walk*, 148.

56. Muir, *Our National Parks*, 462.

huge reservoir behind it. City officials in San Francisco were eager to tap into such a bountiful source of clean water. The dam would also provide an excellent source of clean hydroelectric power. Furthermore, the reservoir would open up recreational opportunities such as boating, fishing, and swimming.

Since the Hetch Hetchy Valley was in Yosemite National Park, the application for the dam was initially turned down. But San Francisco city officials along with Pinchot and his supporters did not give up. A new Secretary of the Interior was persuaded, and the application was approved. Muir and the Sierra Club led a spirited effort to convince Congress to overturn this decision. Muir leveled a searing attack on proponents of the dam: "These temple destroyers, devotees of ravaging commercialism, seem to have a perfect contempt for Nature, and instead of lifting their eyes to the God of the Mountains, lift them to the Almighty Dollar. Dam the Hetch Hetchy! As well dam for water tanks the people's cathedrals and churches, for no holier temple has ever been consecrated by the heart of man."[57] Pinchot insisted that damming the Hetch Hetchy was a matter of right use and wise development. "The first great fact about conservation," explained Pinchot, "is that it stands for development. Conservation does mean provision for the future, but it means also and first of all the recognition of the right of the present generation to the fullest necessary use of all the resources with which this country is so abundantly blessed."[58] Despite Muir's best efforts the Hetch Hetchy dam bill passed by a wide margin in Congress. Muir was stunned by the defeat. But he was convinced that the importance of protecting wilderness would in time prevail. Muir died of pneumonia a year later, but in the ensuing years a number of crucial victories were won in the effort to protect wilderness areas. The losing battle to save the Hetch Hetchy Valley proved to be a stimulus to these efforts.

Muir recognized that in order for the preservationists' protection efforts to triumph they had to get to the root of what was motivating people. They had to expose the "perfect contempt for Nature" in their opponents,[59] and they had to cultivate a love of nature in as many people as possible. In Muir's view the best way to cultivate that love was to get people out into the wilderness.[60] That is why it was so important to him to preserve the most

57. Muir, *Yosemite*, 716.
58. Quoted in Kline, *First Along the River*, 67.
59. Ibid.
60. Muir, *Our National Parks*, 462.

beautiful wilderness areas. Some may question the level of confidence he placed in the ability of nature itself to win people over. But he was convinced that time spent in nature would transform people.

In 1893 President Benjamin Harrison had proclaimed the Sierra of California a forest reserve. Muir expressed his deep conviction the Sierra Forest Reserve "is worth the most thoughtful care of the government for its own sake, without considering its value as the fountain of the rivers on which the fertility of the great San Joaquin Valley depends." He bemoaned that instead "it gets no care at all. In the fog of tariff, silver, and annexation politics it is left wholly unguarded, though the management of the adjacent national parks by a few soldiers shows how well and how easily it can be preserved." Muir was sure that "if every citizen could take one walk through this reserve, there would be no more trouble about its care; for only in darkness does vandalism flourish."[61] Muir's struggle to cultivate such care continues in our own time and place. Only now, with the intensification of human-induced climate change, the stakes are even higher for human beings and all life on Earth.

Aldo Leopold: Loss of Love and Respect for the Land

A sense of environmental loss runs deep in Aldo Leopold's classic work *A Sand County Almanac*,[62] published in 1949, the year after Leopold died while helping his neighbors fight a grass fire. "Part 1: A Sand County Almanac" contains Leopold's "shack sketches," in which he describes experiences on the worn-out 120-acre sand farm on the Wisconsin River that he and his family purchased in 1935 and worked on restoring.[63] Widely respected as a leading conservationist of the twentieth century, Leopold locates the heart of environmental degradation in a loss of love and respect for the land. Leopold's own sense of loss is especially poignant in his essay "Marshland Elegy."[64] There he mourns the destruction of crane marshes, cranes, and other inhabitants of the marshes. The "high priests of progress," charges Leopold, have been oblivious to how human beings and animals, plants and soil "lived on and with each other in mutual toleration, to the mutual

61. Muir, *Our National Parks,* 472.
62. Finch, "Introduction," xx.
63. Ibid., xvi.
64. Leopold, *Sand County Almanac,* 95–101.

benefit of all."[65] These "new overlords" have been intent on turning the marshes into farms, with little regard for the destructive ecological effects. They "knew nothing of cranes, and cared less. What is a species more or less among engineers? What good is an undrained marsh anyhow?"[66]

For Leopold it is inconceivable that "an ethical relation to the land can exist without love, respect, and admiration for the land, and a high regard for its value."[67] Leopold had a significant impact on the emerging science of ecology. In *A Sand County Almanac* it becomes apparent that he uses the term "land" somewhat similar to the way we use "ecosystem." As Leopold defines "land," it is "not merely soil; it is a fountain of energy flowing through a circuit of soils, plants, and animals."[68]

In the foreword to *A Sand County Almanac* Leopold asserts that the primary reason we abuse the land is that "we regard it as a commodity belonging to us."[69] Given this attitude toward the land, it is not surprising that land-use ethics would be dominated by economic self-interest. Since the time of Leopold, we have made only limited progress, if any, in changing our attitude toward the land and in overcoming the dominance of economic self-interest. Leopold emphasizes that any "system of conservation based solely on economic self-interest is hopelessly lopsided. It tends to ignore, and thus eventually to eliminate, many elements . . . that are (as far as we know) essential to its healthy functioning."[70] Such a lopsided system of conservation compromises the health of the land as well as those who inhabit the land. So we must, insists Leopold, "quit thinking about decent land-use as solely an economic problem."[71]

The land will survive the impact of "mechanized" human beings, states Leopold, only if "we see land as a community to which we belong," for then "we may begin to use it with love and respect."[72] What is needed is a new "land ethic," something Leopold addresses in the final chapter of *A Sand County Almanac*. Leopold's land ethic "enlarges the boundaries of the community to include soils, waters, plants, and animals, or collectively: the

65. Ibid., 99.
66. Ibid., 100.
67. Ibid., 223.
68. Ibid., 216.
69. Finch, "Introduction," viii.
70. Leopold, *Sand County Almanac*, 209.
71. Ibid., 225.
72. Finch, "Introduction," viii.

land." In such an ethic, our role as a human being changes "from conqueror of the land community to plain member and citizen of it."[73] To be a citizen of this land community means to love and respect all members of the community and the community as a whole. Leopold urges us to view humans as "fellow-voyagers with other creatures in the odyssey of evolution."[74] He laments that our awareness of our connection with other creatures has not led to a sense of kinship with them. The death of a species is the death of our kin. Leopold's well-known maxim of his land ethic is this: "A thing is right when it tends to preserve the integrity, stability, and beauty of the biotic community. It is wrong when it tends otherwise."[75] In order to fulfill this maxim we need love and respect for the land and a deep sense of kinship with our fellow creatures.

Leopold was convinced that no major change in our ethics would occur "without an internal change in our intellectual emphasis, loyalties, affections, and convictions."[76] A decisive conversion of the heart and mind was needed. Leopold had been raised in a Lutheran family of German descent, but his family had not been active in the church. His wife, Estella, was a devout Catholic, but the church was not a major focus of their family's life. Leopold seldom talked about God and his religious beliefs. But later in his life, when he was confined to bed and awaiting travel to the Mayo Clinic for surgery for a painful tic condition, his youngest daughter, also named Estella, asked her father about his belief in God. As she recalled, "He replied that he believed there was a mystical supreme power that guided the Universe. But to him this power was not a personalized God. It was more akin to the laws of nature."[77]

Despite his lack of belief in a personalized God, he came to see the value of philosophy and religion in cultivating or converting people to an ecological conscience. In his essay "The Ecological Conscience," he acknowledges that "in our attempt to make conservation easy, we have dodged its spiritual implications. The proof of this error lies in the fact that philosophy, ethics, and religion have not yet heard of it."[78] Moved by Leopold's plea for an ecological conscience and new land ethic, Max Otto, a

73. Leopold, *Sand County Almanac*, 204.
74. Ibid., 109.
75. Ibid., 224–25.
76. Ibid., 210.
77. Meine, *Aldo Leopold*, 506.
78. Quoted in ibid., 498.

philosophy professor at the University of Wisconsin, wrote to him, "I wish religious people—*church* people, I mean—could see it to be part of religion to enlist in your cause."[79] Otto's response encouraged Leopold and increased his hope that religion could help motivate people to take real responsibility for the well-being of the land community and all of its members.

For Leopold being a citizen of the land community is an essential part of our core identity, and loving and respecting all members of the land community and the land community as a whole is a core value of human beings. This love and respect are not contingent on the economic benefit of the land and other creatures for human beings. One of my goals in *Coming Home to Earth* is to establish that belief in a personal God does not preclude sharing in the core identity and core value Leopold identifies or enlisting in Leopold's ecological cause. As followers of Jesus, being members of the Earth community is crucial to our core identity; and loving the Earth community and all its creatures is a core value.

Rachel Carson: The Silenced Voices of Spring

As Linda Lear writes in the introduction to the fortieth-anniversary edition of *Silent Spring*, Rachel Carson's "thesis that we were subjecting ourselves to slow poisoning by the misuse of chemical pesticides that polluted the environment may seem like common currency now, but in 1962 *Silent Spring* contained the kernel of social revolution."[80] Carson was compelled to write the book by a letter she received in 1958 from Olga Owens Huckins.[81] Huckins, a former literary editor of the *Boston Post*, had written a favorable review in 1951 of Carson's highly acclaimed book *The Sea Around Us* and knew that Carson had worked for years in the federal Fish and Wildlife Service. Where Huckins and her husband, Stuart, lived on the seashore in Massachusetts, the state had used a mix of fuel oil and DDT sprayed from planes in an effort to eradicate mosquitoes. State officials claimed the mix was harmless. But after repeated sprayings in the summer of 1957, many songbirds in the large bird sanctuary around Huckins' home died.[82] Huckins hoped Carson might intercede with someone in the federal government who could prevent such spraying. Carson knew from experience that gov-

79. Quoted in ibid., 500.
80. Carson, *Silent Spring*, x.
81. Ibid., viii.
82. Lear, *Rachel Carson*, 313–15.

ernment officials and chemical manufacturers were steadfast deniers of the harm being done to wildlife. She compared them to the priest and Levite in the parable of the Good Samaritan, who "choose to pass by on the other side and to see nothing."[83] Rather than intercede with government officials, Carson decided to take her case to the wider public and thus wrote *Silent Spring*. Polluting Earth by using toxic chemicals was an act of human arrogance. Carson wrote to a friend, "There would be no peace for me, if I kept silent."[84]

Although Carson had never been part of the scientific establishment, she was a trained biologist, and in *Silent Spring* she offered a carefully reasoned yet readable scientific case exposing the deadly consequences of DDT and other pesticides. *Silent Spring* succeeded in getting the attention of the wider public, who then helped bring pressure to bear on government officials and chemical manufacturers. *Silent Spring* was a catalyst in the move toward major new laws protecting wildlife and cleaning up our air, water, and land, such as the National Environmental Policy Act (1970), Clean Air Act (1970), Clean Water Act (1972), and the Endangered Species Act (1973).[85]

But Carson was not simply concerned with changing laws. The root of the environmental crisis had to do with our attitude toward nature. She believed that human beings need to wake up to "their kinship with other forms of life."[86] We need to realize that we are not the conquerors of nature; rather, we are part of a vast web of life. Carson wanted us to be aware that although our actions in a given time and place may not have immediate, visible harmful effects, they may have unforeseen—and devastating—consequences for life in the future.[87]

Carson dedicated *Silent Spring* to Albert Schweitzer, who, as she notes, once said that human beings "have lost the capacity to foresee and to forestall." They "will end by destroying the earth."[88] Schweitzer advocated an attitude of "reverence for life"—a deep respect for life, accompanied by awe and wonder. In Carson's writings one senses this deep respect, this awe

83. Carson, *Silent Spring*, 86.

84. Quoted in Lear's introduction to *Silent Spring*, xiv.

85. For a listing and short description of major U. S. federal environmental laws, see https://www.epa.gov/laws-regulations/laws-and-executive-orders#majorlaws.

86. Quoted by Lear in her introduction to *Silent Spring*, xii.

87. Carson, *Silent Spring*, 64.

88. Lear, *Rachel Carson*, 352.

and wonder. For Carson her mother embodied Schweitzer's "reverence for life."[89] She deeply appreciated how her mother, influenced by the nature-study movement,[90] sought to instill respect and love for God's creatures in her children. Linda Lear describes Rachel's mother, Maria, as the "perfect nature-study teacher." She herself had a passion for nature, and the sixty-four acre Carson property was a wonderful laboratory to teach in. As long as the weather cooperated, she and her children spent time outside every day.[91] Of the three Carson children, Rachel, the youngest, especially took to heart her mother's teaching on nature.

Carson's upbringing contributed significantly to her deep understanding of the interconnectedness of all life. In her view, when we acquiesce to practices that cause suffering or destroy other living creatures, we also diminish ourselves, both in a spiritual sense and a physical sense. Carson had a holistic understanding of health. Her ecology of the body emphasized that the well-being of human beings and the well-being of nature are intimately connected.[92] In seeking the well-being of ourselves and all creation, we are being who we were intended to be.

Carson intended her Scripps Commencement address on June 12, 1962, "Of Man and the Stream of Time," to be "a major statement of her views on humankind's relationship with the natural world." She observed that human beings have "long talked somewhat arrogantly about the conquest of nature" and now we have the power to make this boast a reality. According to Carson, "It is our misfortune—and it may well be our final tragedy—that this power has not been tempered with wisdom, but has been marked by irresponsibility."[93] The price of our conquest of nature may be the destruction of ourselves. Carson begins *Silent Spring* with "A Fable for Tomorrow." Toward the end of the fable, when no signs of new life are left in the town, Carson includes this haunting passage: "No witchcraft, no enemy

89. Ibid., 338.

90. Cornell University professors Liberty Hyde Bailey and Anna Comstock popularized the nature-study movement. In Comstock's *Handbook of Nature Study* she emphasizes that nature-study will cultivate in children a "love of the beautiful" and a "sense of companionship with life out-of-doors, and an abiding love of nature." Quoted in Lear, *Rachel Carson*, 14.

91. Lear, *Rachel Carson*, 14–15.

92. Lear, introduction to *Silent Spring*, xvi–xvii.

93. Lear, *Rachel Carson*, 407.

action had silenced the rebirth of new life in this stricken world. The people had done it themselves."[94]

Wendell Berry: A Loss of Affection for the World and Its Creatures

Wendell and Tanya Berry still live in Henry County, Kentucky, on the farm they purchased in 1965. Their farm is located near others that have been in the family for two hundred hundred years. One of Wendell Berry's primary purposes in *The Unsettling of America*, his sharp critique of modern corporate agriculture, published in 1977, is to "show how deeply rooted in our past is the mentality of exploitation."[95] Berry draws a distinction between a mindset of exploitation and a mindset of nurture. As a model of exploitation he lifts up a strip miner. As a model of a nurturer he identifies the "old-fashioned idea" of a farmer—that is, a farmer who lives on and works the land. Berry outlines the characteristics of these two opposing mindsets as follows:

> The exploiter is a specialist, an expert; the nurturer is not. The standard of the exploiter is efficiency; the standard of the nurturer is care. The exploiter's goal is money, profit; the nurturer's goal is health—his land's health, his own, his family's, his community's, his country's. Whereas the exploiter asks of a piece of land only how much and how quickly it can be made to produce, the nurturer asks a question that is much more complex and difficult: What is its carrying capacity? (That is: How much can be taken from it without diminishing it? What can it produce *dependably* for an indefinite time?) The exploiter wishes to earn as much as possible by as little work as possible; the nurturer expects, certainly, to have a decent living from his work; but his characteristic wish is to work *as well* as possible. The competence of the exploiter is in organization; that of the nurturer is in order—a human order, that is, that accommodates itself both to the other order and to mystery. The exploiter typically serves an institution or organization; the nurturer serves land, household, community, place. The exploiter thinks in terms of numbers, quantities, "hard facts"; the nurturer in terms of character, condition, quality, kind.[96]

94. Carson, *Silent Spring*, 3.
95. Berry, *Unsettling of America*, 7.
96. Ibid., 9.

When an exploitive frame of mind predominates, explains Berry, the first casualties are character and community.

This exploitive mindset also reflects a resistance to our limits as human beings and our role in creation. The new guise of evil is a "limitless technology, dependent upon a limitless morality, which is to say upon no morality at all."[97] Berry warns of a dangerous tendency in our society to seek to sever "the umbilical cord fastening us to the wilderness or the Creation."[98] He acknowledges that "there always will be some people willing to do anything at all that is financially or technologically possible, who look upon the world and its creatures without affection and therefore as exploitable without limit."[99]

According to Berry, a loss of affection for the world and its creatures is at the heart of our prevailing mentality of exploitation. He is not convinced that morality, even religious morality, is adequate to motivate us to nurture rather than exploit nature. He lifts up Aldo Leopold as a model of someone motivated by affection. He is inspired by the efforts of Leopold and his family to restore their exhausted sand farm in Sauk County, Wisconsin: "To do this was morally right, of course, but the motive was affection. Leopold was an ecologist. He felt, we may be sure, an informed sorrow for the place in its ruin. He imagined it as it had been, as it was, and as it might be. And a profound, delighted affection radiates from every sentence he wrote about it." Berry fears that without such affection for the land, "the nation and economy conquer and destroy the country."[100]

In Berry's essay "Getting Along with Nature" he observes that Americans have a tendency to define our relationship to nature as one of opposition. This relationship of opposition has shaped the ways we think and act: "We have opposed the primeval forests of the East and the primeval prairies and deserts of the West, we have opposed man-eating beasts and crop-eating insects, sheep-eating coyotes and chicken-eating hawks. In our lawns and gardens and fields, we oppose what we call weeds." More and more people "are beginning to see that this opposition is ultimately destructive

97. Ibid., 79.
98. Ibid., 130.
99. *It All Turns on Affection*, 36.
100. Ibid., 33.

even of ourselves."[101] We are discovering that in diminishing nature we are diminishing ourselves.[102]

Instead of a way of life that diminishes us, affirms Berry, Jesus offers his followers a life-giving alternative, the abundant life (John 10:10).[103] Sadly we have responded to this offer with what Berry calls an "economics of extinction."[104] Too many of us have equated the abundant life "with a bigger car, a bigger house, a bigger bank account, and a bigger church."[105] In our relentless pursuit of the American Dream—our notion of the abundant life—we have degraded and destroyed the world and its creatures. The evidences of this destructive behavior are everywhere: "eroded, wasted, or degraded soils; damaged or destroyed ecosystems; extinction of species; whole landscapes defaced, gouged, flooded, or blown up; pollution of the whole atmosphere and of the water cycle; 'dead zones' in the coastal waters; thoughtless squandering of fossil fuels and fossil waters, of mineable minerals and ores; natural health and beauty replaced by a heartless and sickening ugliness."[106]

In Berry's view, these destructive consequences of our way of life expose the colossal failure of corporate industrialism. Berry stresses that there is an "irreconcilable contradiction between the natural world and the engineered world of industrialism." The natural world is "at the mercy of industrial processes," which are the chief cause of massive ecological damage. Berry diagnoses our disease as industrial destructiveness. The symptoms are "climate change, fossil fuel addiction, pollution, poverty, hunger, and the various forms of legitimated violence."[107]

Unlike many in the current ecological movement, Berry does not think industrial destructiveness can simply be healed by a limitless supply of cheap, clean energy. He conjectures that a limitless supply of renewable energy could even accelerate "our destruction of the world by agricultural erosion, chemical poisoning, industrial war, industrial recreation, and various forms of 'development.'" Epic feats of engineering, no matter how well funded, will not solve all of these problems. Instead, Berry maintains,

---

101. "Getting Along with Nature," in *Home Economics*, 9.

102. Ibid., 10.

103. "Limitless Reality," 49–50.

104. Ibid., 54–55.

105. Ibid., 49–50.

106. *It All Turns on Affection*, 22.

107. Ibid., 89.

"feeding a world of people year after year for a long time requires cultures of husbandry fitted to the nature of millions of unique small places—precisely the kinds of cultures that industrialism has purposely disvalued, uprooted, and destroyed."[108]

The cultures of husbandry Berry has particularly in mind are small-scale farms. He deeply appreciates British economist E. F. Schumacher's emphasis on "local production from local resources for local use."[109] In *The Unsettling of America* he levels a forceful critique of the corporate takeover of agriculture and the mechanization of farming.[110] He grieves the loss of so many family farms. For Berry and his wife, Tanya, living on their family farm in Henry County, Kentucky, for more than forty years has been a countercultural act. He views so-called technological advances in agriculture as a regression.[111] As Berry clarifies, "agriculture" does not mean "agriscience" or "agribusiness." It means "cultivation of land."[112] To engage in agriculture entails living on the land, caring for the soil, collaborating with neighboring farmers, and giving thanks for the fruits of the land. The tendency of agribusiness is to exploit the land until it wears out.

A Third Great Commandment

It is sad that we human beings have brought this ecological crisis on ourselves as well as Earth. "The earth lies polluted under its inhabitants" (Isa 24:5). At the root of this ecological crisis is a loss of love for Earth. The consequences appear more and more likely to be fatal.[113] Our way of life is not sustainable. Inspired by a spirit of domination, we human beings have exploited nature, with little regard for our own well-being, let alone the well-being of other creatures, natural systems, and future generations.

To respond to the ecological crisis we need to be transformed at the very core of our being. Our core values are at stake. Jesus identified the two

---

108. Ibid., 89–90.

109. Quoted in *Home Economics*, 186. Schumacher published *Small Is Beautiful: A Study of Economics as if People Mattered* in 1973, four years before Wendell Berry published *The Unsettling of America*.

110. Berry, *Unsettling of America*, 9–10.

111. Ibid., viii.

112. Ibid., 87.

113. In *Nature Reborn* Paul Santmire asserts that "something is wrong, perhaps fatally wrong, with the way we human beings are living on the earth" (3).

greatest commandments as love of God and love of neighbor. For centuries these two commandments have shaped our Judeo-Christian tradition. Love of God and love of neighbor have been core values. We have not been perfect in putting these values into practice. Nevertheless, they have given us a plumb line to discern where we stand in relation to God and neighbor and to guide our actions. We have reached a point, however, where the survival of life on Earth, and hence the survival of human beings, is at stake. It is no longer enough to love God and to love our neighbor—if our concept of neighbor does not include creatures other than human beings. We can no longer afford to focus on social justice and be oblivious to ecological justice. Even a noble concern for justice can lead us astray if it focuses exclusively on human-to-human relations. We need to love Earth and all of its creatures. We may need a third great commandment: "You shall love the creation." My purpose is to affirm that cultivating such love of creation is deeply rooted in our faith and is at the core of our mission as followers of Jesus. Jesus also stressed that you shall love your neighbor as you love your self. That means love of self is also a core value in our tradition. When we wake up to the urgency of the ecological crisis, it should be clear that loving our Earth home is essential to loving our self.

3

Grieving with Earth

Who Will Grieve with Earth?

In a scene from *A River Runs Through It* Norman and Paul Maclean, sons of a strict Presbyterian minister in Missoula, Montana, decide one night to go carousing with their buddies. The younger brother, Paul, comes up with the crazy idea of "borrowing" a boat and "shooting the chutes" on the Blackfoot River. In the group's drunkenness they decide to go along with Paul. But when they get to the river and see the life-threatening whitewater of the chutes, the buddies all back out. The reckless Paul will not be denied, however, and he convinces his reluctant big brother to go with him. The two brothers shoot the chutes and somehow survive, but the boat is totally trashed. When Paul and Norman come home in the early morning hours, their parents are waiting for them. Word has already gotten to them about what has happened. The father asks, "Who gave you the boat?" They answer, "We borrowed it." The father can be hard. But in this moment his demeanor softens, and in his voice is love and deep sadness: "Boys, what have you done?"

When God looks upon Earth and sees what we have done, I wonder if God says, with a voice of love and deep sadness, "My people, what have you done?" The first step in coming home to Earth is to feel remorse for what we have done to Earth. We need to grieve the destructive impact we have had on God's good creation with God and the whole Earth community.

The destructive consequences of our way of life have intensified in the last several hundred years. But the biblical testimony bears witness that destructive human behavior has been an issue from the beginnings of life on Earth. The story of Noah and the flood begins with an expression of God's regret for making humankind: "The LORD saw that the wickedness of humankind was great in the earth, and that every inclination of the thoughts of their hearts was only evil continually. And the LORD was sorry he had made humankind on the earth, and it grieved him to his heart" (Gen 6:5–6).

God's grief is intense. The Hebrew term translated as "grieve" is the same term used to refer to a woman's pain in childbearing in Genesis 3:16 and to a man's toil in farming in Genesis 3:17.[1] The Lord vows, "I will blot out from the earth the human beings I have created—people together with animals and creeping things and birds of the air, for I am sorry I made them" (Gen 6:7). Notice that other creatures also have to pay the price of human evil. It is as if God wants to start over with a creative life experiment gone wrong. As the story goes, God fulfills this vow, yet saves Noah and his family and two of every kind of living thing. When the flood subsides and Noah and his family and the living things have gone out of the ark, the Lord makes another vow: "I will never again curse the ground because of humankind, for the inclination of human heart is evil from youth; nor will I ever again destroy every living creature as I have done" (Gen 8:21). Furthermore, the Lord establishes a new covenant with Noah and all living things: "I am establishing my covenant with you and your descendants after you, and with every living creature that is with you, the birds, the domestic animals, and every animal of the earth with you" (Gen 9:9–10).

God may have vowed never again to destroy humankind and every living creature and made a new covenant with them, but human beings continued to grieve the heart of God. God must have anticipated that human beings could not be left to their own devices. Psalm 78 is a hymn in praise of God's guidance of the people of Israel from the time of Moses until the establishment of the kingdom of David in Jerusalem. The psalmist depicts the pattern that characterized the life of the people of God: sin, followed by punishment, then repentance and, finally, deliverance. Along the way the people of God were rebellious, stubborn, ungrateful, disobedient, disloyal, and unfaithful. On numerous occasions they put God to the test. At times God's anger rose against them. Other times they just made

---

1. *The New Interpreter's Study Bible*, 18.

God sad. Psalm 78:40 is telling: "How often they rebelled against him in the wilderness and grieved him in the desert!" In Isaiah 63:7 the prophet remembers God's mercy: "I will recount the gracious deeds of the LORD, the praiseworthy acts of the LORD, because of all that the LORD has done for us, and the great favor to the house of Israel that he has shown them according to his mercy, according to the abundance of his steadfast love." Then in Isaiah 63:9 the prophet clarifies it was no messenger or angel but God's presence that saved them; in God's love and pity God redeemed them. How did the people of God respond to God's graciousness? "They rebelled and grieved [God's] holy spirit" (Isa 63:10), beginning anew the pattern of sin-punishment-repentance-deliverance.

In Isaiah 51:12–23 we see another example of this characteristic pattern. The Lord promises the exiled people of God that Jerusalem will be restored. Their homes have been destroyed. Their fields have been devastated. They have lost their leaders, and no new leaders stand ready to take their place. They have endured famine, persecution, and the sword. Their children are not thriving. They have experienced the wrath of God. The people of God are wounded, staggering around like drunks, not because of too much wine, but because of their suffering. The Lord says to them, "You have forgotten the LORD, your Maker, who stretched out the heavens and laid the foundations of the earth" (Isa 51:13). The Lord wonders why they are afraid of their oppressor, a mere mortal who must die.

The Lord seeks to revitalize and encourage them: "Rouse yourself, rouse yourself! Stand up, O Jerusalem" (Isa 51:17). Then the Lord asks two haunting questions, "Who will grieve with you?" and "Who will comfort you?" (Isa 51:19) The people of Jerusalem do not have to wait long for an answer: "Thus says your Sovereign, the LORD, your God who pleads the cause of his people: See, I have taken from your hand the cup of staggering; you shall drink no more from the bowl of my wrath." The implication is that the Lord knows their suffering. God grieves with them. God seeks to comfort them. It is uplifting to hear that the Creator of the heavens and the earth grieves with them, that the Creator has not forgotten them, and that they are still God's people. God's act of sharing the grief of the people, lamenting with them, will begin the healing process. As we read in Lamentations 3:31–33, "For the Lord will not reject forever. Although he causes grief, he will have compassion according to the abundance of his steadfast love; for he does not willingly afflict or grieve anyone." Wrath is not God's final intention.

In the biblical tradition grieving or lamenting is considered a significant part of the life of the people of God. Approximately 60 of the 150 Psalms are laments. The psalmists are not afraid to share with God whatever is on their hearts and minds—even what might be considered negative feelings. Terence Fretheim explains that lament psalms do not shy away from the reality that "life is not all sweetness and light; indeed, life is often plagued by sin and evil, suffering and grief—and this for a multitude of reasons, from one's own sinfulness, to abuse inflicted by others, to the experience of injustice in many different realms."[2] The classic prayer of lament is "How long, O Lord?"[3] The psalmists often lament when they do not see God's purposes being fulfilled. They grieve and lament the difference between God's way in the world and our ways in the world. Overcoming this difference is God's purpose.

The lament psalms focus on human expressions of sorrow and grief, but the tradition of lament is extended to the land in the prophetic writings. In Isaiah 33:9a "the land mourns and languishes" in response to the treacherous and destructive behavior of the invading Assyrians, led by King Sennacherib, and to the failure of Judah's partners to protect them from Assyria. In Jeremiah 4:23–26 the prophet describes a vast ecological disaster; the whole creation is devastated: "I looked on the earth, and lo, it was laid waste and void; and to the heavens, and they had no light. I looked on the mountains, and lo, they were quaking, and all the hills moved to and fro. I looked, and lo, there was no one at all, and all the birds of the air had fled. I looked, and lo, the fruitful land was a desert, and all its cities were laid in ruins before the LORD, before his fierce anger." The Lord responds to this ecological disaster by promising not to make a full end of the land. The earth responds by mourning, and even the heavens above grow black. The whole creation is in mourning.

Jeremiah includes several other explicit references to the land mourning. In 12:4 Jeremiah wonders, "How long will the land mourn, and the grass of every field wither?" He draws the conclusion that the animals and birds are being swept away due to the wickedness of the human inhabitants of the land. In 12:10 the Lord asserts that "many shepherds have destroyed my vineyard, they have trampled down my portion, they have made my pleasant portion a desolate wilderness." The shepherds are a metaphor for the many kings who have trampled God's vineyard, Israel, and have

---

2. Fretheim, *Creation Untamed*, 139.

3. See, for example, Ps 13:1.

made the whole land desolate. "Desolate," says the Lord, "it mourns to me" (12:11a). The heart of the Lord goes out to the land, but no one else "lays it to heart" (12:11b). In Jeremiah 23:10 the prophet writes, "because of the curse the land mourns, and the pastures of the wilderness are dried up." The land is full of "adulterers" who are whoring after other gods. Even the prophets and the priests are ungodly. Such behavior curses the land. The people of God and their leaders have adopted a way of life other than the way of the Lord. In response the land mourns.

We see the same language of the mourning of the land in Hosea 4:1–3. This language is set within the context of the Lord's indictment against the human inhabitants of the land. The prophet announces, "There is no faithfulness or loyalty, and no knowledge of God in the land. Swearing, lying, and murder, and stealing and adultery break out; bloodshed follows bloodshed." In response "the earth mourns, and all who live in it languish; together with the wild animals and the birds of the air, even the fish of the sea are perishing." God's creative handiwork is being undone.[4] The languishing and death of living beings are the visible signs of the earth's mourning. The prophet hopes the visible consequences of the earth's mourning will get the attention of the people of God and wake them up to how their crimes against the Lord's creative order have made it impossible for it to operate as God intended.[5] This prophetic tradition of the earth's mourning is an invitation for us today to share in that mourning. To paraphrase Isaiah 51:19, God is asking us, in our time and place, who will grieve with Earth and all of its inhabitants?

Luke's account of Jesus's triumphal entry into Jerusalem reflects the biblical tradition of lament. As Jesus comes near and sees the city, he weeps over it, saying, "If you, even you, had only recognized on this day the things that make for peace!" (Luke 19:41–42) When the risen Jesus looks out over our Earth home and sees what we have done to it and hears Earth and its inhabitants grieving, surely Jesus must be weeping, saying, "If you, even you, had only recognized the things that make for peace with the whole

---

4. In "Therefore the Earth Mourns" Melissa Tubbs Loya asserts that the prophet bears witness to the undoing of creation (60). Earth responds by mourning. Loya seeks to show, however, that Earth is not simply a mourning victim, but also an active agent. The action of Earth "sets in motion all other actions described in the verse. Earth's mourning, then, ultimately leads to the languishing of its inhabitants and the perishing of all creation" (57).

5. Ibid., 61.

Earth community!"[6] Jesus warns the people of Jerusalem that "the days will come upon you, when your enemies will set up ramparts around you and surround you, and hem you in on every side. They will crush you to the ground, you and your children within you" (Luke 19:43–44). The day is surely coming—if it has not already arrived—when we humans of the twenty-first century will wake up and realize that we have been our own worst enemy, wreaking havoc upon ourselves and the whole Earth community. How ironic and tragic that God has fulfilled God's vow not to destroy human beings and all living creatures but that now the way we human beings live threatens to destroy all life on Earth.

The lamenting of Jesus exposes the destructiveness of our human ways, yet at the same time it opens up the heart of God to us. Jesus, the Word made flesh, the one through whom all things came into being, is close to God's heart (John 1:18). Jesus's grief reveals God's grief to us. To share in Jesus's grief is to share in God's grief. It is to take God's grief to heart. Recalling Jeremiah 12:11, when the land mourns to the Lord, the Lord asserts, "The land is made desolate, but no one lays it to heart." The implication is that God has laid the desolation of the land and its grieving to heart and that God wants its human inhabitants to do the same. Surely in the face of the global ecological crisis, God's heart goes out to the grieving Earth community. Surely the Creator is grieving with Earth in its distress and wants us to join in grieving with the Earth community.

In Romans 8:22–23 the Apostle Paul writes that "the whole creation has been groaning in labor pains until now; and not only the creation, but we ourselves, who have the first fruits of the Spirit, groan inwardly while we wait for adoption, the redemption of our bodies."[7] As we grieve the loss of well-being for Earth we are also grieving the loss of our own well-being. In groaning with the Earth community we are also waking up to the negative

6. In the next chapter we will explore in more depth the biblical understanding of peace as *shalom*, which concerns the well-being of Earth and all of its inhabitants, human and nonhuman, in their relationship to God and to one another.

7. In *The Travail of Nature* H. Paul Santmire explores the "ambiguous ecological promise of Christian theology." The title of Santmire's book was inspired by the Revised Standard Version translation of Rom 8:22: "the whole creation has been groaning in travail together until now." Santmire observes that "nature has been in travail throughout most of Western history." The process of giving birth includes both pain and promise. *The Travail of Nature* was published in 1985. The jury is still out on whether a life-giving theology of nature will emerge at the heart of our Christian tradition or whether the promise of various theologies of nature will result in something akin to theological still-birth (ibid., 10–11).

consequences of our behavior toward Earth for ourselves. The well-being of the nonhuman world and the human world are intimately connected. When any inhabitant of Earth, human or nonhuman, suffers, all of the inhabitants suffer.

Our Judeo-Christian tradition has not been consistent in acknowledging the intimate connection between the well-being of human beings and the well-being of other creatures. Our hearts have been constricted by a misguided focus on our own well-being, and we have not been quick to join in grieving with Earth and all of its inhabitants. Anyone who prays in the name of the risen Jesus, the Word made flesh, cannot ignore the groaning creation. Paul stresses that the whole creation is groaning, waiting for the redemption of our bodies. Paul takes for granted that the well-being of all created bodies is a vital concern for God.

In *Rachel's Cry* Kathleen Billman and Daniel Migliore affirm a close link between the prayer of lament and the embodied life. Lament prayers in the Bible are filled with bodily actions. We lament with our whole self. Billman and Migliore express an urgent need for a "spirituality that affirms the value of the body." This need "is evident not only in harmful attitudes toward our own bodies or the bodies of our neighbors but also in destructive attitudes toward our natural environment." More so than at any previous time in the church's history, "the prayer of lament for despised and damaged bodies today must also include concern for the body of nature, ravaged by greed, exploitation, and reckless abuse."[8] Modern factory farming reflects many harmful consequences of our destructive attitudes toward nature and the bodies of our fellow creatures. Sigve Tonstad states that the most piercing wail of nature may be the "agonized squealing of pigs, turkeys, and chickens that lead the line of victims of modern factory farming in the Western world." Their wailing testifies that "the relationship between the human and nonhuman creation fractured by the Fall has in our time become unhinged and intolerable,"[9] and it reminds us how graphic and particular and painful the groaning of creation can be.

Fretheim draws a distinction between penitential psalms, which express sorrow for one's sin, and psalms of the innocent sufferer.[10] In the current ecological crisis Earth and, to a large extent, the poor are innocent sufferers. Their cry could be "How long, O Lord?" Those of us in positions

---

8. Billman and Migliore, *Rachel's Cry*, 107–9.

9. Tonstad, "Creation Groaning in Labor Pains," 147.

10. Fretheim, *Creation Untamed*, 139.

of power and privilege have much to repent of for our role in contributing to the current crisis. In Psalm 51 the psalmist prays, "Create in me a clean heart, O God." Perhaps our prayer needs to be, "Create in me a life-giving way of being, O God."

Love So Deep

God's grieving with Earth is not simply a condemnation of destructive human behavior, but also a sign of God's deep love for Earth and all of its inhabitants. We see the depth of God's love for the whole creation affirmed in Psalm 145:8–9: "The LORD is gracious and merciful, slow to anger and abounding in steadfast love. The LORD is good to all, and his compassion is over all that he has made." Less well known in the Protestant tradition is this moving affirmation of God's love for all things in The Wisdom of Solomon 11:24–26: "For you love all things that exist, and detest none of the things that you have made, for you would not have made anything if you had hated it. How would anything have endured if you had not willed it? Or how would anything not called forth by you have been preserved? You spare all things, for they are yours, O Lord, you who love the living."

Grasping the depth of God's love for Earth is crucial for followers of Jesus in responding to the ecological crisis. Wendell Berry believes "the ecological teaching of the Bible is simply inescapable: . . . If God loves the world, then how might any person of faith be excused for not loving it or justified in destroying it?"[11] God's deep love for Earth, revealed in Jesus Christ and in creation, is the firm ground on which we stand as we respond to the ecological challenges before us.

God's deep love for the world was the firm ground on which German Lutheran pastor and theologian Dietrich Bonhoeffer took his stand in his resistance to Hitler and the Nazi regime. In *Ethics*,[12] which Bonhoeffer wrote while engaged in a conspiracy to overthrow Hitler, he affirms "the central message of the New Testament is that in Christ God has loved the world and reconciled it with himself." Bonhoeffer clarifies that "this

11. Quoted in Hamilton-Poore, *Earth Gospel*, 22.

12. *Ethics* has been referred to as Bonhoeffer's "magnum opus," even though he never completed it (see Clifford J. Green's introduction to the English edition of *Ethics*, 1). His dear friend Eberhard Bethge arranged his manuscript drafts and published the book posthumously. Bonhoeffer worked on *Ethics* from 1940 to 1943, prior to his arrest and imprisonment by the Nazis on April 5, 1943. He was hung by the Nazis on April 9, 1945, just a few days before his concentration camp was liberated.

message presupposes that the world needs reconciliation with God, but cannot achieve it by itself."[13] The world Bonhoeffer speaks of is not some ideal world that we have no experience of. It is the real world, the lost and condemned world, with all its evil and shortcomings. It is precisely this "'evil world' that is reconciled in Christ to God."[14] Bonhoeffer stresses that "there is no part of the world, no matter how lost, no matter how godless, that has not been accepted by God in Jesus Christ and reconciled to God."[15] "Even the lost and condemned world," insists Bonhoeffer, "is being drawn ceaselessly into the event of Christ." Acceptance of the lost and condemned world is a "miracle of divine mercy."[16]

One marvels that Bonhoeffer's strong affirmation of God's love for the world in *Ethics* was written in the early years of World War II when Hitler and the Nazis were at the zenith of their power. During this time Bonhoeffer was banned from publication and public speaking. He was restricted in where he could live. He was dismayed and grieved by the destruction Germany was bringing upon itself and the world. He was horrified by the killing of the Jews and others deemed expendable by the Nazis. To put it bluntly, the world appeared to be going to hell. Yet despite this devastation, Bonhoeffer wrote with passion and clarity of God's love for this world. Bonhoeffer did not engage in any explicit way in what we would call ecological theology or ecological ethics. But his affirmation of the love of God for the world in the midst of the carnage of World War II and the Holocaust offers an inspiring model for the affirmation of the love of God for the world in the midst of the carnage of the current ecological crisis. Part of the challenge for Bonhoeffer and other insightful leaders in Nazi Germany was to wake people up to the destructive path Germany was going down. Part of the challenge in our time is to wake people up to the destructive ecological path we are on. But waking people up is not enough. People have to be moved in the depths of their being to change an entrenched way of life. Such motivation has to be grounded in something as deep as God's love for Earth and all of its inhabitants.

Indeed, the primary task of the church is to proclaim the miracle of God's love, "against which the world so blindly rages."[17] The scope of the

13. Bonhoeffer, *Ethics* (DBWE 6), 66.

14. Ibid., 65.

15. Ibid., 67.

16. Ibid., 66.

17. Ibid.

church's concern is the "eternal salvation of the whole world."[18] The salvation of each individual member of the community of God, human beings, and all creatures is taken into account, but never apart from the community as a whole. Followers of Jesus share a common destiny with the whole Earth community. We have nowhere to retreat from the Earth community in this life or in the life to come. We are who we are as human beings in relationship to God, other human beings, and the rest of creation. In Colossians 1:19–20 we read, "For in [Christ] the fullness of God was pleased to dwell, and through him God was pleased to reconcile to himself all things, whether on earth or in heaven, by making peace through the blood of his cross." Jesus's willingness to die on the cross reveals the depths of God's love. Being loved so deeply by God reconciles all things and incorporates us into the reconciled reality of God and the whole Earth community.

The depth of God's love for this reconciled community then frees us to engage in ethical decision-making and action without fear. Grounded in God's love, we seek to discern the will of God for this reconciled community and embody it in our daily lives. That does not mean, however, that it is obvious what the will of God is in a given context or that Christians have a corner on the will of God. Bonhoeffer points out that "the will of God may lie very deeply hidden among competing possibilities. It is also not a system of rules that are fixed from the outset, but always new and different in each different life circumstance. This is why it is necessary to discern again and again what the will of God is."[19] Knowing that we and the whole world are loved by God, we are freed and called "to actually discern what the will of God may be, what might be right in the given situation, what may please God; for one must, of course, live and act concretely. Intellect, cognitive ability, and attentive perception of the context come into lively play here."[20] We are free to employ the entire array of human abilities. He also warns against being tormented by fear of a wrong decision. Finally, we are to trust our decisions to the judgment of a gracious judge who loves us deeply.[21]

Given the urgency of the ecological crisis, it is imperative in any discernment process that we take into account all members of the community of God, human beings, and all creatures—that is, all whom God loves deeply. Nonhuman as well as human victims of ecological devastation need

18. Ibid., 73.
19. Ibid., 321.
20. Ibid., 323–24.
21. Ibid., 324.

our tears, and they also need us to act with wisdom and courage. Grieving with Earth and its inhabitants in a time of ecological crisis entails lamentation, discernment, and action. All are grounded in God's deep love for us and the whole Earth community.

Precious in God's Sight

Our capacity to grieve with Earth correlates with our capacity to see Earth and all of its creatures as God sees them. Our capacity to see may be limited in comparison with God's; nonetheless, we are created in the image of God and are capable of participating in seeing as God sees.

One of the favorite children's songs in the churches I have served has been "Jesus Loves the Little Children":

> Jesus loves the little children,
> All the children of the world.
> Red and yellow, black and white,
> They are precious in his sight.
> Jesus loves the little children of the world.[22]

This song has been critiqued for its simplistic categories, but the main point is that every child is precious in the sight of Jesus. Jesus loves the diversity of children. The message of scripture is that Earth and all of its creatures are precious in God's sight, and God loves the diversity of creatures.

Fred Bahnson asserts that most of us suffer from what could be called ecological blindness, "an inability to see the rest of the created order that Jesus has already reconciled to himself and an inability to see the harm we're causing it."[23] The only way we can overcome our ecological blindness and learn to see Earth and all its creatures as God sees them is by recovering an intimate relationship with God, other human beings, and the rest of the Earth community. Bahnson takes a cue from Muir, who said that the Lord "must anoint eyes to see, my pen cannot. One can only see by loving."[24] Experiencing God's love for us and the whole Earth community opens our eyes to see as God sees.

22. Lyrics by Clare Herbert Woolston (1856–1927); tune composed by George Frederick Root (1820–95).

23. Bahnson, "Learning to See," in Bahnson and Wirzba, *Making Peace with the Land*, 42.

24. Quoted in ibid., 59.

In the creation account in Genesis 1, when God looks at what God has created, over and over we hear the refrain "And God saw that it was good." Then, according to Genesis 1:31, after God has created human beings and is preparing to rest, "God saw everything that God had made, and indeed, it was very good." "Very" is not a strong enough translation of the Hebrew word *meodh*. A stronger translation would be "exceedingly." God saw everything God had created, and indeed it was exceedingly good—that is, God was delighted with the whole creation. God took delight in the creative process, and God was delighted with the outcome. In that moment God was like an artist stepping back and gazing at a newly finished painting or sculpture. God's delight is also like that of parents who are filled with delight as they gaze on their newborn child or as they watch their children playing happily. God's delight is like that of hikers reaching the top of a mountain and being blessed with awe-inspiring views from on high. God saw it all, and it all delighted God.

"Everything" in Genesis 1:31 means just that—everything from the largest star to the smallest grain of sand, from the king of beasts to the tiniest ant, from the tallest redwood to a blade of grass. Unlike human beings, who have a limited point of view, God takes it all in with a single gaze: "The eyes of the LORD range throughout the entire earth" (2 Chr 16:9).

Another key word in Genesis 1:31 is "indeed." "Indeed" is not a bad translation, but this New Revised Standard Version translation flattens out the meaning of the Hebrew word *hinneh*. In this case the King James Version and the Revised Standard Version provide the best translation: "behold." "Behold" is a visual word. God beheld the whole creation. It is as if God stepped back, took a look at everything God had made, and said, "Yes!"

I had a glimpse of seeing Earth's creatures as God sees them on a safari in Kruger National Park in South Africa. After the International Bonhoeffer Congress in Capetown in 1996, a group of us from the United States went on a three-day safari. Unlike a zoo, there the wild animals run free; and at night human beings are confined within a camp with a high fence to protect them from the animals. By day we traveled in Toyota vans to view the wildlife. One morning we went out early looking for lions. All of a sudden our driver stopped the vehicle, clapped her hands together, and said with delight, "Lions in the road!" The lions did not pay much attention to us. We noticed that a number of young lions in the grassland by the road were engaged in stalking impalas. One young lion started chasing too soon, and the hunt was a failure. But then we watched with delight as one of the young lions hid himself in the grass. As another young, unsuspecting lion neared, the hidden lion sprung up to pounce on him. Then they rolled around and played in the grass like two kittens. Surely God was filled with delight watching them play.

That in which God delights is precious to God. God delights in Earth and all of its inhabitants; and therefore, they are precious in God's sight. To see as God sees is to delight in Earth and all creatures so fully that they become precious in our sight. The preciousness of the whole Earth community shines through in Chief Seattle's famous speech "How Can One Sell the Air?" He begins by affirming that "every part of this earth is sacred to my people. Every shining pine needle, every tender shore, every vapor in the dark woods, every clearing, and every humming insect is holy in the memory and experience of my people."[25] He responds to the offer of the "Great Chief in Washington" to buy the land with these words: "So we will consider your offer to buy our land. It will not be easy. This land is sacred to us. We take our pleasure in the woods and the dancing streams. The water that moves in the brooks is not water but the blood of our ancestors."[26] The selling price is not the issue. The problem is selling land that is sacred to them and in which they take great delight.

Learning to see Earth and all of its inhabitants as God sees them— that is, as they really are—is what I sense Bonaventure, a Franciscan, has in mind with his concept of contuition. Interpreting Bonaventure, Ilia Delio defines "contuition" as the "consciousness of God's presence together with the object of creation itself whether it be a tree, a flower or a tiny earthworm."[27] To contuit one of God's creatures is to perceive it with sharpened senses and to ponder it until the truth of it in relationship to God and the rest of creation becomes clear to us. Bonaventure considered St. Francis a master of contuition. As Fr. Pat Quinn, a Third Order Franciscan, explains, Bonaventure coined the word "contuition" to "describe how St. Francis was able to perceive and participate in God's Kingdom. According to Bonaventure, through Francis' devotion to Christ, especially his ministry to the poor, his passion, and his death and Resurrection, he came to 'contuit' God and Christ's presence diffused through every situation and all

---

25. Seattle, *How Can One Sell the Air?*, 49.

26. Ibid., 50–51.

27. Delio, *Simply Bonaventure*, 63.

creation."[28] Through St. Francis's relationship with Christ, he was enabled to see the created world and all of its inhabitants in, with, and through the eyes and heart of Jesus—that is, as God sees them. Thus, as Delio affirms, "the created world was no longer an illegible book to him; rather, every aspect of creation spoke to Francis of the love of God revealed in Jesus Christ. Francis was able to read the 'words of creation' as the book of God. Earthworms, twigs and branches, poor beggars and lepers, all spoke to him of the love of God manifested in Christ."[29] Francis recognized that all peoples and all creatures are precious in the sight of God. They all have value because they are created and loved by God. God delights in them all. To contuit all God's creatures is to delight in them, to see them as precious. That which we view as precious we are far more likely to respect and care for.

People who have learned to see as God sees will not exploit God's Earth, in which God delights. In Joseph Sittler's 1964 sermon "The Care of the Earth" he asserts that "delight is the basis of right use." He distinguishes between the *enjoyment* of things and the *uses* of things. He affirms the teaching of the Westminster Catechism that the chief end of human beings is "to glorify God and enjoy him forever!"[30] That implies that we can glorify God and enjoy God's handiwork in creation. Glorifying is not "incongruent with abounding joy."[31] For Sittler "to use a thing" is "to make it instrumental to a purpose," whereas "to enjoy a thing" is "to permit it to be what it is prior to and apart from any instrumental assessment of it." Sittler cites Thomas Aquinas: "It is the heart of sin that [human beings] use what they ought to enjoy, and enjoy what they ought to use."[32] Sittler asserts that "abuse is use without grace."[33] The ecological havoc we have unleashed upon Earth is a clear example of such abuse.

In *Last Child in the Woods* Richard Louv does not refer explicitly to "contuition." But he is on a mission to teach us to "tread more lightly on the earth" and to "expand our culture's capacity for joy," and in his view a key to fulfilling that mission is to open up our eyes and hearts to the wonders and delights of the natural world.[34] Louv grieves our loss of connection to the

28. Quinn, "Seeing the Kingdom," para. 3.

29. Delio, *Simply Bonaventure*, 63.

30. Sittler, "The Care of the Earth," in *Evocations of Grace*, 53.

31. Ibid., 55.

32 Ibid., 56.

33. Ibid., 57.

34. Louv, *Last Child in the Woods*, 286.

natural world. The urgency of his mission has increased as our connection to nature has decreased. He is especially concerned that we help children reconnect with the natural world. Crucial to re-establishing that connection is to spend time in nature, both observing it carefully and simply experiencing the joys of playing in it. Louv wants those who were blessed with delight-filled times in nature as children to take up his mission. Louv knows we are more likely to care for and respect that in which we delight.

Louv shares Janet Fout's moving account of the impact of experiences in nature on her: "I still am awed by celestial happenings like comets, eclipses, and meteor showers. And as I gaze on these heavenly wonders, I somehow connect to the countless humans or human-like others who did the same eons before my birth. The infinite cosmos and its mysteries help keep my life in perspective. More than ever, the commonplace of nature fills me with amazement—every bird feather with its one million parts. As a child, I found unfettered joy in nature and still connect with my deepest joy beside a flowing stream or beneath a canopy of stars."[35]

On the Sunday before I began writing the first draft of this chapter, I experienced some of the awe and unfettered joy referred to by Janet Fout when I hiked up Mt. Ellinor for the first time. Mt. Ellinor towers above Lake Cushman, situated in the southeast corner of Olympic National Park in the state of Washington. This hike was recommended by Ben and Lisa Flesher, who provided me a place to stay and a study nook to work on this chapter. It is not a long hike—only three miles to the summit. But it is steep—more than three thousand feet of elevation gain. I had a sense of accomplishment in reaching the top. But the highlight was the view. Clouds blocked the view down toward Lake Cushman, but the view of the Olympic Mountains to the north and west was truly awe-inspiring.

The Fleshers live on Key Peninsula. While writing in my study nook, I could turn and look out over the waters of Puget Sound. Such beautiful views are a reminder of the presence of the Creator. I am likewise reminded of God's presence while walking along the beach on the Oregon coast—and watching wave after wave roll in has a way of putting life in perspective. It humbles me and reminds me who we are in relation to God and to the whole creation. When I have taught on creation in confirmation classes, I have emphasized how amazing it is that the God who created the vast universe cares about and delights in each one of us, our small planet, and the smallest of creatures. Given how precious Earth and all of its creatures

35. Quoted in ibid., 294–95.

are in God's sight, how could God not grieve the ecological havoc we have wrought?

Nothing Can Separate Us

Grief is part of any memorial service I conduct, even those that focus on celebrating the life of the one who has died. Aside from Psalm 23, the most commonly read biblical text is Romans 8:31–39. The final two verses offer a powerful assurance of God's love for the one who has died: "For I am convinced that neither death, nor life, nor angels, nor rulers, nor things present, nor things to come, nor powers, nor height, nor depth, nor anything else in all creation, will be able to separate us from the love of God in Christ Jesus our Lord." This assurance of God's love also applies to the living who are grieving the loss of the one who has died. Paul addresses this assurance to fellow believers, but in Romans 8:21 Paul affirms that the *whole creation* "will obtain the freedom of the glory of the children of God." Thus, God will treat the whole creation precisely as God treats the people of God. Together we groan with the whole creation. Together we are loved by God. The "us" includes Earth and all of its creatures. Nothing can separate the Earth community from the love of God in Christ Jesus.

If nothing can separate Earth and its habitants from the love of God, the implication is that God is present everywhere. Indeed, Martin Luther affirmed that God is present in, with, and under the stuff of life. Luther writes, "God is substantially present everywhere, in and through all creatures, in all their parts and places, so that the world is full of God and He fills all, but without His being encompassed and surrounded by it. He is at the same time outside and above all creatures. These are all exceedingly incomprehensible matters; yet they are articles of our faith and are attended clearly and mightily in Holy Writ."[36] In Luther's view, therefore, God is fully present in the baby Jesus in Mary's lap as well as in a grain of wheat. Luther once said, "If you really examined a kernel of grain thoroughly, you would die of wonder."[37] We might add that God is fully present in the most majestic mountain and in the tiniest grain of sand on an ocean beach, in the brightest star and in the darkest depth of the sea, in the tallest redwood and in every blade of grass, in the most powerful lion and the tiniest insect.

36. Luther, *Werke* (Weimar Ausgabe), 23:134.34–23.136.36; quoted in Santmire, *Nature Reborn*, 82.

37. Luther, *Werke* (Weimar Ausgabe), 19:496; quoted in Santmire, *Nature Reborn*, 70.

In the Lutheran tradition we teach that the sacraments confirm that God is present everywhere. David Rhoads explains that "if we can be assured by Christ's word that Christ is in, with, and under such ordinary elements as grapes and grain and water, then God is indeed in *every* ordinary thing in life. That makes everything (not Sacraments, but) sacramental."[38] The finite is capable of bearing the infinite. John Hart's *Sacramental Commons* illuminates in an ecologically compelling way the reality of God being present in the ordinary things in life. Hart offers a sacramental vision of creation as a commons of divine creativity and human response in interaction with all living and nonliving creation. He identifies natural sacraments as places, events, or creatures in nature that at the same time draw people into relationship with the Spirit and with all living and nonliving creation. Earth serves as a sacramental commons, a means of grace. The "Earth commons" is "Earth as a whole, in which ecosystems are globally related and integrated."[39] One of Hart's key contributions is to affirm that Jesus Christ, the Word of God, works sacramentally not only through the church but also through creation.

A sacramental approach to reality is a relational approach to reality. Descartes taught "I think; therefore, I am." Thinking is one aspect of who we are. But the concept of the thinking self does not adequately take into account the reality of God, other human beings, or the rest of creation. It is divorced from the relational reality that we participate in. I am in relationship to God, human beings, and the creation; therefore, I am. With this relational concept of the self one can emphasize the value of each individual person or creature and of the community of God, human beings, and creatures as a whole. It also allows us to take into account the whole range of capacities of each individual self, such as feeling, willing, and sensing. The concept of the relational self will serve us well as we explore a holistic concept of peace in chapter 4.

Given the complex of relationships in which we live, we can affirm not only that nothing can separate us from God but also that nothing can separate us from other human beings and the rest of creation. It is folly to try to separate ourselves from the relational reality in which we live. Leopold sought to help us see ourselves as members of a community of interdependent parts that includes soils, waters, plants, and animals—a community that he referred to collectively as the land. Members of the

---

38. Rhoads, "Reflections on a Lutheran Theology of Creation," 18.

39. Hart, *Sacramental Commons*, xvii.

community respect every other member as well as the community itself.[40] Wendell Berry clarifies that "in a natural system whatever affects one thing ultimately affects everything. Everything in the Creation is related to everything else and dependent on everything else. The Creation is one; it is a uni-verse, a whole, the parts of which are all 'turned into one.'"[41]

Another way to speak of the interrelatedness of all things is with the concept of kinship. Kinship reflects the reality that nothing can separate us from God, other human beings, and the rest of creation. In the Christian tradition the concept of a sibling relationship has tended to emphasize our brothers and sisters in Christ. The concept of other creatures as kin has not been as prominent. One well-known exception is St. Francis, who defined the relationship of human beings to creation as a sibling relationship. He spoke not just of our kinship with other living creatures but of our kinship with brother sun and sister moon and other "nonliving" members of creation. At the heart of St. Francis's theology was Jesus Christ, the incarnate Word of God, through whom all things were created and through whom all things were reconciled to God. Given our common Creator and Reconciler, St. Francis concluded that we are all kin.[42]

The concept of kinship has been far more prominent in indigenous traditions. In *Nature's Way* Ed McGaa, Eagle Man, who was born on the Oglala Sioux reservation and is a registered member of the tribe, describes how as a child he began to think of creation as his family: "I gradually came to think of the trout and the jackrabbit as members of my extended family. In fact, *all* creatures—two-leggeds, four-leggeds, finned ones, and winged ones—become dearer to me and teach me more the more time I spend with them."[43] Viewing other creatures as extended family is more in tune with nature's way. The natural world tends to be viewed as "an endless resource to be exploited."[44] When we view other creatures as our kin, we are more likely to honor them and to live in balance with the whole Earth community.

This concept of kinship is likewise crucial in George Tinker's indigenous tradition. Tinker offers a distinct perspective in that he is a member of the Osage Nation, a professor of American Indian Cultures and Religious

40. See page 34.

41. W. Berry, *Unsettling of America*, 46.

42. For a more extensive discussion of St. Francis's concept of kinship with creation, see chapter 4 of Nothwehr, *Ecological Footprints*, 74–100.

43. McGaa, *Nature's Way*, 11.

44. Ibid., xii.

Traditions at Iliff School of Theology, and an Evangelical Lutheran pastor of Living Waters Episcopal/Lutheran Indian Ministry in Denver. In "Creation as Kin" he highlights the phrase *mitakuye oyasin*, which may be used to end every prayer or can be a prayer in itself. The usual translation is "For all my relations." "Yet like most Native symbols," explains Tinker, "*mitakuye oyasin* is polyvalent in its meaning. Certainly, one is praying for one's close kin, aunts, cousins, children, grandparents, and so on. And 'relations' can be understood as fellow tribal members or even all Indian people. At the same time, the phrase includes all human beings, all two-leggeds as relatives one of another, and the ever-expanding circle does not stop there. Every Lakota who prays this prayer knows that our relatives necessarily include the four-leggeds, the wingeds and all the living, moving things on Mother Earth."[45]

A sense of kinship extends to our place, our village, where we live—our home. Given the urgency of the ecological crisis, it is more imperative than ever that we recognize we are part of a global village—all Earth is our home. The good news of the life, death, and resurrection of Jesus and the testimony of creation[46] reveal that Earth, our home, is a place of grace, a place where God is fully present. In this place of grace we are engaged in what Wendell Berry speaks of as a "great coauthorship in which we are collaborating with God and nature in the making of ourselves and one another. From this there is no escape. We may collaborate either well or poorly, or we may refuse to collaborate, but even to refuse to collaborate is to exert an influence and to affect the quality of the product."[47] Being a farmer, Berry has a special sensitivity to how we treat the land. Abuse of the land "*cannot* brighten the human prospect. There is in fact no distinction between the fate of the land and the fate of the people. When one is abused, the other suffers. The penalties may come quickly to a farmer who destroys perennial cover on a sloping field. They *will* come sooner or later to a land-destroying civilization such as ours."[48]

45. Tinker, "Creation as Kin," 148.

46. Thomas Berry takes the Christian tradition to task for overemphasizing verbal revelation in scripture to the "neglect of the manifestation of the divine in the natural world" (*Great Work*, 75). He is also concerned that the Christian tradition has so focused on redemption processes that it has lost sight of creation processes. Followers of Jesus would do well to heed both verbal revelation and natural revelation. Both are primary. We need both books: the Book of Holy Scripture and the "Book of Creation." Redemption can never be understood apart from the context of creation.

47. W. Berry, *Home Economics*, 115.

48. W. Berry, *It All Turns on Affection*, 18.

The destiny of Earth and our destiny as human beings are intimately and integrally related. Leaving our Earth home behind is not an option. To exploit Earth is to exploit human beings, and vice versa. To eliminate earthly beauty is to diminish human existence. "We do not serve the human by blasting the mountains apart for mineral resources," remarks Thomas Berry, "for in losing the wonder and awesome qualities of the mountains we destroy an urgent dimension of our own reality."[49] We destroy our home, and in the process we also destroy ourselves.

Sharing in the Sufferings of God for Earth

One of the key themes in Bonhoeffer's *Letters and Papers from Prison* is sharing in the suffering of God. Bonhoeffer seeks a balanced approach to the theme of suffering, neither underestimating nor overestimating its significance. It is one important part of our human experience and God's experience, but not the only part. Bonhoeffer's personal experience in Nazi prison camps confirmed and deepened his theology of suffering. At the same time his understanding of suffering also shaped his experience of it and influenced decisions that led to his suffering in prison.

In Bonhoeffer's view human suffering must be understood from the standpoint of God's self-revelation in the life, death, and resurrection of Jesus Christ. In *Letters and Papers from Prison* Bonhoeffer speaks of the revelation of God as the ground of theological reflection on life and thus also on suffering.[50] In one of his last letters from prison Bonhoeffer stresses that if we are to recognize what God promises and fulfills "we must immerse ourselves again and again, for a long time and quite calmly, in Jesus's life, his sayings, actions, suffering, and dying."[51] The fundamental question followers of Jesus must ask again and again is, who is Jesus Christ for us today?[52]

In *Letters and Papers from Prison* Jesus is identified as the human being for others.[53] Jesus lived as the human beings for others. He viewed life "from below, from the perspective of the outcasts, the suspects, the maltreated, the powerless, the oppressed and the reviled, in short from the

49. T. Berry, *Great Work*, 175.
50. Bonhoeffer, *Letters and Papers from Prison* (DBWE 8), 406.
51. Ibid., 515.
52. Ibid., 362.
53. Ibid., 501.

perspective of the suffering."[54] Jesus died as the human being for others. The cross was the final, supreme act of being there for others. It was a consequence of his way of life. In a suffering world "only the suffering God can help."[55] A God who did not suffer with us would be a God who did not care about us. The resurrection of Jesus confirms that being there for others is God's way in the world. It is God's "Yes" to the life Jesus lived and to his willingness to die for others. The resurrection sends human beings back into "their life on earth in a wholly new way."[56]

The resurrection, therefore, is not about leaving Earth behind to be with the risen Jesus. The risen Jesus is found in our midst, in the midst of human suffering. Like Jesus, followers of Jesus "have to drink the cup of earthly life to the last drop, and only when they do is the Crucified and Risen One with them, and they are crucified and resurrected with Christ."[57] We identify with Jesus by sharing in his suffering for others. Jesus reveals that the sufferings of God embrace the whole of human suffering. To share in the sufferings of God is to share in the sufferings of our fellow human beings. We are to live "fully in the midst of life's tasks, questions, successes and failures, experiences, and perplexities" and to take seriously no longer our "own sufferings but rather the suffering of God in the world."[58]

For Bonhoeffer the overwhelming catastrophes he confronted were the destructive consequences of Nazi rule and the horror of the Holocaust. That was the context in which he responded to the question, who is Jesus Christ for us today? We face an impending ecological catastrophe. In responding to this question, we can still affirm that Jesus Christ is the human being for others, but "others" in our time and place has to include Earth and all of its creatures. For us today Jesus is also the human being for Earth. He suffered and died on the cross for the whole Earth community. The whole Earth community is suffering. Surely the suffering of God embraces the suffering Earth community. A God who did not grieve and suffer with the whole Earth community would be a God who did not care for all God has created and reconciled.

In the midst of an impending ecological catastrophe, sharing in the suffering of God entails sharing in the suffering of Earth and all of its

54. Ibid., 52.

55. Ibid., 479.

56. Ibid., 447.

57. Ibid., 447–48.

58. Ibid., 486.

inhabitants—that is, all our kin. Our experiences of awe and wonder and beauty in nature reveal the presence of God to us. The suffering and death of Jesus reveal that God is also fully present in our suffering and the suffering of the whole Earth community. Our experiences of the suffering of Earth and its creatures, therefore, put us in touch with the presence of God. To be attuned to nature and ecologically literate in our time and place is not just to be filled with awe and unfettered joy; we need to be fully aware that we live, as Aldo Leopold observed, "in a world of wounds."[59]

The Need for Affective Engagement

Affective engagement is critical in the move toward ecological healing. The heart as well as the head must be engaged. Conversation and prayer with our fellow human beings are vital to the healing process; but we also need to get into the woods. We need to spend time contuiting both ecological delights and ecological losses. It takes time to contuit. Affective engagement with ecological losses may entail time spent carefully observing and pondering an oil spill or a clear-cut or a polluted stream or the death of an endangered species until we see that loss as God sees it.

In early 2009 Wangari Maathai traveled with a fact-finding group to the Congo to ascertain whether the practices of a timber company there could be a model for sustainable forestry management. No doubt aware that Maathai was the founder of the Green Belt Movement and a Nobel Peace Prize winner, timber company representatives were proud of their selective cutting practice and wanted to demonstrate it to Maathai and the rest of the fact-finding group. A huge sapele tree was selected and after fifteen minutes of cutting crashed to the ground. When a timber company representative told the group that the tree was likely more than two hundred years old, Maathai had this response:

> Two hundred years! I thought. For all we knew, it might have survived for another two centuries: retaining water and anchoring soil throughout its root system, storing carbon and releasing oxygen, and providing a home for birds, numerous insects, beetles, and other species in its trunk and canopy. Certainly, the fact that it had taken saws several minutes to bring the sapele to the ground showed that it was not ready to come down, not ready to loosen

---

59. Quoted in Lasher, "Religious Humanism of Rachel Carson," 202.

its tenacious grip on the soil, and not ready to stop providing environmental services.

As I watched the tree fall, tears welled in my eyes. The timber company representative noticed that I had become emotional. "Don't worry," he said. "There are millions of other trees out there in the forest."[60]

Maathai, a trained biologist and a person of deep faith, experienced a far deeper affective engagement with the ecological loss of the felling of the tree than the timber company representative experienced. For him it was simply one of millions of trees in the forest. "What stung me the most," shares Maathai, "was the waste involved in the transformation of that two-hundred-year-old sapele." The bulk of the tree was turned into fodder for a kiln used to fire bricks for the homes of the timber company workers. At least, laments Maathai, "the timber company could have constructed their workers' houses from the lumber itself."[61]

When Wendell Berry insists that "it all turns on affection," he too is highlighting how vital affective engagement is in addressing ecological concerns. He emphasizes that the *primary* motive for good care and use of the land will always be affection, because affection engages us entirely. In Berry's estimation, Aldo Leopold and his family's informed sorrow for their exhausted Wisconsin farm is a shining example of affection for the land. Leopold imagined the land "as it had been, as it was, and as it might be. And a profound, delighted affection radiates from every sentence he wrote about it."[62]

The need for affective engagement in the process of ecological healing suggests that faith communities should explore ways of incorporating lament into corporate worship. In Cynthia Moe-Lobeda's book *Resisting Structural Evil* she asks, "Could it be that worship that empowers the people of God for social and ecological healing will include a profound lament for the ways in which our lives unwittingly endanger Earth's life-systems and vulnerable neighbors far and near?" For Moe-Lobeda this question is rhetorical. Communal lament in worship provides an opportunity to name the reality of our own suffering and the reality of the suffering we have inflicted on other human beings and the earth. Communal lament reminds us that "we can lament without drowning in despair." Communal lament in the presence of God assures us that "Sacred Power for healing this beautiful

60. Maathai, *Replenishing the Earth*, 40.

61. Ibid., 41.

62. W. Berry, *It All Turns on Affection*, 33–34.

and broken world is present with, among, and within the stuff of Earth."
God's "saving presence flows instinctively to life's broken places."[63] In communal lament we lament with God and begin to participate in the process
of social and ecological healing. We share in God's suffering for the beautiful and broken world God loves so deeply.

One of the most powerful ecologically focused religious rituals in
which I have participated is called "The River's Lament Walk." Sponsored
by EcoFaith Recovery[64] and the Wilderness Way Community,[65] it is held on
the University of Portland campus overlooking the Portland Harbor area
of the Willamette River. At seven stations along the riverside edge of the
campus, the story of the Willamette River is told as if the river is telling her
own story: "I have many parents—over 350 that have names, and countless
others that are unnamed. All these waters make me who I am. These are
some you may know: the Columbia Slough, Johnson Creek, Tryon Creek,
the Clackamas River . . ." The story of the Willamette River is both rich and
beautiful and full of pain, abuse, and devastation: "By the late 1920s (in a
mere 75 years from the new settlements), I was called an 'open sewer.' The
City Club of Portland called me 'filthy and ugly' . . . In 2000, I was desig-
nated a Superfund site in this area around you, this area called Portland
Harbor." The walk offers no quick cleanup strategy. The primary purpose
seemed to be to engage participants affectively and spiritually. According
to the leaders, "If we are to awake to the crisis at hand, if we are to engage
in the real debate raging over how to clean up the river and who will pay
for it, and if we are to discover the spiritual resources to face the challenges
right here in Portland, Oregon, the story of the Willamette River is a story
we must hear." Toward the end of the walk I remember gazing down on
Portland Harbor, and it dawned on me that my whole way of life was largely
dependent on Portland Harbor commerce that had resulted in its being de-
clared a Superfund site. In that moment I grieved deeply what we had done.

63. Moe-Lobeda, *Resisting Structural Evil*, 262.

64. EcoFaith Recovery is committed to "cultivating spiritual recovery from con-
sumerism to heal the web of life." It is directed by Pastor Robyn Hartwig of St. Andrew
Lutheran Church. See http://www.ecofaithrecovery.org/.

65. Wilderness Way Community is "relationally-focused, practice-oriented, and
rooted in the progressive Christian tradition." This emergent church community meets
on Sunday afternoons at Leaven Project/Redeemer Lutheran in Northeast Portland.
Community members share a vision of "a world where all beings are able to participate
in abundant life, where sharing and sustainability are the norm, and where poverty, violence, and oppression no longer exist." Wilderness Way is lead by Pastor Solveig Nilsen-
Goodin. See http://www.wildernesswaypdx.org/home.

4

The Things That Make for Peace

Biblical Vision of Shalom

We believe in a God who hears our heartfelt cries of grief and sorrow and indeed the distress-filled cries of the whole Earth community.[1] Again and again in the Old Testament the people cry out to God in their distress, God hears their cry, and the Lord, moved by their plight, delivers them.[2] The classic lament psalm begins with expressions of pain and grief and concludes with expressions of praise, thanks, and assurance that God has heard the psalmist's cry of sorrow.[3] Knowing that God hears our cries, we do not grieve as people who have no hope (1 Thess 4:13). The prophet Jeremiah strongly encourages the people of Israel to grieve, to weep and wail freely, because he believes such grief enables them to imagine a new beginning. Expressing grief serves as a prelude to hope.[4]

In Jeremiah 29:11 the Lord assures the people of God in exile: "For surely I know the plans that I have for you . . . plans for your welfare and not for harm, to give you a future with hope." "Welfare" is the translation of the Hebrew word *shalom*. The more common translation of *shalom* is

---

1. Cf. John Chryssavgis' sermon "The Cry of the Earth—the Cry of the Heart," 88–94, and Leonardo Boff's book *Cry of the Earth, Cry of the Poor*.

2. Brueggemann, *Peace*, 26–27.

3. See, for example, Psalm 69.

4. See the section titled "Mourning as Prelude to Hope" in Fischer, *Loving Creation*, 76–80.

"peace." God's intention for the exiles is to give them a future with hope. *Shalom*—their well-being—defines that hope. *Shalom* is God's vision of and commitment to the well-being of Earth and all of its inhabitants. Created in the image of God, we are invited to share in the fulfillment of this vision and commitment. *Shalom* means "peace," but not simply as an absence of war and violent conflict. The biblical vision of *shalom* is a rich concept of peace. *Shalom* refers to well-being of the whole person—mind, body, heart, and soul. It is well-being in all our relationships: with God, with other humans, and with Earth and all its creatures. It entails well-being in our families, neighborhoods, congregations, communities, watersheds, and nations.

Walter Brueggemann identifies *shalom* as the "central vision of world history in the Bible." In this vision of *shalom* "all of creation is one, every creature in community with every other, living in harmony and security toward the joy and well-being of every other."[5] Given the scope of this vision, we can affirm that *shalom* is the central vision of creation's history in the Bible. *Shalom* encompasses all of reality.[6] In Brueggemann's assessment *shalom* functions well as a theology of hope, a promised vision of what will be. This vision of an assured future can keep us from giving up in the face of despair or from giving in to the status quo. At the same time Brueggemann clarifies that the Bible's vision of *shalom* is not romantic.[7] Biblical writers are fully aware of how easily God's will for *shalom* can be compromised or undercut. The movement toward *shalom* is not inevitable. The well-off and the powerful, the "haves" who benefit from things as they are, can fall into the trap of viewing the status quo of injustice and exploitation of the "have-nots" as an acceptable way of life. For this reason, insists Brueggemann, the "haves" are particularly held accountable for *shalom*.[8] The "haves" do indeed seem more culpable than the "have-nots" for undercutting the move toward *shalom*. Nonetheless, in Jeremiah 6:13–14 the Lord takes everyone to task: "For from the least to the greatest of them, everyone is greedy for unjust gain; and from prophet to priest, everyone deals falsely. They have treated the wound of my people carelessly, saying, 'Shalom, shalom,' where there is no *shalom*."[9] The point is that we cannot depend on human beings to be faithful to the task of pursuing *shalom*.

5. Brueggemann, *Peace*, 13.
6. Ibid., 15.
7. Ibid., 19.
8. Ibid.
9. I have inserted *shalom* for "peace" in the NRSV translation.

What we can count on is God's fidelity to the vision of *shalom*. The psalmist's vision of *shalom* in Psalm 85 gathers together what Brueggemann refers to as "Israel's remarkable vocabulary of fidelity (steadfast love, faithfulness, righteousness, peace)." The process of enacting steadfast love, faithfulness, and righteousness and moving toward *shalom* is God's salvific work. The new order of *shalom* will be "marked by the neighborly engagement of ground and sky, heaven and earth, God and people."[10] Apart from *shalom*, social and ecological chaos or disorder would reign. When Jesus speaks of "the things that make for peace," he means anything that contributes to *shalom*.

The prophet Isaiah's vision of the peaceable kingdom provides one of the most beautiful pictures of *shalom* in the Bible:

> The wolf shall live with the lamb,
>> the leopard shall lie down with the kid,
> the calf and the lion and the fatling together,
>> and a little child shall lead them.
> The cow and the bear shall graze,
>> their young shall lie down together;
>> and the lion shall eat straw like the ox.
> The nursing child shall play over the hole of the asp,
>> and the weaned child shall put its hand
>> on the adder's den.
> They will not hurt or destroy
>> on all my holy mountain;
> for the earth will be full of the knowledge of the LORD
>> as the waters cover the sea. (Isa 11:6–9)

Shalom in the peaceable kingdom fulfills God's intention for creation. In Isaiah's vision of *shalom* full knowledge of the Lord will not be limited to head knowledge. In fact, it will fill the whole person. It will fill the whole Earth community. It will be more of a relational knowledge. Peaceful, nonviolent relationships will be the norm, not the exception. God will be at peace with human beings and all creatures, human beings will be at peace with one another and with other creatures, and all creatures will be at peace with other creatures. There can be no peace among the peoples of Earth if human beings are not at peace with Earth. There can be no peace with God

10. Brueggemann, *Peace*, 6.

if human beings are not at peace with one another and the whole Earth community. How can we be at peace with God whom we have not seen if we are not at peace with human beings and the Earth community whom we have seen?[11] In Isaiah 11:3–5 the prophet emphasizes that the peace he envisions will be a just peace. Justice and equity will reign in the peaceable kingdom—that is, God, human beings, and all creatures will be given their due.

This beautiful vision of peace on Earth in Isaiah is a compelling one; but the reality is that, at the very least, creatures need to eat to live. In the process of living we cannot avoid killing other life. "Violence" has often been used as a general description of all killing, consumption, and destruction on Earth. A distinction needs to be drawn between (1) killing, consumption, and destruction essential for the flourishing of life, and (2) exploitive killing, indulgent consumption, and wanton destruction that diminishes life. "Violence" refers to the latter. On the one hand, God abhors violence. Violence is abusive and gratuitous. It does not respect the abused. The abused have no intrinsic value in the eyes of the perpetrator of violence. Such violence is disgusting. On the other hand, necessary killing, consumption, and destruction are part of the creation in which God delights. God affirms the intrinsic value of each creature, even those sacrificed so that others may live. In one way or another, all life will be sacrificed for the sake of other life. Dying that others might live is central in the process of redemption and the process of creation. To some this sacrificial dimension is a scandal in both processes.[12] But sacrifice is essential to the flourishing of life. God does not want necessary sacrifice to lead us to disgust with self, humanity, or nature. Such sacrifice should not be conflated with gratuitous violence. Otherwise, as Pastor Stuart Holland commented to me, "the victims of violence are just 'collateral damage' of a greater good. This allows us to trivialize the bruised, the bloodied, and the broken."

Colossians 1:15–20 affirms the central role of Jesus's sacrifice on the cross in reconciling all things to God and establishing *shalom*. Jesus Christ is identified as the "firstborn of all creation" (1:15). "In him all things in heaven and on earth were created" (1:16). "In him all things hold together" (1:17). All the fullness of God was pleased—that is, delighted—to dwell in him (1:19). This passage comes to a climax in verse 20: "Through him God was pleased to reconcile to himself all things, whether on earth or in

---

11. Cf. 1 John 4:20.

12. T. Berry, *Christian Future*, 90.

heaven, by making peace through the blood of his cross." The reconciliation of all things to God and the establishment of *shalom* require a major sacrifice—Jesus sacrifices his life on the cross. If we take Colossians 1:20 seriously, Jesus sacrifices his life not just for sinful human beings but for the whole creation. There is no individual redemption apart from our relationships to God, other human beings, and the creation. Archbishop Desmond Tutu delights in Jesus's desire to embrace all creation. God's supreme work, asserts Tutu, "is to reconcile us to God and to one another and, indeed, to reconcile us to all of God's creation."[13] Our great work as human beings is to participate in God's reconciling work.

The groaning of the whole creation in Romans 8:18–25 can be interpreted as a universal longing for *shalom* and universal hope for salvation. This passage expresses Paul's vision of universal salvation that includes other creatures and embraces the whole creation. Human beings together with all creation wait for the redemption of our bodies (8:23). We do so in hope. In hope we are saved (8:24). Such a powerful vision of salvation for all God has created precludes any concept of salvation that leaves Earth and its inhabitants behind.

The book of Revelation may seem an unlikely source of support for an understanding of salvation that embraces the whole Earth community. Revelation has been a favorite of proponents of rapture theology and those who look forward to leaving Earth behind. Many Lutherans have been put off by the complicated imagery in Revelation and have simply ignored it. This is a mistake. Revelation 21 and 22, the final two chapters of the Bible, provide a compelling vision of the fullness of salvation that does not leave Earth behind but includes it.[14] In Revelation 21:1–4 John prophesies,

> Then I saw a new heaven and a new earth; for the first heaven and
> the first earth had passed away, and the sea was no more. And I
> saw the holy city, the new Jerusalem, coming down out of heaven

13. Tutu, foreword to *The Green Bible*, I-14.

14. J. Richard Middleton offers *A New Heaven and a New Earth* as a "small contribution" toward a holistic eschatology grounded in Scripture. He also explores ethical implications of such an eschatology, and he investigates "what happened to the biblical vision of the redemption of the earth in the history of Christian eschatology" (15–16). Middleton is convinced that the Bible teaches the "new heaven and new earth depicted in Revelation 21–22 as the final destiny of redeemed human beings, rather than an otherworldly life in heaven hereafter" (12). Upon receiving and reading a copy of his book, I was encouraged to discover a kindred spirit on a holistic understanding of salvation that embraces our Earth home. His in-depth study of the scriptural grounding of holistic salvation is much more than a small contribution.

from God, prepared as a bride adorned for her husband. And I
heard a loud voice from the throne saying,

"See the home of God is among mortals.
  He will dwell with them;
       they will be his peoples,
           and God himself will be with them;
       he will wipe away every tear from their eyes.
  Death will be no more;
       mourning and crying and pain will be no more,
           for the first things have passed away."

The first heaven and first earth pass away—they die. But they are resurrected in a new creation. The first line of Revelation 21 echoes Isaiah 65:17,
where the Lord announces, "I am about to create new heavens and a new
earth." Immediately in Isaiah 65:18 the Lord affirms that a joy-filled Jerusalem will be part of that new creation. God's holy city and God's people will
not be left behind. Likewise, in Revelation 21:1–4 salvation is not about
leaving Earth behind and going to heaven to be with God. A select group
of human beings will not be raptured to heaven, as we see depicted in the
Left Behind series. If there is any rapture here, it is God who is raptured to
Earth.[15]

In Revelation, John envisions that God's presence on Earth will bring
the fullness of salvation. There will be no more weeping, suffering, and
death. All things will be made new. Revelation 22:5 affirms that God, the
author of the tree of life, will provide for the healing of the nations. Salvation is a healing process. It entails the healing of mind, body, heart, and
soul; the healing of relationships between God, human beings, and all creatures; the healing of the community and the nation; and the healing of our
watersheds, ecosystems, and the whole Earth community. Salvation is not
about getting to heaven; it is about healing leading to *shalom*. It is not about
leaving anything behind but about moving all things toward *shalom*. God
initiates the process of salvation, and we are invited to participate in it. We
do not have to be anxious about getting to heaven or about our individual
salvation. We are to be free of this anxiety so that we can focus on what God
is doing here on Earth and fully participate in that work.

15. Cf. Rasmussen, "Baptized Life," 188. Barbara Rossing speaks of "rapture in reverse" (*Rapture Exposed*, esp. 141–58).

Following Jesus in Making Peace

The resurrection of Jesus affirms that God cares for us and for the whole Earth community. Our Christian hope in the resurrection does not offer us an ultimate escape route out of this life's tasks and difficulties into eternity.[16] Instead, our hope in the resurrection sends us back into the world to immerse ourselves in caring for God, human beings, and Earth. Those whose primary religious concern is their individual salvation have less incentive to care for the well-being of other human beings, let alone for the well-being of Earth. Given that God has reconciled all things in Christ, human beings participate with other creatures in a single community in Christ.

Jesus Christ for us today is the one who seeks *shalom* for this community. Seeking *shalom* with the Earth community, therefore, is not just an option for followers of Jesus; it is intended to be a way of life. We are to follow Jesus in seeking *shalom*. In Matthew 6:33 Jesus teaches his disciples, "Strive first for the kingdom of God and his righteousness, and all these things will be given to you as well." The kingdom of God is Jesus's alternative vision of a transformed Earth and thus of *shalom*. To strive first for God's kingdom is to make seeking *shalom* the focus of our life and ministry. Following Jesus toward *shalom* bears the hope of being led out of ecological exile. For those who do not recognize that we are in ecological exile, the first step in following Jesus is to wake up to the reality and urgency of the ecological crisis.

Properly understood, Jesus's vision of *shalom* should drive us back into the world. To conceive of Jesus's saving work apart from the concrete and material—the stuff of life—makes no sense. Jesus embodied *shalom* in his thoughts, words, and deeds. As his followers, we are to do the same. We do not do so in some idealized setting. Jesus actualizes his vision of *shalom* in an imperfect setting, in the midst of this life. The process of seeking *shalom* begins here and now, right where we are.

In first-century Palestine Jesus was not confronted with a global ecological crisis. He did not lay out a road map for us to follow in addressing the ecological crisis. That is why Bonhoeffer was insistent that we continually ask the question, who is Jesus Christ for us today? Bonhoeffer conceived of Jesus as the human being for others.[17] By "others" he meant other human beings. Given the horrific atrocities perpetrated against the Jews, it was crucial for Bonhoeffer to affirm that "others" included the Jews. Given

---

16. Bonhoeffer, *Letters and Papers from Prison* (DBWE 8), 447–48.

17. Ibid., 501.

the ecological atrocities we have perpetrated, it is crucial for us to extend the understanding of "others" to include Earth and other creatures in their distress. Jesus is not only the human being for other human beings but also the human being for other creatures and the created order.

Jesus may not have addressed ecological issues explicitly, but as Brian McLaren reminds us, he displayed an awareness and appreciation of God's love and care for Earth and all of its inhabitants. In a prayer of thanksgiving for "this good Earth," McLaren highlights this awareness and appreciation:

> We thank you, God, for speaking to our world through Jesus. He told us that, just as you care for sparrows, you care for us. He reminded us that you give the wildflowers their natural beauty and you wish to clothe us with beauty in a similar way. He taught us that wisdom is hidden in the growth of the smallest seed, in the turning of the seasons, in every corner of your amazing creation. He taught us to see every creature as beloved by you, God our Creator, and he called us to live with your love pulsing in our hearts. So let us learn to see and love this good Earth as Jesus did, and to care for it and enjoy it and rejoice in it, so that the Earth may indeed be filled with the glory of God as the waters cover the sea.[18]

Rejoicing in the wonders of creation, learning to see each creature as beloved by God, and recognizing the goodness of the Earth community are all crucial in seeking *shalom* with Earth and all of its creatures. Learning to see every creature as God sees them is a form of contuition.

However, not all gospel texts portray Jesus as a lover and appreciator of all creatures. The account of the Gerasene demoniac in Luke 8:26–39 shows demons begging Jesus to cast them out and send them into a herd of swine. Jesus does so, and the whole herd of swine rushes down a steep bank into the sea and perishes. The demoniac is healed. But obviously the pigs do not fare well, and the swineherds lose their livelihood. This gospel text portrays Jesus in a way that leads to some of the ecological ambiguity in the Christian tradition. Jesus's cursing of the fig tree in Mark 11:12–14 may also cultivate a measure of ecological ambiguity. We would do well to heed Brueggemann's caution about developing romanticized versions of the Bible's vision of *shalom*. For those of us for whom biblical authority is crucial, we need to dare to say a new word; the ecological crisis is that urgent. We need to speak with clarity where there has been ambiguity. Even if God's delight in and love for Earth and all of its inhabitants is deeply

18. McLaren, "Good Earth," 168.

embedded in the tradition, the tradition may not have given a clear, consistent ecological witness. The reality is the followers of Jesus have much work to do in making peace with Earth in our time and place.

Within the Lutheran tradition in the United States, Joseph Sittler stands out as a theologian who recognized early on the need for an understanding of Jesus Christ that leads to healing and renewal in our relationship to Earth. In 1954, eight years before Rachel Carson published *Silent Spring*, he wrote an essay entitled "A Theology for Earth." In this essay he affirms that human beings ought to stand alongside nature as a cherishing brother or sister. Instead, we tend to plunder what we have a responsibility to tend. Psalm 104 teaches us that "the trees and the birds, the grass and the cattle, the plump vine and wine that gladdens the hearts of [humankind] are all bound together in a bundle of grace."[19] Our gracious God wants tender care to define our relationship with Earth and all of its creatures.

In Sittler's view it is blasphemous the way human beings "strut about this hurt and threatened world as if they owned it."[20] In Jesus Christ God has revealed a very different way of being human, based not on controlling the created world but on caring for it. The power of grace revealed in Jesus Christ is needed to diagnose, judge, and heal us so that we can live as God intends in relation to nature as well in relation to God and other human beings. Jesus embodies God's will to restore the whole creation to "wholeness, joy, and lost love"[21]—namely, *shalom*. God's faithfulness becomes concrete in the body of Jesus Christ.[22] In Sittler's assessment the traditional center for Christian ethical reflection is the reality of God and God's will "as embodied in and illuminated by Jesus Christ."[23] He stresses, however, that center does not mean the entire content for ethics. Since everything is related to everything else, followers of Jesus, while holding to Jesus Christ at the center of our lives, remain open to insights from various fields as we explore our relationship with nature.

Sittler is a strong proponent of an earth-friendly interpretation of Jesus Christ.[24] In a very different theological and social context, Ivone Gebara

19. Sittler, "A Theology for Earth," in *Evocations of Grace*, 28–29.

20. Ibid., 46.

21. Ibid., 29.

22. Sittler, *Structure of Christian Ethics*, 11.

23. Sittler, *Evocations of Grace*, 180.

24. Cf. Santmire's account of an "earth-friendly" Christology in *Nature Reborn*, 41–43.

offers us a provocative, earth-friendly interpretation of Jesus. In *Longing for Running Water* she articulates her ecofeminist perspective on what it means to follow Jesus in seeking the health and dignity of suffering human beings and suffering Earth. She is leery of attempts by followers of Jesus to absolutize or eternalize their religious formulations. For Gebara, knowing is not primarily a matter of rational cognition. What defines us first and foremost as human beings is not our ability to think but our relatedness—to God, to one another, to Earth and all of its creatures, and to our selves. Knowing is first and foremost a matter of experiencing. To know is to experience.[25]

Thus, Gebara's ecofeminist perspective stresses speaking of Jesus out of our own relational experiences. That is why she begins her account of Jesus by sharing her own personal journey with Jesus. While Gebara could affirm Sittler's emphasis on of the centrality of Jesus and of the value of the body for our faith, she makes very clear that she has "neither the desire nor the ambition to build a new Christology to be discussed by professional theologians," nor does she wish to "create a new ecofeminist theological treatise on Jesus."[26] From Gebara's perspective Jesus's teachings do not provide a body of eternal truths or a political program. Instead, his proposal for universal brotherhood/sisterhood offers an "orientation to life itself, a road that needs to be continually built, to be laid out in the light of the unexpected and expected events of every day, in the light of encounters with the outcast."[27] The connection with a vision of *shalom* becomes apparent inasmuch as we recognize, as St. Francis did, our sibling relationship with all created things.

What Gebara is most interested in is dialogue with the gospel among the followers of Jesus. From her point of view Jesus has an "open, inclusive, affectionate, dialogical, and provocative centrality."[28] The gospel frees us to raise challenging questions for the gospel. Based on her encounters with afflicted neighbors and the afflicted environment in urban areas of Brazil, she raises a series of such questions:

> My question for the Christian faith, and especially for the gospel of Jesus, has to do with the growth of our ecological sensibilities and our struggle against society's patriarchal structures. My question for the gospel has to do with the devastation of the planet, the

25. Gebara, *Longing for Running Water*, 48.

26. Ibid., 174.

27. Ibid., 42.

28. Ibid., 179.

elimination of so many species, and the destruction of so many human groups, among whom the most directly affected are the poorest of the economically poor. My question for the gospel of Jesus has to do with the manner in which his "way" has been locked within a rigid dogmatic structure that is prepared to exclude those who have doubts or uncertainties and to repress freedom of thought in the name of some monolithic truth. In the final analysis, my questions have to do with the complicity of religious institutions in social injustice and the use of the gospel of Jesus to serve the interests of a privileged elite.[29]

Gebara recognizes that Jesus and the gospels do not have a great deal to say about ecological salvation.[30] But the orientation to life embodied by Jesus and witnessed to in the gospels allows us "to introduce the issue of ecological salvation."[31]

Gebara identifies three fundamental touchstones of Jesus's orientation to life. The first is a stance in favor of the poor and outcast. The second is firm resistance to oppressive powers. And the third is a lack of dogmatism. She views them as beacons for our journey as followers of Jesus.[32] Another fundamental value, the gospel value of bodily well-being, especially for the poor, showed Gebara that following Jesus "required a 'religion' that started from the body: an incarnated religion, one rooted in human flesh and in the flesh of the earth."[33] Jesus focused on the recovery of health and dignity for suffering human beings. What we are discovering in our time is that the health and dignity of human beings are intimately related to the health and dignity of all life. Thus, Gebara maintains that for the sake of human beings and the rest of life "we need to abandon a merely anthropocentric Christianity and open ourselves up to a more biocentric understanding of salvation. To Jesus' humanistic perspective, we need to add an ecological perspective."[34]

In Jesus's life and ministry he constantly pressed the boundaries of who was considered included in the scope of God's love and concern. In Luke 15:2 the Pharisees and the scribes grumble about him, saying, "This

---

29. Ibid., 175.

30. Sallie McFague's ecological model of salvation with its emphasis on the body inspires Gebara's use of this term. See especially McFague, *Body of God*, 180–82.

31. Gebara, *Longing for Running Water*, 183.

32. Ibid., 176.

33. Ibid., 177.

34. Ibid., 183.

fellow welcomes sinners and eats with them." Sinners were excluded from
the religious community. It was assumed God was against them. To eat with
someone in the time of Jesus was to communicate full acceptance of them.
By eating with people who had been excluded from the religious community Jesus was demonstrating God's love and acceptance of them. In Matthew 25:40 Jesus teaches his followers, "Inasmuch as you have done it to the
least of these, you have done it unto me." Given our emerging ecological
sensibilities, the time has come for us to extend our conception of the scope
of God's love and of the least of these among us. Since God delights in and
deeply loves all creation, and since all things have been reconciled to God
in Christ, why would the least of these not include plants and animals?
Why would we not treat them with the love and respect they are due? Why
would they not be considered our neighbors?

The parable of the Good Samaritan shows the extensiveness of God's
love by pressing the limits of who is considered a neighbor. The current
ecological crisis compels us to expand the scope of our concept of the
neighbor to include nonhuman creatures.[35] Earth and all of its creatures
are like the victim alongside the road in the parable of the Good Samaritan.
Earth is wounded. Earth is dying. The magnitude of the ecological crisis
may tempt us, like the lawyer in the parable, to seek to limit the scope of
our concern. But to ignore the suffering of the Earth community is to pass
by on the other side. We ourselves are victims in this case—even though
we often seem oblivious to our wounded condition. Our own well-being is
intimately connected to the well-being of Earth. If we ignore the well-being
of suffering Earth, then we ignore our own well-being. There are two foci in
the second greatest commandment: love of neighbor and love of self. Love
of neighbor, broadly understood, embraces the whole Earth community.
But as suggested earlier, to highlight the pressing need to care for wounded
Earth, it may be time to speak of a third great commandment: "You shall
love the creation."[36] For followers of Jesus, love of Earth needs to join love of
God and love of neighbor as the core values we live by. We are commanded
to love our neighbor as our self. This command implies that love of self is
also a core value for followers of Jesus.[37] What we are waking up to in our

35. Diane Landau maintains that in an age of climate change we need to recognize
"that the great commandment to care for the neighbor is now a global imperative—and
one that cannot be fulfilled in the absence of care of creation" ("Editors' Preface," in *Holy
Ground*, 16).

36. See chapter 2, pages 40–41.

37. One of the challenges for Gebara has been to convince the women among whom

time is that love of self compels us to love Earth. If we fail to care for the whole Earth community, we are sealing our own fate as well as the fate of all life on Earth.

No Salvation Apart from Earth

Although Dietrich Bonhoeffer was preoccupied with the struggle against Nazism in Germany and did not focus on ecological concerns in his life and writings, his vision of the community of God, human beings, and all creatures provides followers of Jesus with a firm theological foundation from which to address ecological issues. He articulates this vision in the following passage from *Ethics*:

> *Human beings are indivisible wholes, not only as individuals in both their person and work,* but *also as members of the human and created community* to which they belong. It is this indivisible whole, that is, this reality grounded and recognized in God, that the question of good has in view. "Creation" is the name of the indivisible whole according to its origin. According to its goal it is called the kingdom of God. Both are equally far from us and yet near to us, because God's creation and God's kingdom are present to us only in God's self-revelation in Jesus Christ. *To participate in the indivisible whole of God's reality is the meaning of the Christian question concerning the good.*[38]

This theological vision of the community of God, human beings, and all creation is an ecological vision of reality. This vision reveals how intimately connected God, human beings, and other creatures are in this life and will be in the life to come.

In this vision of community Bonhoeffer takes seriously the individual, but individuals can never be isolated from the human community and created community to which they belong. Bonhoeffer conceives of human beings as relational or social selves. It is an abstraction to conceive of an individual relationship to God or to seek an individual good apart from the communities to which we belong. The belief that individuals can get to heaven and leave Earth behind is also a product of abstract thinking.

---

she works to value their own well-being. The Christian emphasis on serving others and denying oneself had contributed to this tendency to devalue one's self (*Longing for Running Water*, 179).

38. Bonhoeffer, *Ethics* (DBWE 6), 53.

Salvation embraces the whole community of God, human beings, and creation.

The movement from a focus on God and humanity to a focus on God, humanity, and creation is a major paradigm shift in theological reflection. In the Christian tradition, with this paradigm shift, we are finally catching up with St. Francis and biblical writers who witnessed to God's love of the creation. As is the case with any major paradigm shift, this one is being resisted by many and outright rejected by some. Inasmuch as this shift in our thinking requires major changes in our way of life, virtually all of us who enjoy the privileges of our current lifestyle are likely to resist in some measure. What is encouraging, however, is to witness a quickening of this paradigm shift in our Christian traditions and other religious traditions, which has the potential to break down divisions that have separated us for decades and centuries. The ecological crisis has the potential to unite us. All humanity needs to wake up to the need to care for our Earth home. Our life and all life on the planet depend on it.

One prime example of this quickening is Pope Francis's recent release of his encyclical *Laudato Si': On Care for Our Common Home.*[39] *Laudato Si'* means "praise be to you." He begins by praising God for our common Earth home, which "is like a sister with whom we share our life and a beautiful mother who opens her arms to embrace us." According to Francis, our sister, Mother Earth, "now cries out to us" because we have plundered her at will.[40] The devastating consequence is that our Earth home "is beginning to look more and more like an immense pile of filth."[41] We are in need of "global ecological conversion."[42] In addressing the ecological crisis one key figure the pope turns to is St. Francis of Assisi, from whom he took his name when elected pope. St. Francis is the "example par excellence of care for the vulnerable and of an integral ecology lived out joyfully and authentically." For St. Francis "every creature was a sister united to him by bonds of affection."[43] Pope Francis appeals not just to his fellow Catholics but to all people to enter into dialogue about protecting our common Earth home

39. This encyclical was released in June 2015. It is encouraging to see the spiritual leader of the largest Christian church body in the world so strongly appealing for Catholics, the broader church community, and all people to join together in caring for our common Earth home.

40. Pope Francis, *On Care for Our Common Home*, 7.

41. Ibid., 19.

42. Ibid., 8.

43. Ibid., 12.

and shaping its future.[44] He affirms that all creatures share our ultimate destiny in the fullness of God. They are "moving forward with us and through us towards a common point of arrival, which is God, in that transcendent fullness where the risen Christ embraces and illumines all things."[45] Clearly Pope Francis does not teach that our Earth home and nonhuman creatures will be left behind. He lifts up a paradigm of salvation that embraces the whole community of God, human beings, and all God's creatures.

As might be anticipated, John Muir was one of the first in the chorus of prophetic voices exposing the negative consequences of the old paradigm of salvation. When he came upon a dead bear in Yosemite, he leveled a sharp critique of Christians' concept of a "stingy heaven" that had no room in it for their nonhuman kin: "Not content with taking all of earth, they also claim the celestial country as the only ones who possess the kinds of souls for which that imponderable empire was planned." God's charity, asserted Muir, "is broad enough for bears."[46] The old paradigm of salvation reflects our spiritual arrogance.

Wendell Berry was especially concerned that the old paradigm of salvation gives free rein to the industrial economy to dominate the earthly realm. In analyzing the history of religion in Kentucky, Berry critiques religion that divorces itself "from even the biblical concerns with economy and economic behavior, the daily 'housekeeping' by which we make our livings and lives." Speaking of practitioners of such displacing religion in Kentucky, Berry explains that "along with our eagerness to secure earthly places for ourselves—deeded boundaries that would belong to us, our heirs, and assigns forever—we brought along this juiceless and desiccating Protestantism (mostly) that deferred all sanctity and worth to Heaven. It was a strictly 'spiritual' religion that made a rule of despising the earth and earthly life. The odd result of this religion was to make our earthly life and economy strictly materialistic."[47] "Materialistic" refers here to the view that Earth and all of its inhabitants and resources are at our disposal to use and abuse as we see fit. This displacing religion identified by Berry abandons Earth to the whims of human beings. This attitude toward Earth is far different from an incarnational attitude that affirms the value of the material creation. When Sittler states that God is an "undeviating materialist," he

44. Ibid., 8 and 13.

45. Ibid., 51.

46. Quoted in Nash, *Loving Nature*, 124.

47. Berry, *It All Turns on Affection*, 70.

is lifting up God's deep love for all creation and God's affirmation of the goodness of creation.[48] Accordingly, human beings are called to love and respect Earth and all of its inhabitants. The new paradigm will not let us abandon Earth to human domination and abuse. The new paradigm provides for peace understood as *shalom*—peace that entails the well-being of the whole Earth community.

Peace with the whole Earth community is essential to peace among the peoples of Earth. In Pope John Paul II's 1990 World Day of Peace message, "Peace with God the Creator, Peace with All of Creation," he stated unequivocally that our disrespectful attitude toward nature threatens world peace. World peace is threatened, he stressed, not merely by violent conflict and injustice among peoples and nations but also by the lack of "*due respect for nature.*" We cannot continue to plunder our natural resources if we want life to thrive on Earth. We need a better understanding of "*the relationship between human activity and the whole of creation.*"[49] We are integrally related to the rest of creation. What happens in one part of our ecosystem has consequences for the other parts and for future generations. Our lack of respect is manifested in various forms of ecological pollution.

One of the saddest consequences of the old paradigm of salvation is our loss of a sense of Earth as our home. With this old paradigm, we view Earth at best as a temporary home. In *Replenishing the Earth* Wangari Maathai comments on an old American song used often for funerals in Kenya that reflects this loss: "This World Is Not My Home." The first line is, "This world is not my home, I'm just a-passing through." Maathai acknowledges that the vision of a better world beyond this one may be a source of comfort at funerals for those who have lost a loved one, but she is concerned about the attitude toward Earth such a vision cultivates. This vision of Earth not being our home can encourage the faithful to "ignore the bounty the Lord has given them on this planet. Even though they say they cannot be bothered with earthly things, they still need food, clean drinking water, and air to breathe. They are, therefore, not being honest with themselves. Surely, to be able to respond to a planet that is being destroyed and may soon not be able to sustain them, the faithful would help themselves if they were to sing: 'This world *is definitely* my home,' and 'I'm *not* just passing through.'"[50] We

48. Sittler, "A Theology for Earth," in *Evocations of Grace*, 29. See also chapter 1, page 2.

49. Pope John Paul II, "Peace with God the Creator," 1 and 5.

50. Maathai, *Replenishing the Earth*, 122–23. "This World Is Not My Home" was composed by American gospel music writer Albert Brumley.

cannot just expect other people and God to fix everything for us. We need to take responsibility for our Earth home and our lives.

Kenyan funerals are not unique in cultivating this attitude that the Earth is not our home. As a pastor since 1985 I have been with many families in the aftermath of a loved one's death and presided over many funerals and memorial services. One of the most frequent comments I hear is that at least the one who has died is in a better place. Clearly a funeral or memorial service is not the right time to make an issue out of such comments. My strategy has been to emphasize that nothing, not even death, can separate us from God's love in Christ Jesus (Rom 8:38–39). Surely, however, given the urgency of the ecological crisis, we need to join Maathai and others in challenging any paradigm of salvation that diminishes our sense of Earth as our home and diminishes our motivation to care for Earth and all of its inhabitants.

It is encouraging in our time to witness an impressive chorus of diverse voices affirming a new paradigm of salvation embracing Earth as well as humanity, though we have already seen that this new paradigm of salvation is rooted in the biblical vision of *shalom* and in key texts such as John 3:16, Romans 8:18–25, Colossians 1:15–20, and Revelation 21:1–4. Psalm 36:6 affirms, "You save humans and animals alike, O LORD." In Psalm 74:12 the psalmist speaks of God "from of old, working salvation in the earth." One implication is that salvation is an ongoing process. Repeatedly in Isaiah the Lord proclaims salvation to the ends of the earth (45:22; 49:6; 52:10; 62:11). In Isaiah 65:17 and 66:22 God's intention to make a new heaven and a new earth is first announced. Given the biblical roots of this new paradigm, perhaps it would be more accurate to assert that this paradigm is being renewed or is re-emerging in a chorus of diverse voices.

Sittler was a pioneering voice among Lutherans in the United States for a paradigm of salvation that embraces the whole creation. In his view we make a mistake when we conceive of salvation or redemption as a historical drama that leaves Earth untouched. Through Jesus Christ God was pleased to reconcile all things, whether on Earth or in heaven. Salvation embraces the whole creation. Sittler asserts that "salvation is an ecological word."[51] Salvation restores right relations that have been corrupted. More precisely, salvation is the restoration of the whole matrix of relations we call creation. Historical categories are part of the matrix, but they are not

---

51. Sittler, "Ecological Commitment as Theological Responsibility," in *Evocations of Grace*, 82.

adequate to articulate the full reality of salvation. For Sittler our paradigm of redemption/salvation must be as relational as our concept of creation. My personal salvation must embrace the salvation of everything, for as Sittler emphasizes, "I am no-thing apart from everything."[52]

Steven Bouma-Prediger offers a more encompassing paradigm of salvation than has been common in his evangelical tradition. His evangelical theology of care for the earth affirms "God's wide redemptive embrace."[53] The good news is that nothing is beyond the scope of God's salvation. Bouma-Prediger highlights five key aspects of what God's good future will look like:

1. God's good future is earthly.

2. God will dwell with us and with all our creaturely kin.

3. The separation between heaven and earth is overcome.

4. Evil and its consequences are no more.

5. We inhabit a most unusual city.[54]

He offers this description of this most unusual city:

> The holy city is precisely that—holy—for God is everywhere. There is no temple, no set-apart place, for God himself is the temple. A person has replaced a building. Thus, nothing in this city is profane; nothing is not sacred; all is for the service of God. And this city is a gardened city. In this city flows the river of life, watering (among other things) trees that line its banks. These trees, descendants of the tree of life (Gen 2), provide fruit year-round, sustenance in every season, and their leaves are a healing balm for the nations. People of all kinds stream into this city, whose gates never close and whose light never ceases. Kings and paupers, friends and enemies, nations both holy and heathen—they bring their glory and honor to the city (cf. Isa. 60).[55]

God's good future is embodied in this most unusual holy city here on Earth. God dwells in this city with all the inhabitants. All is well. God's vision of *shalom* is fulfilled. Bouma-Prediger's shorthand description of God's good future is simply "a world of shalom."[56]

---

52. Sittler, *Essays on Nature and Grace*, in *Evocations of Grace*, 179.

53. Bouma-Prediger, *For the Beauty of the Earth*, 171.

54. Ibid., 107–9.

55. Ibid., 108–9.

56. Ibid., 109.

Denis Edwards, a Catholic priest and associate professor in systematic theology at Flinders University and the Catholic Theological College of South Australia, seeks a paradigm of salvation not limited to the individual being justified before God. Edwards insists that "salvation is a bigger concept than simply the forgiveness of sins." He explains that "nonhuman creatures, and the universe itself, do not sin. Yet they will be transfigured by the saving love of God in Jesus." Earth and nonhuman creatures have suffered the consequences of human sin, and so they are in need of healing. Human salvation must be understood within the "broader ecological and cosmic framework of salvation."[57] Forgiveness is part of the saving process, but salvation embraces the whole of creation, including our "interpersonal relationships, our bodily selves, political and social systems, the Earth's biological community and God."[58] As followers of Jesus, we cannot ignore the ecological crisis, because the well-being of Earth and all of its creatures is at stake. A paradigm of salvation "based on God's action in the death and resurrection of Jesus, tells us that we have reason for hope that our actions directed toward love, justice, and care for the Earth and its creatures have meaning in terms of God's final transformation of all things in Christ."[59]

In *Christ of the Celts* J. Philip Newell clarifies that God saves us not by separating us from creation but by integrating us with all people and the whole creation. The Celtic tradition emphasized that creation was the sanctuary of God. Surely, concludes Newell, God's saving grace embraces the whole sanctuary of God.[60] Using a birth image from second-century theologian Irenaeus, Newell affirms that "life comes forth directly from the womb of God's being." The whole universe is born of God's being. According to Newell, "Irenaeus teaches a gospel that leads not into a separation from creation but into a harmony with the Heart of the universe."[61] Only a heartless God would leave behind Earth—born of God's own being—in the process of salvation. Given the oneness of the body of reality, Newell asks a series of rhetorical questions about what it means to seek healing and salvation: "How can I claim to be whole as a father if my son is suffering? How can we claim to be well as a people if other nations are in pain? How can we be healthy as a human race if the body of the earth is infected?" To offer the

57. Edwards, *Jesus the Wisdom of God*, 149.

58. Ibid., 150.

59. Ibid., 151.

60. Newell, *Christ of the Celts*, 110–11.

61. Ibid., 37.

hope of salvation apart from the rest of humanity and the rest of the Earth community "contradicts everything we know about the interrelatedness of life and well-being."[62]

Ivone Gebara lifts up a paradigm of salvation that views human beings as citizens of Earth and the cosmos and that does not diminish the value of our present life. We participate in the extraordinary process of life's evolution. Gebara emphasizes that we are creatures of the earth and the soil and thus we "feel an urgent need to rebuild [the earth], to stop harming our own body, to stop exploiting and destroying it."[63] The new heavens and the new earth "are always on the way: They were coming to be yesterday, they are coming to be today, and they will be on the way tomorrow. Heaven is not opposed to earth; it does not present itself as something superior or as the final aim of our efforts, the place in which we will at last enter into a state of divine peace and harmony."[64] This perspective values our present life, with its struggles and possibilities, and all life on Earth. Gebara observes that we can say very little about what is traditionally called life after death. What we can report, she says, is "that out of the dissolution of one living form there arise thousands of others; that one life nourishes a sequence of others; and that in the end our living is part of the process, part of the dissolution and recomposition of life."[65] Gebara acknowledges that some readers may be disappointed that she does not say more about heaven, angels, the loving embrace of the Father at the gates of paradise, and joyful reunions with loved ones. We can hope for such things, but they are something like dreams: intimations of a reality that we cannot be certain of. What we can do is live life and seek the well-being of Earth and all of its inhabitants here and now.

Sallie McFague's ecological model or paradigm of salvation, with its focus on the well-being of the body, also places emphasis on the present realities of life. Like Bonhoeffer and Gebara, McFague offers us a radical, this-worldly paradigm of salvation. Otherworldliness neglects our intimate connection to Earth. Our bodies are our bond with all of God's creatures.[66] McFague's ecological model highlights our unity with each body on the planet. It compels us to take seriously the suffering of human bodies

62. Ibid., 109.

63. Gebara, *Longing for Running Water*, 90.

64. Ibid., 161.

65. Ibid.

66. Rasmussen, *Earth Community, Earth Ethics*, 309.

and the suffering of Earth and its creatures. It keeps us from substituting otherworldly salvation for this-worldly oppression. For McFague, salvation—that is, the liberating, healing, inclusive love of God—is the *direction* of creation, and creation is the *place* of salvation. McFague wants to know where in creation salvation is at work here and now. "Creation as the place of salvation," clarifies McFague, "means that the health and well-being of all creatures and parts of creation is what salvation is all about—it is God's place and our place, the one and only place."[67]

In listening to this chorus of diverse voices affirming a paradigm of salvation embracing both humanity and Earth, a number of distinctive characteristics of this paradigm have emerged. First of all, it is universal or cosmic in scope. It is inclusive of all things created and reconciled by God in Christ. Secondly, it is ecological. It is attentive to the ecosystems that we participate in. It is also ecological in recognizing Earth as our home. Thirdly, it is communal. It views us as members or citizens of the community of God, human beings, and all God's creatures. Each member of the community is valued, as is the community as a whole. Fourthly, it is holistic. Salvation is a healing process leading to *shalom*. This healing process is concerned with the well-being of the whole person—mind, body, heart, and soul. It entails well-being in all our relationships to God, other humans, and Earth and all of its inhabitants. It leads to *shalom* in our families, neighborhoods, congregations, communities, watersheds, and ecosystems. Fifthly, it is this-worldly. For God so loved *this* world. Our focus is not on some other world apart from this world. The focus is on God's saving work in this life on Earth. Sixthly, this paradigm of salvation is radical. It gets us back to the roots of who God created and reconciled us to be as witnessed to in the two books: the book of scripture and the book of creation. The seventh characteristic of the paradigm is that it is relational. This characteristic stands out as a major emphasis in the voices affirming this Earth-embracing paradigm. Over and over again our connectedness with other creatures and the whole creation is stressed. A relational understanding of the self emphasizes both the value and the dignity of each member of the relational reality as well as of the relational reality as a whole.

There is no escape from this relational, interconnected reality in which we participate. We can either work with God or against God in seeking to move this reality toward *shalom*. Salvation is the process of moving toward *shalom*. It is a healing process—a holistic healing process. As we

67. McFague, *Body of God*, 180–82.

have already highlighted, it entails healing of mind, body, heart, and soul. It includes healing in our relationships to God, other humans, and the whole Earth community. Establishing justice with Earth and all of its inhabitants is an essential part of this healing process.

A holistic approach to healing also takes into account the role of beauty in the healing process. John Muir once said, "Everyone needs beauty as well as bread, places to play in and pray in where nature may heal body and soul alike."[68] That sheds light on why Muir was so committed to setting aside places of natural beauty such as Yosemite and why he was so passionate in his efforts to preserve the Hetch Hetchy Valley within Yosemite. Appearances count. Beauty in nature can be visual. It can also be auditory. I wrote the first draft of this chapter in a cabin near the McKenzie River. With the windows opened, I could hear the sound of the rushing waters of the river—a soothing, healing sound. Each morning I would walk along the McKenzie to the local store to pick up a newspaper. I was blessed with both the visual and auditory beauty of the river.

For Leopold it was the song of the Río Gavilán, a river in Chihuahua, Mexico, that played a healing tune: "The song of a river ordinarily means the tune that waters play on rock, root, and rapid. The Rio Gavilan has such a song. It is a pleasant music, bespeaking dancing riffles and fat rainbows laired under mossy roots of sycamore, oak, and pine." Leopold adds that "this song of the waters is audible to every ear." But he also heard other music in the hills rising up on either side of the Río Gavilán, "by no means audible to all. To hear even a few notes of it you must live here a long time, and you must know the speech of hills and rivers. Then on a still night, when the campfire is low and the Pleiades have climbed over rimrocks, sit quietly and listen for a wolf to howl, and think hard of everything you have seen and tried to understand. Then you may hear it—a vast pulsing harmony—its score inscribed on a thousand hills, its notes the lives and deaths of plants and animals, its rhythms spanning the seconds and the centuries."[69] There is beauty and healing power in this vast pulsing harmony—the heartbeat of life. Leopold laments that the song of most rivers has been "marred by the discords of misuse."[70]

68. Quoted in the editors' preface to *Holy Ground*, 11.

69. Leopold, *Sand County Almanac*, 149.

70. Ibid. In 1967, when Tom McCall became governor of Oregon, the Willamette River was a river "marred by the discords of misuse." See my brief account of McCall's efforts to lead the cleanup of the Willamette on page 5.

In Matthew 6:28–29 Jesus displays his awareness of the power of beauty in the healing process. He invites his followers to "consider the lilies of the field, how they grow; they neither toil nor spin, yet I tell you, even Solomon in all his glory was not clothed like one of these." This passage in the Sermon on the Mount addresses the issue of worrying about our lives, specifically about what we will eat and drink and what we will wear. The need is for emotional and spiritual healing. Considering the beauty of the lilies is part of the healing process Jesus encourages. In effect, he advocates contuition—that is, gazing at the lilies of the field until one sees them as God sees them. Comparing how God sees the lilies of the field to how God sees us will help us come to realize that we have nothing to worry about— God delights in us, and God cares for us.[71]

We might not anticipate that a self-professed urban ecofeminist such as Ivone Gebara would be a proponent of "salvation through beauty." By her own admission her ecofeminism "has little contact with the world of forests, with the mysteries of the jungle, with the power of rivers and waterfalls, and with the eruptions of volcanoes." Her ecofeminism is based on the experiences of her urban neighbors with limited access to green things and to clean air and water. Nonetheless, her ecofeminism is "pregnant with health: not health as we understood it in the past, but the health of a future that promises deeper communion between human beings and all living creatures." She strongly believes "beauty is important in healing people. It might be the beauty of sounds, of colors, of words, of faces, of food and drink, or of embraces."[72] Obviously, she is not advocating an aesthetic appreciation of the beauty of nature apart from a concern for the suffering of the poor and oppressed and for the suffering of the Earth community. Holistic healing will take into account both beauty and bread. We need daily beauty as well as daily bread.

Making Peace with Earth

Those who take to heart the paradigm of no salvation apart from Earth will be in the forefront of making peace with Earth. In addressing the ecological crisis the followers of Jesus have a public role to fulfill. In the Lord's Prayer we pray, "Your kingdom come. Your will be done on earth as in heaven." We need to specify more precisely our role in the process of fulfilling God's

71. Cf. 1 Pet 5:7: "Cast all your anxiety on [God], because [God] cares for you."

72. Gebara, *Longing for Running Water*, vii.

intention for *shalom* in the reconciled community of God, human beings, and all creation. What are the things that make for peace with Earth that God is calling us to do? Given a paradigm of salvation that fully embraces Earth, how are we to relate to Earth?

James Gustafson responds to the question of how human beings are to relate to nature or the earth by laying down five typologies.[73] The first is despotism. Nature is "exploited arbitrarily by humans for whatever ends they choose or perceive to be of immediate benefit to them."[74] Humans function in effect as gods. This approach is utilitarianism in the extreme, and it is characteristic of the exploitive corporate industrialism and agri-culture that Wendell Berry rails against in his writings.[75] Strip mining is a prime example of despotism run amok. Despotism also reflects the attitude that Chief Seattle and many other Native Americans perceived in the Euro-pean invasion of their homelands.

Gustafson identifies the second way as dominion. Nature is viewed as a gift from God to be used for human well-being.[76] The inspiration for this approach is a particular interpretation of Genesis 1:28, where God gives dominion to human beings "over the fish of the sea and over the birds of the air and over every living thing that moves upon the earth." This dominion approach was the prevailing mindset of many of the European immigrants, especially those with religious sensibilities. They believed they were claim-ing a gift God had given them. This mindset would also appear to under-gird the prevailing notion of property ownership. My property is a gift for me to use for my well-being and the well-being of my family, friends, and other human beings I choose to benefit.

The third approach Gustafson describes is stewardship. Human be-ings, created in the image of God, are caretakers of nature for God. God remains the owner.[77] Human beings are responsible to God for their care-taking. In Gustafson's assessment stewardship has been the preferred way of understanding our human responsibility for nature in the Judeo-Christian tradition. This approach has helped mitigate the influence of those who be-lieve God has authorized them to dominate or lord it over nature. Genesis 1:28 is interpreted as an exhortation to care for the creation, not dominate

---

73. See Gustafson's full discussion of this typology in his *Sense of the Divine*, 79–106.

74. Ibid., 79.

75. See discussion of Berry's critique in chapter 2, pages 37–40.

76. Gustafson, *Sense of the Divine*, 91.

77. Ibid., 92.

it. In many ways Aldo Leopold and Wendell Berry reflect this stewardship approach to the land.

Gustafson refers to the fourth approach as subordination. In this form human beings are in the service of other forms of life. Nature is viewed with deep reverence. Gustafson questions whether anyone actually embodies this approach in its pure form. Albert Schweitzer, with his "reverence for life" ethic, probably came closer than any other.[78] This fourth approach is also reflected in those who practice some form of nature mysticism. Some of the writings of John Muir go in that direction. Those who advocate for the intrinsic value of the natural world manifest aspects of subordination, although they do not necessarily view human beings as subordinate to nature. Human beings also have intrinsic value.

In Gustafson's typology the final way of relating to nature is participation. Gustafson acknowledges that this approach sheds the "most light on my interpretation of the place of the human between God and the natural world."[79] According to Gustafson, "Human beings participate in the patterns and processes of interdependence of life in the world."[80] God is the ultimate power who works through these processes of interdependence. As human beings we are dependent on these processes, but through our intentional participation in them we have some impact on them. These processes make human well-being and the well-being of other creatures possible but do not guarantee their well-being. "Bad things" can happen to individual humans and creatures. This participatory approach assumes that humans respect nature. It allows us to affirm the intrinsic value of human beings and nature, which implies that "we can and should intervene for the sake of humans and nature itself."[81]

A participatory approach to ecological ethics fits well with an Earth-embracing paradigm of salvation. As members of the community of God, human beings, and other creatures, we participate in the process of salvation, of moving this community toward *shalom*. Given the current ecological crisis, our specific focus is on making peace with Earth. We need to be careful not to exaggerate or to underestimate our role. As the reality of the ecological crisis attests, human beings have a significant impact, for good

78. Ibid., 97–98.
79. Ibid., 99.
80. Ibid., 103.
81. Ibid.

or for ill, on the well-being of Earth and its inhabitants. The survival of life on Earth is at stake.

In making peace with Earth the followers of Jesus have at least a two-fold task: (1) to engage in a ministry of reconciliation, and (2) to establish ecological justice. God has given us this ministry of reconciliation. In 2 Corinthians 5:17–19 Paul writes, "So if anyone is in Christ, there is a new creation: everything old has passed away; see, everything has become new! All this is from God, who reconciled us to himself through Christ, and has given us the ministry of reconciliation; that is, in Christ God was reconciling the world to himself, not counting their trespasses against them, and entrusting the message of reconciliation to us." In Jesus Christ God has established us in the reconciled reality—that is, the community—of God, human beings, and other creatures. In gratitude for being included in this community we respond by engaging in a ministry of reconciliation. One aspect of our ministry is to proclaim the good news of the reconciliation of all things with God through Christ. In Mark 16:15 Jesus commissions his disciples: "Go into all the world and proclaim the good news to the whole creation." Most ancient authorities do not include the longer ending of Mark (16:9–20); it is not present in the earliest and most dependable Greek manuscripts of the Gospel. Nonetheless, it is encouraging that someone in the early church recognized that the scope of the good news of salvation embraced the whole creation. Proclamation in word and deed of the universal scope of the good news is a primary task in the ministry of reconciliation. In relation to other creatures, caring deeds will be vital. But even with human beings, deeds often speak louder than words. The most powerful proclamation will be when our words match our deeds.

Worship rituals are a vital part of our ministry of reconciliation. In the Christian church we have tended to focus our worship on God-human and human-human relationships. We have not given adequate attention to God-creation and human-creation relationships.[82] We have a serious liturgical deficit that in many ways reflects the lack of care for Earth in our larger culture. A number of congregations and church bodies in Oregon and around the country have at least begun to give more attention to Earth and its creatures in worship. I learned that even the smallest gesture can make a difference. Several years ago a retired couple from a sister Evangelical Lutheran congregation began attending our congregation. We were a little hesitant to encourage them to keep coming. We seek to avoid luring

---

82. Rhoads, "Reflections on a Lutheran Theology of Creation," 21.

members away from sister congregations. But they kept coming, so finally I went to visit them. I asked them what had brought them to St. Andrew. I am not sure what response I expected—perhaps something they were mad about at their previous congregation. I know I did not expect what the woman told me. She said, "You prayed for other creatures in the prayers of the church." Apparently, we had included a petition for other creatures and had continued to do so from time to time. She was also aware that both pastors were actively involved in addressing ecological concerns. It turns out that this woman had a particular interest in animal rights and valued being part of a church community where care for animals was expressed in worship.

Another way we engage in a ministry of reconciliation with Earth and all of its inhabitants is to preserve wilderness areas. We need to recognize that we live in a vast wilderness, the universe, which is "*somewhat*" hospitable to us.[83] Wendell Berry strongly affirms the importance of preserving wilderness areas, even small ones in unexpected places. "Every farm should have one," he advocates. "Wildernesses can occupy corners of factory grounds and city lots—places where nature is given a free hand, where no human work is done, where people only go as guests."[84] Going to the wilderness to escape the ugliness and dangers of our daily life is an act of futility.[85] We cannot escape from our place in the interconnected reality of which we are a part. But going to a wilderness area as a guest is a small act of reconciliation. Setting aside a wilderness area, however small it may be, is an act of reconciliation. These acts of reconciliation bring healing to ourselves and to the whole Earth community.

There is no formula for engaging in a ministry of reconciliation. We have explored several acts of reconciliation in which we can engage in the regular flow of our lives. We have not yet looked at radical acts of reconciliation that may involve major sacrifices. Jesus's death on the cross is the central example of such a radical, sacrificial act of reconciliation. The depth of the ecological crisis will likely require major sacrifices in our way of life. We will look more closely at that possibility in chapter 6. In any case no one can prescribe the precise form the ministry of reconciliation will take. In the process of discerning what acts of reconciliation we are called to engage in we will need to be attentive to the matrix of relationships of which

83. Berry, *Home Economics*, 138–39.

84. Ibid., 17.

85. Cf. ibid., 18.

we are a part. We may need to experiment or use a measure of ecological imagination.

A wonderful example of ecological imagination was Wangari Maathai's proposal for people of faith to plant a tree during the Easter season as a sign of gratitude for the tree that gave its life to serve as the cross of Jesus. It was a fitting act of ecological imagination for a woman of deep faith in Jesus who led the Green Belt Movement. In a symbolic way a new tree of life replaces the tree of death. Maathai also asserts that the planting of a tree reflects a "new consciousness of the nature of the salvation that Christ offered." She cites John 3:16—for God so loved the world—to affirm that "redemption is consequential to the whole world" and not, therefore, just for a select group of human beings.[86] This creative act of reconciliation bore witness that there is no salvation apart from Earth.

A second task for followers of Jesus in making peace with Earth is to establish ecological justice. Walter Brueggemann emphasizes that justice (*mishpat*) is a "real and indispensable component of *shalom*."[87] Given a vision of peace (*shalom*) as the well-being of the whole community of God, human beings, and other creatures and the well-being of each member of the community, we need a concept of ecological justice that fits with this vision. Ecological justice reigns in the created community when the goodness of each member is affirmed, the rights of all members are respected, all members have the opportunity to thrive as God intended, and relationships are equitable.

James Martin-Schramm defines "justice" as the "social and ecological expression of love."[88] Justice must entail a special concern for the poor, a rough calculation of freedom and equality, and a passion for establishing equitable relationships. The key ethical aims of justice are (1) to relieve the worst conditions of poverty, powerlessness, exploitation, and environmental degradation, and (2) to provide equitable distribution of burdens and costs. Martin-Schramm identifies four norms of ecological justice: sustainability, sufficiency, participation, and solidarity. This ecological justice ethic focuses on human-caused problems that threaten the well-being of human and natural communities. Both human and natural communities are ethically important.[89]

86. Maathai, *Replenishing the Earth*, 132–34.

87. Brueggemann, *Peace*, 3.

88. Martin-Schramm, *Climate Justice*, 28.

89. Ibid., 26.

Martin-Schramm defines "sustainability" as the "long-range supply of sufficient resources to meet basic human needs and the preservation of intact natural communities."[90] Sustainability compels us to give consideration to the well-being of future generations and the planet as a whole. Our way of life in the present ought not to jeopardize the well-being of future generations or the well-being of the planet. Doing ecological justice requires us to develop a sustainable way of life.

The second norm is sufficiency. This norm stipulates that "all forms of life are entitled to share in the goods of creation"; they are to have their basic needs met.[91] Equitable sharing is necessary to ensure each life form receives what is sufficient to provide for their well-being. The reason humans are to share with plants and animals is that they are valued in God's eyes. God saw that everything God had made was good. This principle of sufficiency is the basis for critiquing wasteful and harmful consumption.

The third norm is participation. I have used "participation" as a general description of the role of human beings in the community of God, humans, and other creatures. Martin-Schramm uses "participation" in a narrower way here. This norm focuses on "respect for and inclusion of all forms of life in human decisions that affect their well-being."[92] The concern is for the voiceless, both human and nonhuman. Often the voices of poor and oppressed human beings are not heard when decisions that affect their own well-being are at stake. Nonhuman creatures are voiceless in decisions that affect them other than any observations we may have of their suffering.

The fourth and final norm is solidarity. Solidarity highlights the "communal nature of life in contrast to individualism" and encourages "individuals and groups to join in common cause with those who are victims of discrimination, abuse, and oppression." Solidarity challenges us to share in the plight of the powerless, to listen to the poor, and to recognize our interdependence with the rest of creation.[93]

Martin-Schramm uses these principles of ecological justice in his effort to develop a just climate policy. He stresses that our response to global climate change must take into account human rights. He is especially concerned about the impact of climate injustice on those living in poverty. In his conversations with colleagues at a consultation on climate change

90. Ibid., 28.
91. Ibid., 30.
92. Ibid., 33.
93. Ibid., 35.

convened by the Lutheran World Federation, this theme emerged: "All over the world, those who are the most affected and least able to adapt to global climate change are also those who have least contributed to the problem."[94] We face the real prospect of massive waves of climate refugees fleeing rising sea levels, drought, famine, and conflict caused by climate change.

The concern for potential climate refugees is commendable. It is clearly unjust for those who have contributed the least to the problem to be most affected by it. Their rights as human beings need to be taken into account as we seek to address global climate change. It is also crucial to take the rights of nonhuman life into account in any just climate policy. The accelerated rate of extinction of animal and plant species suggests that they are paying a heavy price for human behavior. They have done nothing to contribute to the problem of climate change. Martin-Schramm's four ecojustice principles are broad enough in scope to take the rights and well-being of nonhuman creatures into account along with humans. Unless we take into account as fully as possible the rights and well-being of all creatures, human and nonhuman, we are not going to be able to develop a just climate policy that turns us in the direction we need to go. We need to make peace with all life on Earth. We need to learn to view other creatures as our kin. This is not some nice ideal. Our radical interconnectedness with other creatures is a practical reality that we have ignored for too long. Human beings and all God's creatures are now paying the price.

The point is not to diminish the special concern for the poor and marginalized. In Pope John Paul II's 1990 World Day of Peace message he states that we will not find our way to a proper ecological balance unless we directly address "structural forms of poverty."[95] In *Affluenza* the authors observe that a disproportionate number of people in poverty live in areas contaminated by carcinogens. One of the most famous areas is Louisiana's "Cancer Alley," where petrochemical companies release a toxic mix of pollutants into the air and water.[96] Martin-Schramm notes that a key finding of the Intergovernmental Panel on Climate Change's Fourth Assessment Report is that "the impacts of global climate change will fall disproportionately on those who bear the least historical responsibility for causing the problem and have the least financial capacity to respond."[97] Environmental

94. Ibid., xi.

95. Pope John Paul II, "Peace with God the Creator," 11.

96. De Graaf et al., *Affluenza*, 86.

97. Martin-Schramm, *Climate Justice*, 121.

racism can increase the level of injustice.[98] To live in poverty and to be a person of color can be a double whammy when being victimized by environmental degradation. As Wangari Maathai affirms, "All human beings have a right to a clean and healthy environment. We all seek it, but it is often only the wealthy who have the means to create and enforce that right. Those who are poor and marginalized don't have the same options."[99]

While taking a class on community organizing, Lyndsay Moseley, who helped launch the Sierra Club's national faith partnerships initiative, became involved in a case of drinking water in a low-income community being contaminated by illegally dumped toxic chemicals. She learned that human well-being and environmental well-being are inextricably linked: "Taking part in a coalition of residents, union leaders, environmentalists, and church folks to demand clean water for the neighborhood, I discovered how citizen action can bring victory against tremendous odds. And as I saw how the fate of that Knoxville community was joined to the fate of the Earth, I began to understand God's call to care for creation is the same as God's call to love our neighbors."[100] Our neighbors are, in fact, a vital part of that creation and cannot arbitrarily be separated from it.

Thus, we do not want to pit the needs of poor and marginalized human beings over against the needs of nonhuman creatures. The realities of ecological degradation compel us to broaden the scope of our concern. *Accelerated Climate Change: Sign of Peril, Test of Faith*, a 1994 World Council of Churches publication, called for an integrated and twofold response: (1) to distinguish "luxury emissions of the rich" versus "survival emissions of the poor"; and (2) to view nature as "co-victim with the poor."[101] All God's creatures, human and nonhuman, have a right to a clean and healthy environment. No creature has a right to a clean and healthy environment at the expense of another.

In order to establish ecological justice in the whole community of God, humans, and other creatures, we need to extend natural rights to other creatures. In *Loving Nature* James Nash "recognizes the instrinsic value of all God-created being" and affirms the biotic rights of nonhuman creatures, but he does so with "plenty of trepidation and confusion." He

98. Cf. my discussion of James Cone's analysis of environmental racism in chapter 5, pages 111–12.

99. Maathai, *Replenishing the Earth*, 168.

100. Moseley, "Editors' Preface," in *Holy Ground*, 11.

101. Cited in Martin-Schramm, *Climate Justice*, 24.

highlights four troublesome problems with extending such rights. First of all, recognizing nonhuman rights, including those of microorganisms, may "trivialize the very concept of rights and diminish human rights." Second, asserting nonhuman rights "could lead to a host of absurdities." Third, recognizing nonhuman rights "creates countless complications and dilemmas in determining and balancing rights." Finally, in a number of cases it will be hopelessly impractical to show respect for nonhuman rights.[102] Nash's trepidation and confusion are understandable, but the urgency of the ecological crisis compels us to take some risks. Extending rights to nonhuman creatures (or should we say *recognizing* their rights?) could be viewed as a necessary experiment or act of ecological imagination. Nash's troublesome points suggest that we may need to keep improvising as we go. As with any paradigm shift there is some shaking out that will have to happen along the way.

We—that is, the whole community of God, humans, and other creatures—are in this together. We privileged human beings have caused tremendous degradation to Earth and its inhabitants. We have triggered so much sorrow and suffering. We have been as enemies to the Earth community. By engaging in a ministry of reconciliation and seeking to establish ecological justice, by pursuing the things that make for peace, we participate with God in healing Earth's wounds and in making God's vision of *shalom* a reality for all of Earth's inhabitants. Not one is to be left behind. Even as we now cry out to God in distress, we live in the firm hope of God's deliverance. And we look to the day when we will join together with the whole Earth community in praising God with a chorus of "*shalom*"!

---

102. Nash, *Loving Nature*, 173–74.

5

Conversion to Earth

Ecological Enlightenment Is Not Enough

The urgency of the ecological crisis has heightened the need for a great ecological awakening. Thích Nhất Hạnh compares the distress cries of Earth to ringing bells trying to wake us up from the unsustainable dream destroying our planet. "The bells of mindfulness," he writes, "are sounding. All over the Earth, we are experiencing floods, droughts, and massive wildfires. Sea ice is melting in the Arctic and hurricanes and heat waves are killing thousands. The forests are fast disappearing, the deserts are growing, species are becoming extinct every day, and yet we continue to consume, ignoring ringing bells."[1] He describes us as "sleepwalkers, not knowing what we are doing or where we are heading." We know our Earth home is in danger. We know our way of walking has a destructive impact on all of life. Yet we keep acting as if what we do each day has no bearing on the well-being of Earth. "The American dream," he asserts, "is no longer even possible for Americans."[2] It is an unsustainable way of life.

A key purpose of this chapter is to wake us up to our need for ecological repentance. We need to turn from our unsustainable way of life and take up a sustainable way of life, and we need to do it now. It is time for a major ecological conversion. The Second Great Awakening led to active involvement by many Christians in a variety of reform movements, including the

1. Nhất Hạnh, "Bells of Mindfulness," 25.
2. Ibid., 27.

effort to abolish slavery. The hope is that an ecological awakening will moti-vate followers of Jesus along with many others to engage in an urgent effort to care for Earth and all of its inhabitants. A change of ecological mindset is not enough. A major conversion of our hearts is essential.

Aldo Leopold was a catalyst for such an ecological enlightenment. His strategy was to focus on educating not condemning. According to Rob-ert Finch, Leopold was "convinced that most environmental mistakes are due, not to some inherent baseness in human nature, but to ignorance."[3] Leopold's educational efforts and especially the land ethic he puts forth in *A Sand County Almanac* were a major contribution to the conservation movement in this country. Furthermore, followers of Jesus can agree with Leopold that condemnation is not a desirable strategy in cultivating care for the earth. "Indeed, God did not send the Son into the world to condemn the world, but in order that the world might be saved through him" (John 3:17). But it is telling that what most moved fellow farmer and nature writer Wendell Berry was not Leopold's ecological knowledge or even his land ethic but the way Leopold and his family cared for an exhausted Wisconsin farm and brought it back to life.[4] For Berry it was Leopold's "experiential knowledge" rather than his "expert knowledge" that made the decisive dif-ference. Expert knowledge has "no cultural depth or complexity." It focuses on immediate, practical economic and sometimes political results. Such knowledge has its place, but it does not take into account adequately the distinction between experimental knowledge and experiential knowledge. Experience focuses on the meaning of events and thus is able to move us toward wholeness.[5]

In Berry's view, during the Enlightenment, as the Industrial Revolu-tion was revving up, a fundamental shift occurred in the relationship of humankind to the rest of creation. The "dominant minds" began to "see the human race, not as a part or a member of Creation, but as outside and opposed to it." Berry acknowledges that the Industrial Revolution was only partly responsible for this fundamental shift; but "when the wheels of the industrial revolution began to revolve, they turned against nature, which became the name for all of Creation thought to be below human-ity, as well as, incidentally, against all once thought to be above humanity. Perhaps this would have been safe enough if nature—that is, if all the rest

3. Finch, "Introduction," xx–xxi.

4. See page 38 above, and Berry, *It All Turns on Affection*, 32–33.

5. Berry, *Unsettling of America*, 168.

of Creation—had been, as proposed, passively subject to human purpose." "Of course," Berry adds, "it never has been."[6] The dominant minds of which Berry speaks lost sight of the well-being of the rest of creation and were overconfident in the power of the human mind to provide for human well-being. Dominant minds have been a major factor in leading us into the ecological mess we are in. It is a mistake to assume that dominant minds will necessarily lead us out of it.

Sittler, who was widely admired for his powerful, creative mind, also warns against a misplaced confidence in the human mind. In his retirement, the Lutheran School of Theology at Chicago provided him with an office so that even though his eyesight was limited he had a place to "brood"—we affectionately called him "Old Brooder." During my seminary days we looked forward to the times when he would come down from his office and share his broodings during chapel. We were also amazed at how many hymns he knew by heart, another sign of the power of his mind. Nonetheless, Sittler challenged the fundamental Enlightenment conviction that human happiness is attainable and is to be sought "in the strength of rational thought and action."[7] Any efforts at ecological reform have to take into account the whole person—mind, body, heart, and spirit—and the whole reconciled relational reality in which we participate with God, other humans, and the rest of creation.

Ecological enlightenment is not enough to motivate most people to engage in radical ecological reform. We do need, of course, to increase our knowledge of the ecological crisis. We need to pay attention to scientists such as James Hansen and other experts who can shed light on the problems we face and offer possible solutions. In addressing the ecological crisis, good science and sound policy are crucial. But in order to motivate people to engage in the needed reforms, the heart as well as the head must be changed.

From Dieter Hessel's perspective, what we need in the Christian community is nothing less than an ecological reformation of the church.[8] This ecological reformation will focus our attention on the imperiled Earth community. It will reorient liturgy, theology, ethics, and mission. It will embody a commitment to ecojustice. The central challenge will be to

6. Berry, *Home Economics*, 70.

7. Sittler, *Evocations of Grace*, 147.

8. Hessel, "The Church Ecologically Reformed," 185–206. Hessel's essay is in many respects a *tour de force*.

promote the rebuilding of sustainable communities. Hessel envisions the church as the body of Christ dedicated to working in human communities and natural communities to fulfill God's will.[9] According to Hessel, any adequate Christian theology will have a holistic vision of salvation that encourages "human participation in social history and the natural world as one unified reality with a destiny of *shalom*."[10] Hessel concludes with an "agenda for earth community ministry"; he lays out the "earth-community responsibilities" for churches to undertake. The agenda for earth community ministry is impressive.[11] But not even a well-designed ecological agenda or program is enough unless the heart is fully engaged and the will is reformed or redirected.

Bartholomew I, the "Green Patriarch" of the Orthodox Church, is recognized for his leadership and insight in addressing the theological, ethical, and practical issues related to the ecological crises of our time. In June 2002 he delivered the closing address for the fourth international and interreligious symposium on the Adriatic Sea. In this address he clarifies that we often speak of the environmental crisis, but the real crisis lies in the human heart.[12] The root cause of our difficulties is human selfishness and sin. "*What is asked of us*," stresses Bartholomew, "*is not greater technological skill but deeper repentance*." In his view "the root cause of our environmental sin lies in our self-centeredness and in the mistaken order of values that we inherit and accept without any critical evaluation." Bartholomew acknowledges that lectures and international conferences such as the one he was addressing may have a role to play in awakening our ecological consciences, but finally, "what is truly required is a baptism of tears."[13] A crucial aspect of that baptism of tears is naming the ecological sin of which we need to repent.

---

9. Hessel specifies eight steps toward an ecologically reformed church. See his discussion of these steps in ibid., 187–202.

10. Ibid., 205.

11. Ibid., 205–6.

12. Bartholomew I, *Cosmic Grace, Humble Prayer*, 305. In *Nature Reborn* Santmire makes a similar point: "The fatal flaw in human history is located in the human heart, not in the finitude of the earth, nor in some imagined fallenness of the earth" (44).

13. Bartholomew I, *Cosmic Grace, Humble Prayer*, 306.

Naming Our Ecological Sin

Motivating people to fully engage in major ecological reform will require a radical conversion. Followers of Jesus believe that repentance is a necessary part of the conversion process. Repentance begins with a genuine heartfelt acknowledgment of our sin. Psalm 51 is the classic psalm of repentance used on Ash Wednesday. In Psalm 51:1 the psalmist petitions God: "Have mercy on me, O God, according to your steadfast love; according to your abundant mercy blot out my transgressions." This prayer provides a pattern for ecological repentance. We do not simply attribute ecological problems to other people, but we first acknowledge how greed and violence in our own hearts have made us complicit in the ecological crisis.[14]

When it comes to ecological sin, all of us who have enjoyed the privileges of our way of life need to take the ecological log out of our own eye. We need to preach to the choir—that is, the "ecologically enlightened"—as well as to the ecologically blind. None of us is eager to make the most difficult but necessary changes in our way of life. We tend to dabble in Earth care. But the time for dabbling is past. We need to wake up to our central role in the ecological devastation that is upon us. Brian Swimme and Thomas Berry point out that our whole society is in a state of shock and denial that our Western civilization is the principal cause of the extensive ecological damage our Earth home is suffering: "We are unable to move from a conviction that as humans we are the glory and the crown of the Earth community to a realization that we are the most destructive and the most dangerous component of that community."[15]

Even an ecologically minded farmer like Wendell Berry admits that he has not been an innocent observer in the destructive consequences of strip mining on the Cumberland Plateau. Berry lives beside the Kentucky River. The river's watershed has been negatively impacted by silt and pollutants from the strip mines. The water's not safe to swim in and the fish are not safe to eat. Native black willows are gone. Erosion of the banks has worsened. "Every time I have turned on a light switch," confesses Berry, "I have given my support to the coal economy and thus abetted and implicitly consented to the desecration of my home river."[16]

14. Fischer, *Loving Creation*, 82.

15. Swimme and Berry, *Universe Story*, 254.

16. Berry, *It All Turns on Affection*, 93–94.

Leopold, another paragon of ecological enlightenment, exposes his complicity with other Forest Service officers in Arizona in the "extinguishment" of the last grizzly bear on Escudilla Mountain. This grizzly bear, known as Old Bigfoot, hibernated in a den in a rockslide high up on the mountain. When the weather warmed each spring, he would emerge from his den, descend the mountain, bash in the head of a cow, eat his fill, and then climb back up to his stomping grounds. There, comments Leopold, he "summered peaceably on marmots, conies, berries, and roots." One year a government trapper showed up and offered to slay any destructive animals. Bigfoot was mentioned. With the blessing of the Forest Service officers and other residents, the trapper went after Bigfoot. His usual methods (traps, poison, and so on) did not work. Finally he "erected a set-gun in a defile through which only the bear could pass, and waited. The last grizzly walked into the string and shot himself." The government trapper had a sense of satisfaction that "he had made Escudilla safe for cows." What he did not realize is that "he had topped the spire off an edifice a-building since the morning stars sang together." When a local rancher plowed up a dagger engraved with the name of a captain in Coronado's entourage, Leopold and his Forest Service cohorts made disparaging remarks about the Spaniards "who, in their zeal for gold and converts, had needlessly extinguished the native Indians." It never occurred to them, confesses Leopold, "that we, too, were the captains of an invasion too sure of its own righteousness."[17]

In the Pacific Northwest our most infamous ecological sin has been our failure to adequately care for our salmon populations. In "A Prayer for the Second Coming of the Salmon," David James Duncan clarifies that Pacific salmon "are not just 'canaries in a coal shaft.' They're the signature wild creature of the Northwest—a creature upon which millions of humans, fauna, and megafauna depend for their very existence. A 'modern Northwest' that cannot support salmon is unlikely to support 'modern Northwesterners' for long."[18] Efforts to save the salmon have come to a head in the battle over removing four dams on the Snake River. What terrifies Duncan is the *unwillingness* of Northwesterners to give up a mere four deadly dams (out of two hundred dams on the Columbia-Snake River Basin). He asserts that "no person, no family, no country, and no civilization in history has remained viable for long without engaging in corrective acts of self-criticism,

17. Leopold, *Sand County Almanac*, 134–37.
18. Duncan, "Prayer for the Second Coming of the Salmon," 184–85.

self-sacrifice, and restoration."[19] The viability of the Christian community also depends on our willingness to engage in such corrective acts.

The church, therefore, needs to be willing to name its own ecological sin. Unless we do so, our proclamation on care for Earth will lack integrity, and we will come across as hypocritical. But there is a second part to Matthew 7:5; taking the log out of our own eye will allow us to "see clearly to take the speck out of your neighbor's eye." In the case of ecological sin it is as if we all have logs in our eyes.

In Nazi Germany Bonhoeffer was appalled by the virtual silence of the church on the Jewish question. Atrocious, destructive Nazi policies went unchecked. In "The Church and the Jewish Question," published in April 1933, shortly after Hitler came to power, he identified three possible ways for the church to act against the state when the state is not fulfilling its responsibilities: (1) to question whether the state is fulfilling its legitimate responsibilities—that is, to name the sin; (2) to aid the victims of the actions of the state; and (3) to engage in direct political action—it may be necessary to "seize the wheel itself."[20] The third way is necessary especially when the state ignores the church's naming of the state's failure to fulfill its proper responsibility.

With our Earth home under assault, it would be appalling for the church to be silent on the ecological question. The fear of being considered hypocritical can stifle the church's willingness to speak up. But when it seems we are heading over an ecological cliff, the church needs to exercise its prophetic voice and join the chorus of those yelling "Stop!" It is not just government leaders who need to be called to account. Corporations are often some of the worst perpetrators of ecological degradation. When the churches themselves degrade the environment, they need to listen to the prophetic voices of ecologically minded people from within or without the church calling them to account.

In naming the reality of ecological sin and in our eagerness to move toward *shalom* Santmire warns us that just as we ought not to minimize the evils of "Hiroshima and Dresden, of Dachau and Buchenwald, of apartheid and killing fields," we ought not to minimize the presence of evil in the groaning in travail of the whole creation. Radical evil is an unavoidable mystery in life.[21] "The shadow of the cross," observes Santmire, "falls upon

---

19. Ibid., 197.

20. Bonhoeffer, *Berlin: 1932–1933* (DBWE 12), 365–66.

21. Santmire, *Nature Reborn*, 59.

the entire cosmos, not just on us human beings."[22] Santmire's warning is a reminder of the presence of radical evil in all of life, including the ecological crisis. The cost of resisting radical evil can be heavy, as Bonhoeffer and all who resisted the Nazis discovered. Resisting radical evil is not for the faint of heart. Those in power who benefit most from our established way of life will not give up their power and privileges easily. It is not likely, for example, that major oil companies will lead the effort to move us beyond fossil fuels. We ourselves will not be eager to give up our way of life. In the face of radical ecological evil a silent church could be viewed as a timid church or a church that does not care.

Wangari Maathai's way of naming sin and salvation is to name places where we see heaven and hell on earth. "If we can acknowledge hell in the charcoal pit in the middle of the Congo," she asserts, "so we can likewise recognize heaven in a clean, deep river full of fish and surrounded by banks lush with vegetation and wildlife; or healthy, well-nourished children eager to learn and work hard for the future; or a citizenry deeply engaged in its society and community, animated by an acknowledgment that all of the Source's handiwork is worth preserving."[23] Presumably, strip-mined mountains in the Appalachians would be a place where we see hell, and in the clear rushing waters of the Upper McKenzie River here in Oregon we could recognize heaven. Maathai also finds it helpful to use documents such as the Earth Charter[24] as a mirror to reveal the best of our sacred traditions and as an alternative to a presumed divine mandate "to do whatever we wish to the planet, because 'life' here is merely transitory and meaningless."[25]

Bartholomew I identifies our original ecological sin not as any legalistic transgression but precisely as "our refusal to accept the world as a sacrament of communion with God and neighbor." This original ecological sin has hindered our ability to fulfill our noble human vocation: "to participate in God's creative action in the world." We have given in to a "theory of development that values production over human dignity and wealth over human integrity. We see, for example, delicate ecological balances being upset by the uncontrolled destruction of animal and plant life or by a reckless

22. Ibid., 24.

23. Maathai, *Replenishing the Earth*, 75.

24. The Earth Charter, an initiative of more than six thousand international organizations, was adopted on June 29, 2000. It is an effort in ecological enlightenment and consciousness-raising. See my assessment of it in chapter 7, pages 171–72.

25. Maathai, *Replenishing the Earth*, 180.

exploitation of natural resources."[26] We are under the illusion that such development leads to human well-being. But ultimately, it will be destructive of humankind as well as the rest of creation. "The plain truth," confesses Bartholomew, "is that we have been given the opportunity to enjoy and use God's creation, but instead we have chosen to exploit and abuse it."[27] The ecological crisis is so acute that "our way of life is humanly and environmentally suicidal."[28] In an address at an environmental symposium in Santa Barbara in 1997, building on the concept of crimes against humanity, Bartholomew spoke in forceful terms of ecological crimes or crimes against the natural world:

> To commit a crime against the natural world is a sin. For human beings to cause species to become extinct and to destroy the biological diversity of God's creation; for human beings to degrade the integrity of the earth by causing changes in its climate, by stripping the earth of its natural forests, or by destroying its wetlands; for human beings to injure other human beings with disease; for human beings to contaminate the earth's waters, its land, its air, and its life, with poisonous substances—all these are sins.[29]

The process of healing begins with confessing our ecological sin, asking for forgiveness for the harm we have caused to God's creation, and praying that God will transform our minds and hearts to care for our Earth home as God intended.

One of the most destructive ecological sins is our inordinate trust in the powers of technology. According to Bonhoeffer, the problem with technology in the modern West is that it "has freed itself from every kind of service. Its essence is not service but mastery, mastery over nature. A wholly new spirit has produced it, the spirit of violent subjection of nature to thinking and experimenting human beings." The triumph of technology has been made possible by the "liberation of reason for domination over creation." The dominant minds mentioned by Wendell Berry have been unleashed, and nature has paid the price. Bonhoeffer goes so far as to say that "technology has become an end itself. It has its own soul; its symbol is the machine, the embodiment of violation and exploitation of nature."[30]

26. Bartholomew I, *Cosmic Grace, Humble Prayer*, 46.

27. Bartholomew I, "Orthodox Church and the Environmental Crisis," 33.

28. Ibid., 36.

29. Ibid., 221.

30. Bonhoeffer, *Ethics* (DBWE 6), 116–17.

A primary fruit of our inordinate trust in the powers of technology is what Wendell Berry calls the exploitive industrial economy. In the essay "Two Economies," he observes that this industrial economy "has been accompanied by an ever-increasing hurry of research and exploration, the motive of which is not 'free enterprise' or 'the spirit of free inquiry,' as industrial scientists and apologists would have us believe, but the desperation that naturally and logically accompanies gluttony."[31] He is startled by the extent to which the "industrial economy depends upon controlled explosions—in mines, in weapons, in the cylinders of engines, in the economic pattern known as 'boom and bust.'" He characterizes an explosive economy as one that "sets no limits on itself."[32] Berry calls for a conversion to the Great Economy—what Jesus referred to as the Kingdom of God. The Great Economy "conserves and protects its goods. It proposes to endure."[33] Uncontrolled consumption and cutthroat competiveness are a recipe for ecological disaster. The ideal in the Great Economy, if we intend to survive and preserve Earth and all of its inhabitants, has to be "the maximum of well-being with the minimum of consumption."[34]

Bonhoeffer did not express much hope of overcoming the violent subjection of nature and reversing the triumph of technology. Thus far he has proven to be a prophet. To be silent in the face of the "violent subjection of nature" is not a faithful or responsible option. It needs to be exposed, and the spirit of domination must be resisted. Technology has a role to play in our world, but it is idolatrous and foolish to put excessive trust in technology. Our use of technology is measured by whether it leads to *shalom* in the community of God, human beings, and all creation, a community ruled by serving, not by dominating.[35] We have been particularly inept in anticipating the destructive consequences of technology. Or worse yet, perhaps we have just not cared enough for the well-being of future generations of human beings, let alone for the well-being of our Earth home, to give up our love affair with technology. In either case, whether it is ineptitude or a lack of care, our survival and the survival of life on Earth are at risk.

---

31. Berry, *Home Economics*, 68.

32. Ibid., 69.

33. Ibid., 60.

34. Ibid., 72.

35. Cf. Bouma-Prediger, *For the Beauty of the Earth*, 64. In *Sanctorum Communio* (DBWE 1) Bonhoeffer speaks of the community of God being ruled by serving (63).

We privileged human beings need to wake up to the reality that "the world has enough for everyone's need, but not enough for everyone's greed." In the theological and ethical literature addressing ecological concerns this quotation from Gandhi is repeated almost as often as Thoreau's "In wildness is the preservation of the world"—or "salvation of the world," as those with a theological bent like to paraphrase it. Human greed has been and continues to be a major factor in the degradation of our Earth home and in making people reluctant to adopt necessary changes to our way of life. Gandhi's quotation also highlights the reality that Thích Nhất Hạhn stressed: not everyone in the world can adopt the American way of life.[36] It is not a sustainable way of life for Americans or anyone else. We do not have adequate resources, nor can Earth absorb the negative ecological consequences that would ensue.

The African Church Leaders Statement on Climate Change and Water of 2008 bluntly states, "Unless decisive action is taken immediately, climate chaos will lead to increased human suffering and social upheaval condemning millions of people to hunger, disease, misery and death. Our pursuit of 'happiness and high quality of life' need not endanger other peoples, nations, communities, species and future generations that are also entitled to survival and happiness. The earth has enough resources to satisfy everyone's need, but not enough resources for anyone's greed."[37]

Bartholomew I is candid in his assessment of the depth of sin at the root of ecological degradation: "We are faced with extremely self-centered and greedy behavior of people in relation to the natural environment. Such conduct betrays their indifference toward natural beauty and natural habitats."[38] This behavior also betrays a serious lack of awareness of how such indifference compromises the conditions for human survival as well as the conditions for the rest of life on Earth. It is not easy to turn such deep-seated behavior around. Given the urgency of the ecological crisis, it almost feels like trying to turn the Titanic at the last minute. The truth is that a privileged way of life can be very alluring. We are drawn to the glitter of it, especially when the negative consequences are not immediately visible to us. We cling to affluence for dear life, as if our survival and well-being were at stake.

36. See page 99 at beginning of this chapter.
37. Quoted in Hayhoe and Farley, *Climate for Change*, 123.
38. Bartholomew I, *Cosmic Grace, Humble Prayer*, 53.

An ugly reality of ecological degradation is that the powerful and privileged are most responsible for causing it and the poor and marginalized suffer the most devastating consequences from it. John Carr, Secretary of the Department of Social Development and World Peace of the U.S. Conference of Catholic Bishops, states that the "real 'inconvenient truth' is that those who contributed the least to climate change will be affected the most; those who face the greatest threats will likely bear the greatest burdens and have the least capacity to cope or escape."[39] This truth applies to poor and marginalized individuals as well to poor and marginalized nations. It helps explain why "developing nations" would want "developed nations" to shoulder greater burden for greenhouse gas mitigation. The developed nations have benefited the most from these emissions and are the primary polluters. The developing nations have tended to suffer the worst of the ecological consequences. They should not have to shoulder an unfair, disproportionate burden.

This truth mentioned by John Carr is not simply an inconvenient truth. It is sin, a collective sin. All but the poor and marginalized in this country have reaped the benefits of this unbalanced situation. We are participants in this collective sin. Ivone Gebara labels this unbalanced situation as evil. Human evil, she asserts, is the "millennial thirst for individual power and our millennial hunger to eat more and more while preventing others from consuming their rightful share." Human evil is the "excessive desire to take possession of life and make it our own. It is the appropriation of goods—and also of other persons, whom they regard to be of secondary importance—by individuals and groups, the self-appointed proprietors of the earth."[40] Our want and greed trump the basic needs of the poor and marginalized and the well-being of Earth. This is, of course, a very short-sighted way of living. Consumed by our greed, we fail to grasp how our own well-being is compromised by our insatiable desires. We have this deep-seated human tendency to seek pleasure and well-being at the expense of other human beings and creatures without recognizing that we are all in this together.[41]

---

39. Quoted Hayhoe and Farley, *Climate for Change*, 123.

40. Gebara, *Longing for Running Water*, 168.

41. I am a fly fisherman. Even the most conscientious fly fisherman, who uses barbless hooks and practices catch-and-release, who thinks rainbow trout are the most beautiful creatures on Earth, still seeks pleasure at the expense of another creature. I have yet to catch a fish that did not fight being caught.

This unbalanced situation becomes apparent in a dramatic way when the full costs of war, including ecological costs, are counted. In war as in everyday life, the poor and marginalized, Earth and its creatures tend to bear the brunt of the damage. Usually, in calculating the costs of war, we only count the dead. We rarely mention, observes Gebara,

> the destruction of the environment, the death of animals, the poisoning of natural springs, and the destruction of the present and future means of survival of those who have not died. We do not mention the deaths of birds and other animals, the forests that were burned, or the flowering fields that were trampled. We do not speak of the filthy and poisoned water where once there was a beautiful lake or river.
>
> The starry sky, obscured by poisonous clouds of war, is forgotten. The air, which has been made almost unbreathable by gases used in chemical warfare, is rarely mentioned. Women who have been raped and killed, or who have cared for the wounded, go unremembered. We do not mention the interdependence of all life systems, even though it is present everywhere.[42]

War demonstrates the lengths the powerful and the privileged will go to in their efforts to have what they want and to maintain their way of life.

Environmental racism is a brazen example of the unbalanced situation that exists in our communities, our nation, and our world. James Cone defines "environmental racism" as the "unequal protection against toxic- and hazardous-waste exposure and the systematic exclusion of people from environmental decisions affecting their communities."[43] Cone maintains that blacks and the poor of all races tend to get more than their fair share of the bad and less than their fair share of the good in life. He takes to task middle-class and white environmentalists who have been skilled "in implementing the slogan 'Not In My Backyard' (NIMBY)," which has led government leaders and corporations to use poor neighborhoods as dumping grounds for toxic wastes.[44] Some black leaders have not wanted to get caught up in environmental issues and lose sight of the struggle against racism. Cone warns blacks and other poor and marginalized peoples that ecology cannot be left to middle-class and elite environmentalists. Ecology affects every aspect of our lives. "A clean, safe environment," asserts Cone,

---

42. Gebara, *Longing for Running Water,* 28.
43. Cone, "Whose Earth Is It, Anyway?" 28.
44. Ibid., 28–29.

"is a human- and civil-rights issue that affects the lives of poor blacks and other marginalized groups. We therefore must not let the fear of being distracted from racism blind us to the urgency of the ecological crisis. What good is it to eliminate racism if we are not around to enjoy a racist-free environment?"[45] Naming environmental racism for what it is—collective sin—provides an opportunity for people of all colors to fight for human rights for all and for a just and sustainable planet.

In responding to ecological sin, doing nothing is not an option. Too much is at stake for us to pass by on the other side of suffering human beings and the rest of the suffering Earth community. In Bartholomew's "Call to Action" at the first international symposium in Patmos on September 25, 1995, he highlighted these four words: "*We cannot remain idle.*"[46] When it comes to the ecological crisis, sins of omission can be as deadly as sins of commission. In Bartholomew's view even ecological harm caused by negligence constitutes a grave or mortal sin. To maintain truthfulness and integrity in our relationships to God, humanity, and the created order, we need to name environmental degradation for what it is—nothing less than sin. Once we have named it, then we need to do something about it, discerning as best we can what God is calling us to do. We dare to act knowing that God desires to make peace with Earth and all of its inhabitants, including us. We need not fear acting, with due humility, in the context of God's cosmic grace. We are part of the bundle of grace that includes God, human beings, and the whole creation.

Our focus has been on ecological sin as what we have done or left undone that abuses, degrades, or destroys Earth and its inhabitants. We have highlighted the various ways we have failed to care for the whole Earth community in the way God intends. Failing to care for Earth and all of its inhabitants is not simply a moral failure; it is blasphemous. To ignore or neglect or abuse that which God has created, delighted in, and loved is to show irreverence toward God, which is blasphemy, a sin against God.[47] We are destroying what God created and dearly loves—that is blasphemous. We are not showing reverence to God. We are disrespecting God. For Bartholomew I, the presence of God in all created beings and things implies that "*the thoughtless and abusive treatment of even the smallest material and living creation of God must be considered a mortal sin. An insult toward the*

---

45. Ibid., 29.

46. Bartholomew I, *Cosmic Grace, Humble Prayer*, 155.

47. Sittler, *Evocations of Grace*, 84.

natural creation is seen as—and in fact actually is—an unforgivable insult to the uncreated God.[48] We can be filled with gratitude that God is not done with us yet.

Metanoia: A Call to Ecological Conversion

Bartholomew I has issued a call to people of faith "to proclaim the need to change people's lifestyles and attitudes, to preach what is called in spiritual terms *metanoia* or repentance."[49] In this time of ecological crisis a call for *metanoia* can be viewed as a call to ecological conversion. What does ecological conversion entail? And what will motivate people to engage in ecological conversion?

Conversion entails leaving behind an old way of life and adopting a new way of life. One can break with a past tradition and take up a new tradition; or perhaps one has strayed from the heart of a tradition and returns to its roots; or one may reject certain elements of a tradition and arrive at a new formulation of the tradition. Conversion entails a sense of rupture and new direction, and yet the new place one arrives at feels like "home."[50]

The Protestant Reformation stressed the need for conversion. Returning to our biblical roots, the reformers issued a call to conversion through the preaching of the gospel of Jesus Christ. The conversion called for—to faith in God and love toward the neighbor—is no longer radical enough. Faith in God and love of the neighbor are central, but somehow much of the tradition lost sight of the importance of the rest of the Earth community. Our loss of love for Earth, or simply our neglect of the well-being of the whole Earth community, has contributed to the ecological mess we find ourselves in. We cannot continue in the conversion business as usual. A new conversion paradigm is needed—or perhaps it is more a matter of getting back to the roots of our tradition in a renewed way.

In the first half of the decade of the 1970s I was a high school student in Portland, Oregon. Oregon, the most unchurched state in the union, was a hotbed of the Jesus movement. On several Sunday evenings I remember going with my high school youth group from Mt. Carmel Lutheran Church to Maranatha Church. Maranatha was a central gathering point for youth involved in the Jesus movement. The focus was on developing a personal

---

48. Bartholomew I, *Cosmic Grace, Humble Prayer*, 130; italics in original.

49. Bartholomew I, "Orthodox Church and the Environmental Crisis," 40.

50. Rasmussen, "Introduction" of *Earth Habitat*, 7.

relationship with Jesus. We were encouraged to accept Jesus into our heart. Looking back, I appreciate the focus on the role of the heart in our life of faith. But I never felt comfortable with the "me and Jesus" approach. It was an inwardly focused experience. It was as if it did not matter what was going on in the rest of the world. Ironically, in the early 1970s, with Tom McCall as governor, Oregon was also a hotbed of the environmental movement.

When I first encountered Bonhoeffer's concept of *metanoia* or conversion in a "Modern Thought and Christian Consciousness" course at Pacific Lutheran University, it was a breath of fresh air. Bonhoeffer took our personal relationship with Jesus seriously. But he taught that our relationship with Jesus was not intended to turn us inward, away from the world, but outward, toward the world.

For Bonhoeffer *metanoia* was a conversion from a focus on one's self to a focus on God and other human beings. Becoming a Christian, being converted, does not mean becoming "religious in a certain way, making oneself into something or other (a sinner, penitent, or saint) according to some method or other. Instead it means being human, not a certain type of human being, but the human being Christ creates in us. It is not a religious act that makes someone a Christian, but rather sharing in God's suffering in worldly life. That is μετάνοια [*metanoia*], not thinking first of one's own needs, questions, sins, and fears but allowing oneself to be pulled into walking the path Jesus walked."[51] That path is an existence for others. The church focuses not on its own self-preservation but is open to the world. *Metanoia* results "in vicarious solidarity with the world in its need."[52] *Metanoia*, the process of conversion, leads us into an existence for others as followers of Jesus and as the church.

According to Bonhoeffer daily personal intimacy with Jesus Christ, the human being for others, is crucial to the process of conversion. By orienting ourselves daily to the image of the incarnate, crucified, and risen Jesus Christ we allow ourselves to be called to conversion.[53] In one of his

---

51. Bonhoeffer to Eberhard Bethge, July 18, 1944, in *Letters and Papers from Prison* (DBWE 8), 480.

52. De Gruchy, "Editor's Introduction to the English Edition," in ibid., 27.

53. Bonhoeffer to Ruth Roberta Stahlberg, March 23, 1940, in *Conspiracy and Imprisonment: 1940–1945* (DBWE 16), 41. In this letter Bonhoeffer explicitly mentions the image of the crucified. The image of the crucified is crucial to identifying with Christ in his sufferings. The next sentence of my discussion of Bonhoeffer's concept of conversion includes a quotation from Bonhoeffer with a reference to the life as well as the death of Jesus; and in Bonhoeffer's discussion of ethics as formation, for example, he stresses that

final letters from prison to Eberhard Bethge, Bonhoeffer asserts that we "must immerse ourselves again and again, for a long time and quite calmly, in Jesus' life, his sayings, actions, sufferings, and dying in order to recognize what God promises and fulfills."[54] In a letter from prison written to Bethge on July 20, 1944, the day after the failed assassination attempt on Hitler's life, he affirms that

> one only learns to have faith by living in the full this-worldliness of life. If one has completely renounced making something of one-self—whether it be a saint or a converted sinner or a church leader (a so-called priestly figure!), a just or an unjust person, a sick or a healthy person—then one throws oneself completely into the arms of God, and this is what I call this-worldliness: living fully in the midst of life's tasks, questions, successes and failures, experiences, and perplexities—then one takes seriously no longer one's own sufferings but rather the suffering of God in the world. Then one stays awake with Christ in Gethsemane. And I think this is faith; this is μετάνοια [*metanoia*]. And this is how one becomes a human being, a Christian. (Cf. Jer. 45!). How should one become arrogant over successes or shaken by one's failures when one shares in God's suffering in the life of this world?[55]

For Bethge this letter was the most important one from his teacher, confessing partner, and best friend; and this insight into *metanoia* as "living fully in the midst of life's tasks, questions, successes and failures, experiences, and perplexities" and "taking seriously no longer one's own sufferings but rather the suffering of God in the world" was the crucial insight.

It would be a mistake to assume that for Bonhoeffer sharing in the suffering of God in the world in an existence for others rules out a love of self. Living for others does not call for a neglect of or lack of love for the self. The second greatest commandment is this: "You shall love your neighbor as yourself." Love of neighbor presumes a love of self. Like Ivone Gebara, Bonhoeffer recognized that this commandment has two poles of love: love of neighbor and love of self.[56] How can we care for others unless we care for our self? In Bonhoeffer's letter of October 9, 1940, to Bethge, about the

---

"formation occurs only by being drawn into the form of Jesus Christ, by *being conformed to the unique form of the one who became human, was crucified, and is risen*" (*Ethics*, 93).

54. Bonhoeffer to Eberhard Bethge, August 21, 1944, in *Letters and Papers from Prison* (DBWE 8), 515.

55. Ibid., 486.

56. See Gebara, *Longing for Running Water*, 179.

time he began writing his *Ethics* and as his involvement in the conspiracy against Hitler continued to intensify, he expresses his belief that "a great deal of the exhaustion and sterility in our ranks is rooted in the lack of 'self-less self-love.' Since this topic has no place in the official Protestant ethic, we arrogantly disregard it and become work obsessed, to the detriment of the individual and of the whole. It belongs, however, to that humanum for which we are redeemed."[57] Bonhoeffer implies, therefore, that love of self is a core value of the reconciled reality of God and the world in Jesus Christ in which we participate as human beings. Bonhoeffer alludes to "selfless self-love" once again in a letter to Bethge dated May 6, 1944. He asserts that "too much altruism is oppressive and demands too much." Love of self "can be less self-seeking, less demanding."[58] Seeking to be a selfless person can be another example of trying to make something of oneself. Furthermore, each of us is a creature of God in whom God delights and whom God loves. God wants us to be cared for. God suffers in the world for each one of us.

Bonhoeffer provides us with a radical concept of conversion that gets us back to the roots of our faith. But it is not radical enough for us today. It lacks an explicit, focused emphasis on love of Earth or love of creation. Nonetheless, his affirmation of God's deep love for the world in *Ethics*, his emphasis on this-worldliness in *Letters and Papers from Prison*, and the ecological trajectory of his vision of the community of God, human beings, and all creatures help open us up to a concept of conversion that embraces the whole Earth community and the rest of creation. Daily personal intimacy with the creation as well as with Jesus Christ is crucial in the process of conversion. Jesus Christ for us today is not only the human being for others but also the human being for Earth. Existence for others includes existence for the whole Earth community.

In his brief introduction to *Earth Habitat* Larry Rasmussen, who was deeply influenced by Bonhoeffer's ethics, asserts that *"conversion to Earth"* is crucial to Christianity's role in the interreligious, global human vocation of Earth-keeping.[59] Rasmussen develops this call to conversion to Earth in depth in two major works: *Earth Community, Earth Ethics*, published in 1996, and *Earth-Honoring Faith*, published in 2013. Rasmussen believes humanity has arrived at a radical turning or tipping point. We can

---

57. Bonhoeffer to Eberhard Bethge, October 9, 1940, in *Conspiracy and Imprisonment: 1940–1945* (DBWE 16), 78.

58. *Letters and Papers from Prison* (DBWE 8), 375.

59. Rasmussen, *Earth Habitat*, 7.

either change or perish—those are our choices. In "The Baptized Life" he identifies two major tipping points in Earth-human relations. The first was the Industrial Revolution, during which human beings in industrial nations moved from an "organic, ever-renewing, land-based economy to an extractive, non-renewing, industrial economy."[60] We are now poised for the second tipping point, "an ecological reformation, a leap of human ingenuity." This second tipping point is actually a "counter-tipping point—a tip toward Earth-honoring faith rather than Earth-abusing faith."[61]

In *Earth Habitat* Rasmussen clarifies that *conversion to Earth* means to measure "all Christian impulses by one stringent criterion: their contribution to Earth's well-being."[62] In *Earth Community, Earth Ethics*, "a work about the earth and its distress," Rasmussen restates this criterion, pleading for fidelity to Earth: "Our most basic impulses and activities must now be measured by one stringent criterion—their contribution to an earth ethic and their advocacy of sustainable earth community."[63] In *Earth-Honoring Faith* he observes that Christianity and the other faiths of the world[64] are in need of a "conversion to the realities of the tough new planet."[65] Our greatest work as people of faith is "effecting the hard transition from a time of, on balance, a destructive human presence on the planet to a time of mutual enhancement in the community of life."[66] Some may question whether Rasmussen overemphasizes the conversion to Earth. My sense is he is simply calling for us to participate in what God is up to with Earth. Wendell Berry affirms that "the care of the earth is our most ancient and most worthy and, after all, our most pleasing responsibility. To cherish what remains of it, and to foster its renewal, is our only legitimate hope."[67] The testimony of Scripture is that God's home is with Earth and all its inhabitants. Focusing on the well-being of Earth is a matter of caring for God's home, our home, and the home of our kindred creatures.

60. Rasmussen, "Baptized Life," 182, quoting Thomas Berry, *Evening Thoughts*, 107.

61. Ibid., 184.

62. Rasmussen, introduction to *Earth Habitat*, 7.

63. Rasmussen, *Earth Community, Earth Ethics*, xii.

64. Some indigenous faiths may be an exception, but they too are having to adjust to the hard realities of the tough new planet caused by human beings and traditions that have lacked earth-honoring faith.

65. Rasmussen, *Earth-Honoring Faith*, 7.

66. Ibid., 8.

67. W. Berry, *Unsettling of America*, 14.

The call to ecological conversion, therefore, involves a turning away from an excessive focus on the self and one's own kind and a turning toward God, other human beings, and the whole creation. A conversion to Jesus Christ for us today is a conversion to God, neighbor, and other creatures. This process of conversion or repentance will include genuine sorrow and contrition over our contribution to environmental degradation in its many forms.

The call to ecological conversion is an invitation to faith in God as creator, reconciler, and sustainer of all that exists. Martin Luther emphasized that faith is active in love toward the neighbor. People of faith will love the neighbor. He is describing an ethical reality. For us today faith will also be active in care for the creation. People of faith will care for the creation. That is an essential part of the description of ethical reality.

The preface to *The Green Bible* marvels at the amazing relevance of the Bible in discerning our role in caring for creation: "It is almost as if it [the Bible] were waiting for this moment to speak to us. With over a thousand references to the earth and caring for creation in the Bible, the message is clear: all in God's creation—nature, animals, humanity—are inextricably linked to one another. As God cares for all of creation, so too we cannot love one dimension without caring for the others. We are called to care for all God has made."[68] Selecting creation care passages to print in green, as is the practice of *The Green Bible,* is a somewhat arbitrary venture. Nonetheless, *The Green Bible* is a sign that care of Earth is deeply rooted in our faith, that we are rediscovering and renewing something at the core of who we are as human beings.

In exploring our call to ecological conversion, keeping in mind Bonhoeffer's appeal for selfless self-love, we have arrived at a quadrilateral of core values of our faith: love of God, love of neighbor, love of creation, and love of self. Followers of Jesus will live by these core values. That is a description of ethical reality. That is a description of ecological reality. How can we worship and love God and yet ignore or destroy what God has created? We are discovering that to destroy the rest of the Earth community is to destroy ourselves. All four of our core values compel us to engage in a major ecological conversion.

The church's primary vocation is to preach and teach for conversion to God, other human beings, and all creation. Such preaching and teaching will include calling sin by its rightful name, including individual, corporate,

68. Preface to *The Green Bible,* I-15.

and ecological sin. It will also include the proclamation of the reconciliation of God, human beings, and the whole creation in Christ—that is, God's love for everything God has created. Ecological preaching and teaching shapes and forms individuals and the community of faith.

Surely worship life and prayer life will be shaped by this ecological focus. Sallie McFague highlights the role of prayer in the process of conversion: "In prayer a reversal occurs: we do not talk about God and the world but begin to see ourselves and the world in God. We begin to see human life and the world from the divine perspective, from a broader and more inclusive point of view than we are otherwise capable of holding. We begin to recognize who we are in the scheme of things from the perspective of the Creator and Redeemer of everything that is. We are no longer the center (a definition of sin); we know God is the Center (a definition of salvation)."[69] McFague's description of the role of prayer bears striking similarities to the concept of contuition explored in chapter 3.[70] Prayers of lament are especially vital in helping us express genuine sorrow and contrition.

A faithful, responsible church will not ignore or give short shrift to nonhuman creation. The church is also called to participate in the effort to establish ecological justice. The church as church does not have privileged expertise or knowledge on the best strategies or techniques to address the most pressing ecological issues. Nonetheless, the church does have a role to play. Part of the challenge is discerning what a particular church's role should be in a given time and place. A local church with a wetland, for example, surely needs to pay attention to restoring its wetland as one part of its role. No responsible person or community, institution or nation, corporation or church can ignore the reality of the ecological crisis. We need to engage in responsible action with boldness and with a sense of humility.

An Appeal for Ecological Humility[71]

Today Bonhoeffer is often celebrated as an example of a modern Christian martyr, and his conspiratorial activity against Hitler and the Nazis tends to

69. McFague, *Life Abundant*, 9.

70. See pages 54–55.

71. Portions of this section were included in "Bonhoeffer's Appeal for Ethical Humility," a lecture I delivered at Pacific Lutheran University for the "Commemoration of Dietrich Bonhoeffer: Lutheran Pastor and Resister, 1906–1945." This commemoration, sponsored by the Lutheran Studies Program, was held on April 9, 2015, the seventieth anniversary of Bonhoeffer's death.

be looked upon with favor. It is striking, however, that he deliberately sought to avoid justifying his actions. From his standpoint any attempt to justify his involvement in the conspiracy would have been the height of ethical arrogance. In fact, according to Eberhard Bethge, Bonhoeffer "would have accepted the charge that what he had done was not a 'good response' to the challenges of the times, but a very tardy one." It was one thing to give an account of his actions in the conspiracy; it was another thing to try to justify his actions. In Bonhoeffer's view "the responsible position was not to take this justification into his own hands, before, during, and after his actions."[72] Only God could ultimately judge his actions. In the extraordinary situation Bonhoeffer found himself in, he felt compelled to act as he did, but only with a profound sense of ethical humility.

This sense of ethical humility permeates Bonhoeffer's *Ethics*. His appeal for ethical humility applies not only to extraordinary situations but also to more ordinary situations in life. In *Ethics* he is reflecting on his extraordinary involvement in the conspiracy, although he cannot do so explicitly. At the same time he is looking forward to the rebuilding of life in Germany after the demise of Hitler and the Nazis, to the end of the war and a return to more ordinary times. The intent of Bonhoeffer's *Ethics* is both to encourage us to participate in bold ventures of responsibility and to instill in us a deep sense of humility as we engage in ethical reflection, decision-making, and action.

Bonhoeffer's concern for ethical humility pervades the central concepts he employs to develop his ethics. Responsible action is one of those central concepts. In Bonhoeffer's view, ethical humility is built into the structure of the responsible life. Responsible persons are free to live and make decisions, but that freedom is always conditioned by our obligation to God and to our neighbor.[73] Our obligation to God and neighbor is fulfilled by "responsible action"—that is, action on behalf of or in the place of others. Thus, we never engage in responsible action or make ethical decisions in isolation. The community of God is built upon the actions of responsible persons on behalf of or in the place of others.

Bonhoeffer's appeal for ethical humility is, in effect, a call for us to remove the log of ethical arrogance from our own eye so that we can see

72. Bethge, *Dietrich Bonhoeffer*, 830.

73. *Ethics* (DBWE 6), 257. Bonhoeffer is building on Paul's understanding of freedom in Gal 5:13: "For you were called to freedom, brothers and sisters; only do not use your freedom as an opportunity for self-indulgence, but through love become slaves to one another" (NRSV).

clearly the ethical pitfalls into which we and others are falling. In particular, Bonhoeffer alerts us to the danger of the quest for moral certainty and to the limitations of one-principle or one-theme ethical approaches, whether philosophical or theological. The point is not to discourage us from engaging, if necessary, in bold ventures of responsibility, such as Bonhoeffer did in the conspiracy against Hitler, but to lead us to acknowledge our ethical limitations and to recognize that the ultimate judgment and fulfillment of our ethical ventures are in the hands of God. In the final analysis Bonhoeffer's ethical courage, for which he is so admired, grew out of his profound sense of ethical humility; for he was confident that he and his co-conspirators were not acting on their own but in the presence of the God of history who can transform even our mistakes and shortcomings into good.

We have already noted the limits of Bonhoeffer's ethics for an ecological ethic; in an ecological ethic a more explicit focus on love of Earth and the whole creation is needed.[74] Nonetheless, his appeal for ethical humility can serve us well as a catalyst for an appeal for ecological humility. In an appeal for ecological humility the structure of the responsible life must be understood in relationship to God, other human beings, and the creation. God is not simply the God of history, but the God of the whole creation. Ecologically responsible persons are free to live and make decisions, but that freedom is conditioned by our obligation to God, human beings, and the rest of creation. Responsible action, therefore, needs to fully take into account Earth and other creatures. Jesus Christ for us today is the human being for Earth and *all* its inhabitants. It is not possible for us to engage in responsible action in isolation from the whole community of God, human beings, and the rest of creation. We are acting not only in the presence of the God of history but also in the presence of the God of the whole creation. We need to be bold in employing our capacities as human beings to seek the well-being of our fellow human beings and fellow creatures—our kindred. At the same time we need to be aware of our limitations as human beings. One of the key insights of the story of Adam and Eve is that from the very beginning we human beings have had a deep-seated tendency to resist our God-given limits. These limits are intended for our well-being and the well-being of the whole Earth community.

The need to accept our limits as human beings is crucial to any appeal for ecological humility. Accepting our limits is emphasized again and again by those seeking to develop an ecological ethic for our time. Like

74. See pages 12, 50, 62, 79.

Bonhoeffer, Ivone Gebara affirms that we have a limited grasp of reality. She appeals for a "more open-ended attitude toward all established concepts." We need to recognize that "none of these concepts is more than a perspective, a tentative point of view adopted in order to deal with everyday life and with the broader sweep of history." Our limited grasp of reality is "almost always based on our own limited experience." The temptation is to absolutize our knowledge. Being clear on how partial our knowledge is enables us to respect and be open to "the great variety of approaches to reality."[75] Gebara's appeal for a more open-ended attitude implies that as followers of Jesus our approach to reality is one contribution to the process of seeking the well-being of humanity and the rest of creation. Jesus was sent into the world not to make all human beings Christians but to help us become the human beings God created us to be—that is, persons who live by the four core values: love of God, love of neighbor, love of creation, and love of self.

Wendell Berry laments "the fairly recent dismantling of our old understanding and acceptance of human limits." True intelligence is to recognize that our intelligence and our world are limited. Instead, we operate under the delusion that we are intelligent enough to fix the bad consequences of our misuse of intelligence. This delusion leads to the illusion of unlimited economic growth.[76] Larry Rasmussen also highlights this illusion. "We still imagine," he observes, "that we can have infinite growth on a finite planet. Even the notion of limits offends our way of life and its values. The biblical notion that just enough is enough, rather than either poverty or riches, doesn't register with us."[77] Rasmussen points to how sure we tend to be of the goodness of our way of life. We are so enamored with our way of life that we will go to tremendous lengths to justify and preserve it.

This certainty concerning our way of life is a form of pride—what the Greeks called *hubris*. Bartholomew I, quoting Euripides, stresses that such hubris is a symptom of "the desire to become greater than the gods."[78] Such hubris can lead, as Wendell Berry maintains, to "too great a human confidence in the power of 'mine own hand.'"[79] Berry is drawing on the Lord's instructions to Gideon in Judges 7:2: "The troops with you are too many for me to give the Midianites into their hand. Israel would only take the credit

75. Gebara, *Longing for Running Water*, 69–70.

76. Berry, *It All Turns on Affection*, 19.

77. Rasmussen, "Earth-Honoring Faith," 24.

78. Bartholomew is quoting the classical Greek tragic poet Euripides (*Cosmic Grace, Humble Prayer*, 315).

79. Berry, *Home Economics*, 56.

away from me, saying, 'My own hand has delivered me.'" Berry does not dismiss the power of human beings, but our power needs to be tempered by an awareness of our limits. We must realize that "we are at once limited and unendingly responsible for what we know and do." He further explains, "We cannot know the whole truth, which belongs to God alone, but our task nevertheless is to seek to know what is true."[80]

Along similar lines, John Paul II and Bartholomew I, in their "Common Declaration on Environmental Ethics" of June 10, 2002, assert that "we must regain humility and recognize the limits of our powers, and most importantly, the limits of our knowledge and judgment. We have been making decisions, taking actions, and assigning values that are leading us away from the world as it should be, away from the design of God for creation, away from all that is essential for a healthy planet and a healthy commonwealth of people."[81] They stress the need for a new way of life and a new culture of life. For Wendell Berry a key to cultivating a healthy way of life and a healthy culture of life "is actual conversation, actual discourse, in which people say to one another in good faith fully and exactly what they know, and acknowledge honestly the limits of their knowledge."[82] Such conversation gives him hope even as we struggle with the devastating ecological consequences of our individual and collective human behavior.

An appeal for ecological humility does not mean that scientists should hold back in sharing the results of their scientific studies. The best scientists have a sense of humility built into their approach. They marvel at the complexities of the universe and life on earth. Their task is to offer the best possible theory or explanation of the evidence that is available to them. New evidence may require a new explanation. They also realize they do their work as part of a community of scientists. But as James Hansen stresses in *Storms of My Grandchildren*, such humility does not entail reluctance to contradict authority, be it political or religious authority. If scientists "keep two sets of books," one they believe and one to please the authorities, it will compromise their work. According to Hansen, scientists "should be clear and blunt" about what they think, "even if authorities do not like it"—otherwise they "will not do very well in science."[83]

80. Berry, *It All Turns on Affection*, 27.
81. Bartholomew I, *Cosmic Grace, Humble Prayer*, 309–10.
82. Berry, *It All Turns on Affection*, 87–88.
83. Hansen, *Storms of My Grandchildren*, 60.

Hansen is issuing an appeal similar to Wendell Berry's for honest conversation and discourse that is crucial to addressing the urgent ecological issues we face. Hansen's particular concern is with climate change. An appeal for ecological humility could be interpreted as a plea to look at both sides of the climate-change issue. We need to be willing to look at all sides of an issue in the search for truth. But Hansen warns against a "balanced" perspective that distorts the truth.[84] Sometimes there are not two sides of an issue if one side is being manipulated for political purposes that are not in tune with the well-being of human beings and the whole Earth community. The vast majority of the climate science community thinks the preponderance of the evidence supports the theory that our way of life is triggering catastrophic climate change. The call for a balanced perspective can be used to perpetuate inaction—the status quo. The status quo will allow fossil fuel companies, for example, to continue to make massive profits. The status quo will also allow we who live a privileged lifestyle to avoid having to making any significant changes in our way of life. An appeal for ecological humility does not entail going to sleep at the wheel. Again, as David James Duncan has said, "No person, no family, no country, and no civilization in history has remained viable for long without engaging in corrective acts of self-criticism, self-sacrifice, and restoration."[85]

Four-hundred-meter runners often talk about "hitting the wall" as they round the final turn and head into the home stretch. If they expend too much energy in the first three hundred meters, they will have nothing left for the final one hundred. We are in mortal danger of hitting an ecological wall, only in this case we are not talking about a race but our life. Unlike running the four hundred meters, where only one runner has to pay the price of expending too much energy, when we hit the ecological wall, the consequences will be global for human beings and for the rest of life. We cannot violate our God-given limits with impunity. Living within our limits as human beings is the path to ecological healing and wholeness—the path to well-being for our Earth home and all who dwell in it. As we head for home, ecological humility is essential. Six centuries ago, in Julian of Norwich's *Showings*, she summed up our human condition in seven words: "Without this humility we cannot be saved."[86] These prophetic words remain so true for us today.

84. Ibid., 57.

85. Duncan, "Prayer for the Second Coming of the Salmon," 197.

86. Julian of Norwich, *Showings*, 306.

6

Taking Up Our Ecological Cross

The Need to Sacrifice Our Way of Life

BEFORE PRESIDENT GEORGE H. W. Bush went to the Earth Summit in Rio de Janeiro in 1992, he announced to the press corps that the American way of life is not up for negotiation. Given the tremendous ecological degradation the way we live has caused, what is not negotiable in 2016 is that the American way of life must change. Even the ecologically enlightened face radical adjustments far beyond what they will be comfortable making. Our way of life has an allure and a momentum that are hard to resist—but at this critical point we have no choice, and no time to waste.

President Bush's comment is a symptom of the arrogance Rachel Carson referred to in her Scripps Commencement address.[1] Such an arrogant attitude reflects our incomplete awareness of how fully human beings are part of nature. Human beings have had a tendency to conceive of nature as something set apart from the human environment. This tendency makes no sense when our well-being is so dependent on the natural world. We often talk as if the things human beings construct are not part of nature: our homes, our automobiles, our computers, and other modern conveniences. Since human beings built them and human beings are full participants in nature, they are all part of nature. The question is whether what we build contributes to our well-being and the well-being of Earth and all of its inhabitants. It is becoming ever clearer that our way of life with all of

1. See page 36.

its devices is not an effective strategy for sustainable living. In fact, it is a destructive strategy.

In her address Carson mentioned that human beings have long talked "somewhat arrogantly about the conquest of nature."[2] She acknowledges we now have the power to fulfill that boast. The way of life we have arrived at could be viewed as the result of our efforts to conquer nature. Carson warns that the price of that boast may be the destruction of human beings as well as all life on Earth. Given the imminent climate catastrophe we face, our destruction is not simply a possibility; it is virtually a sure outcome if we persist in pursuing our unsustainable strategy for living. Human beings have the power to inflict tremendous damage on the natural world, but we cannot set ourselves outside of nature. So connected are human well-being and the well-being of the natural world that in destroying the natural world we are destroying ourselves.

Even when human beings are made aware of the consequences of ecological degradation for our own survival, we still have a tendency to resist making the necessary changes in our lifestyle. EcoFaith Recovery, mentioned in chapter 3,[3] is "a growing network of faith-based people and institutions within the Christian tradition in the Pacific Northwest, waking up to the enormity of the ecological-economic-spiritual crisis before us" and seeking to address this resistance to ecological lifestyle changes. Eco-Faith Recovery is "fed by the deep waters of the Christian faith tradition, the environmental and eco-justice movements, and the 12-step recovery movement." They recognize the addictive elements that characterize our consumptive way of life. Drawing on insights from the 12-step movement, "EcoFaith Recovery acknowledges that not only have our 'lives become unmanageable,' but for those of us in the 'developed' world, our entire way of life has become unsustainable—individually, institutionally and globally. Therefore, we acknowledge our need on every level of our personal and public lives to go into 'eco-faith recovery,' share our stories in community, discover our collective power, and turn to a higher spiritual power in order to effectively face this crisis with creativity and imagination."[4]

2. Quoted in Lear, *Rachel Carson*, 407. See also earlier comments on Carson on pages 34–37.

3. See page 65.

4. EcoFaith Recovery, "About Us: On either side of the river is the tree of life . . ." See http://www.ecofaithrecovery.org/about/.

Al Gore has also noticed the addictive pattern of our consumptive way of life, but that does not explain for him "the full complexity and ferocity of our assault on the earth." Gore wonders "how so many thinking and caring people can unwittingly cooperate in doing such enormous damage to the global environment and how they can continue to live by the same set of false assumptions about what their civilization is actually doing and why." The unhealthy ways individuals relate to our Earth home cannot explain the scope and the violence of the assault on it. Gore has come to the conclusion that something "has gone terribly wrong in the way we collectively determine our mutual relationship to the earth."[5] EcoFaith Recovery also recognizes the collective nature of the violence done to the Earth community, which is why in addition to insights from the 12-step movement they stress the need to draw on the deep waters of the Christian faith and of the environmental and ecojustice movements in addressing what they view as an institutional and global as well as individual crisis.

In Romans 7:15 the Apostle Paul laments his incapacity to do what he wants: "For I do not understand my own actions. For I do not do what I want, but I do the very thing I hate." It is hard to understand why followers of Jesus, filled with gratitude for God's creative and reconciling activity in the world, would not respond to the ecological crisis in a constructive, caring way. Thus far our response has been tepid at best. We may long to do what God wants us to do and what we want to do, but we are so enamored with and stuck in our old way of life that we do not fulfill this longing.

What is needed is a radical change in the way we live. This change is radical in at least two senses: (1) it will transform the whole person—mind, body, heart, and soul—and the whole community; and (2) it will get back to the roots of God's intentions for the community of God, human beings, and the rest of God's creatures—the community of life. The scope of our concern is not simply for the community of life as it is manifested here and now. We are to take into account generations yet to come who are to be included in this community of life. Taking a cue from some of our indigenous kin, we need a "seventh-generation strategy."[6] In *Our Responsibility to the Seventh Generation* indigenous people from Canada, Mexico, and India share their insights into sustainable development. They stress that the current model of development is unsound and cannot be sustained. In order to ensure the survival of humanity, "we cannot simply think of our survival; each new

5. Gore, *Earth in the Balance*, 226.

6. See previous reference to seventh-generation thinking in chapter 2, page 21.

generation is responsible to ensure the survival of the seventh generation."[7] No generation will survive that does not take into account our relationships to Earth and all of its creatures. Climate scientist James Hansen concludes *Storms of My Grandchildren* with a reference to seventh-generation thinking. In his final sentence he states, "It is a paradigm of almost all religions and of humanists that Earth, creation, is an intergenerational commons, the fruits and benefits of which should be accessible to every member of every generation."[8] Sadly, although this paradigm is rooted in the Christian tradition, it has been sorely neglected and not commonly put into practice. The Christian tradition is not alone in this respect, as the current state of the ecological crisis indicates.

Resistance to the radical change needed in our way of life is not surprising given the sacrifices this change will require. Bartholomew I identifies sacrifice as the "missing dimension" in addressing the ecological crisis. The fundamental obstacle impeding our work for the environment, asserts Bartholomew, is this: "how to move from theory to action, from word to deeds."[9] We may teach that we belong to a community of God, human beings, and all creation. We have enough technical scientific knowledge and a fairly good idea of how to do what needs to be done. Nonetheless, we are negligent in putting that teaching and knowledge into action. What is lacking is a willingness to sacrifice. Bartholomew highlights that "*sacrifice is primarily a spiritual issue and less an economic one. In speaking about sacrifice, we are talking about an issue that is not technological but ethical.*"[10]

Bartholomew stresses that sacrifice is to be willing and voluntary.[11] An appeal for sacrifice is not an appeal for those who have been abused to overlook or put up with abusive behavior. In "*La Causa* and Environmental Justice," Kevin O'Brien's study of the environmental impulse in the advocacy work of César Chávez, he clarifies that Chávez drew a distinction between "unjust and involuntary sacrifice" for the sake of oppressive growers and sacrifice "for the sake of justice and a better future."[12] Sacrifice cannot be understood apart from human dignity. Chávez's concern for the human dignity of farm workers led him to address environmental justice

7. Clarkson et al., *Our Responsibility to the Seventh Generation*.

8. Hansen, *Storms of My Grandchildren*, 270.

9. Bartholomew I, *Cosmic Grace, Humble Prayer*, 305.

10. Ibid., italics in original.

11. Ibid., 306.

12. O'Brien, "*La Causa* and Environmental Justice," 156.

concerns. According to O'Brien, Chávez's perspective critiques ecological ethicists who emphasize "nonanthropocentric thinking rather than the centrality of human dignity."[13] O'Brien observes that those who advocate a nonanthropocentric approach have tended to shy away from calls to sacrifice in response to urgent environmental concerns. Surely we need to take seriously this emphasis on human dignity. We also need to emphasize the dignity of each creature. In my view what is needed is a God-centered approach focused on discerning the will of God and a Christ-centered approach focused on following Jesus, each of which emphasizes the dignity of all, human and nonhuman. This is in effect a single approach since Jesus, the one we are called to follow, committed his life and ministry to discerning and doing the will of God.

In *The Gospel according to the Earth* Matthew Sleeth observes that we are a generation with an aversion to words like "*discipline, denial, sin, restraint, obedience, or sacrifice.*" This aversion impacts our willingness to make necessary changes in our way of life. One church advised Sleeth not to use the word *sacrifice* at all: "Talk about that, and you'll lose everybody. Appeal to their common sense." For Sleeth, however, not talking about sacrifice makes no sense at all for followers of Jesus. In his view "the illogical marvel that Jesus introduced to the world is sacrifice. From his first night in a stable to his last hours on the cross, Jesus was all about sacrifice. His life was a sacrifice." Sleeth notes that Gandhi identified "religion [or worship] without sacrifice" as one of the seven deadly social sins.[14] He tells a humorous and at the same time inspirational story about hearing a "little old lady" give the commencement address at his wife Nancy's college graduation ceremony more than thirty years ago. A highly intelligent young man who would serve as an emergency room physician for a number of years, Sleeth was frankly unimpressed with her delivery style. Her simple message boiled down to this: "Love God, and give your life to others. Nothing else matters." That little old lady was Mother Teresa.[15] Initially, Mother Teresa heard God's call to work with those dying on the streets of Calcutta. The Missionaries of Charity, the order she founded, now ministers to the forgotten and the destitute all over the world. In a time of ecological crisis, we must be willing to sacrifice both for the forgotten human beings and for the forgotten creatures of the world.

13. Ibid., 152.

14. Sleeth, *Gospel according to the Earth*, 185.

15. Ibid., 184.

A Way of Life for Followers of Jesus

In Mark 8:34–36 Jesus tells his disciples and the crowd gathered with them, "If any want to become my followers, let them deny themselves and take up their cross and follow me. For those who want to save their life will lose it, and those who lose their life for my sake, and the sake of the gospel, will save it. For what will it profit them to gain the whole world and forfeit their life?" Jesus draws a sharp contrast between an old, self-centered way of life that ultimately results in forfeiting our life and a new way of life that participates in the process of salvation. This new way of life is characterized by sacrifice—giving our lives for others. In an ecological age this way of life entails giving our lives for other human beings and other creatures, especially for the suffering and most vulnerable among us. This sacrificial way of life does not preclude selfless self-love.[16] Those who attend to their own basic needs will be able to care for others.

Jesus was put to death on the cross because of the way he lived. He willingly accepted death as a consequence of his faithful obedience to God. But death is not the purpose of this sacrificial way of life. Like Jesus, we give that others may have life and have it abundantly (John 10:10). By giving of ourselves fully in the midst of life, by taking up our ecological cross, we participate with God in the process of moving Earth and all of its inhabitants toward *shalom*.

In leaving behind our old way of life for this new way of life, the first thing we need to sacrifice is the spirit of domination that infects our minds. We have to give up the power to lord it over and dominate other creatures and weak and marginalized human beings. The same mindset that will engage in strip mining and permanently destroy a mountaintop ecosystem will have few qualms about what happens to the local human inhabitants. God intended for all creatures, not just human beings, to be fruitful and multiply. All creatures have an impact on the created order. Other creatures have been content to make that impact within the limits God has given them. Many human beings have not been content to live within our God-given limits. "Dominion" has been interpreted as a license to dominate. The consequences for other humans, other creatures, and ourselves have been disastrous and threaten to become more devastating in a hurry. We need to give up this license to dominate.

16. See previous discussion of Bonhoeffer's concept of "selfless self-love" in chapter 5, page 115.

In Mark 10:35–45 James and John come to Jesus with a request: "Grant us to sit, one at your right hand and one at your left, in your glory." This request comes from a spirit of domination, a desire to lord it over others. When the other ten disciples heard this request, they got miffed; they did not appreciate James and John trying to get one up on them. Jesus called them all together and said to them, "You know that among the Gentiles those whom they recognize as their rulers lord it over them, and their great ones are tyrants over them. But it is not so among you; but whoever wishes to become great among you must be your servant, and whoever wishes to be first among you must be slave of all. For the Son of Man came not to be served but to serve, and to give his life a ransom for many."

Jesus contrasts two very different ways of life here. One is governed by a spirit of domination. The other is governed by a spirit of service. The power to lord it over others is alluring, as James and John's request reflects. It is not easy to give up this power and the way of life commensurate with it. But that is precisely what we must sacrifice when we take up this new way of life and follow Jesus in serving others. Like Jesus, we are content to give our lives as a "ransom for many." For us today the many includes all our kindred, both human and nonhuman. All things, whether on Earth or in heaven, were reconciled to God through Jesus Christ, by making peace through the blood of his cross (Col 1:20). "If Jesus did not die for white-tailed deer, redheaded woodpeckers, blue whales, and green Belizean rain forests," asserts Steven Bouma-Prediger, "then he did not die for you and me."[17] The term "ransom" suggests that a sacrificial way of life can be costly. It cost Jesus his life. But once again, the purpose of this way of life is that all may have life and have it abundantly.

David James Duncan identifies the salmon as the Pacific Northwest's "living image of sacrifice." They are a "living gospel in themselves"—and thus, no more salmon, no more sermon.[18] The salmon was also an ancient symbol of Christ's sacrifice in the Celtic world. It was found in Celtic Christian art and poetry. The fish had been a symbol of Christ in the early church. But the Celts were more specific. Newell explains why the salmon served as such a powerful symbol of Christ for the Celts: "The salmon, strong and glistening with vitality, swims hundreds of miles in the open sea and climbs thousands of feet in the torrents of mighty rivers to give birth to new life.

17. Bouma-Prediger, *For the Beauty of the Earth*, 116.
18. Duncan, "Song of Salmon," 92–93.

And in spawning new life, it dies. Christ, the Salmon of Wisdom, the One who gives himself for the birthing of new life."[19]

In the course of my formal education, one of my professors—I cannot recall which one—defined "holy" as "fulfilling the purpose for which you were made." A salmon is holy when it has spent itself completely for the end for which it was made. In Duncan's "Song of Salmon" he offers this colorful description of the holiness of the salmon:

> Salmon are holy because they're the life's blood and beloveds of fisherfolk, and the first disciples of Christ were fisherfolk, so it's the trade of Peter, James, and John we're fighting to defend here. Salmon are formidably holy, because the commercial fisherman Peter guards the Pearly Gates. Salmon are holy because, when their flesh feeds even the most intractable salmon-haters among us, they are literally "loving their enemies and doing good to those who hate them." Salmon are holy because, when they feed their young bodies to kingfishers and otters and eagles; and their large ocean-going bodies to seals, sea lions, and orcas; and their magnificent, sex-driven, returned-to-the-river bodies to bears and Indian tribes and sport and commercial fishers and fly fishers; and finally even their spawned-out, nitrogen-rich bodies to salmon-berry bushes, sword ferns, cedar trees, and wildflowers, they have served us from one end of their lives to the other as a kind of living gospel in themselves.[20]

Spending ourselves completely for the end for which we were made is one definition of holiness. A sacrificial way of life is one in which we spend ourselves completely for the end for which we were made. When we abuse Earth and its inhabitants, both human and nonhuman, we are being unholy; and we are inflicting our unholiness on them. We affirm their holiness and our own when we treat them in accordance with the end for which they were made.

Here in the Pacific Northwest the salmon is a signature creature. Billions have been spent on efforts to save the salmon. The amount spent has been a source of controversy, and not everyone cares whether the salmon is saved. But enough people care about these impressive creatures that the money has been spent and will continue to be spent until a sustainable solution is arrived at. As impressive as a salmon may be, holiness is not a category reserved for them or for some other magnificent creature, such as

19. Newell, *Christ of the Celts,* 90.
20. Duncan, "Song of Salmon," 92.

a tall redwood tree in Northern California. Leopold affirms the "holiness" of the draba flower: "Draba plucks no heartstrings. Its perfume, if there is any, is lost in the gusty winds. Its color is plain white. Its leaves wear a sensible woolly coat. Nothing eats it; it is too small. No poets sing of it. Some botanist once gave it a Latin name, and then forgot it. Altogether it is of no importance—just a small creature that does a small job quickly and well."[21] Even this most seemingly insignificant creature is just as holy as a salmon or a redwood insofar as it gives its life for the purpose for which God created it.

Taking up our ecological cross and adopting a sacrificial way of life does not have to be a dramatic undertaking. We have no formula for a sacrificial way of life, especially not in the midst of unprecedented ecological challenges. In caring for the Earth community there are many small jobs that need to be done well. The call to care for Earth and all of its inhabitants is an essential part of following Jesus today. Whether we should care for Earth is no longer an issue to be debated. But each of us has to discern the specific ways God is calling us to embody that care in our daily lives.

Caring for the Earth community is a message to be proclaimed to the whole creation (Mark 16:15). Not all followers of Jesus are ready to adopt Earth care as an essential part of Christian discipleship. That means we have work to do. Our words and deeds need to make as clear as possible how vital caring for the whole Earth community is to our way of life as followers of Jesus. We are called to make concrete sacrifices each day to care for Earth and all of its inhabitants and to contribute to the process of moving the community of God, human beings, and all God's creatures toward *shalom*. Our contributions may seem small, but they need to be decisive. This is not the time to dabble in discipleship. This is not the time to fit a little Earth care every now and then into the course of our busy lives. The ecological crisis is upon us.

Following Jesus is a personal as well as a communal vocation. Our communal vocation is lived out as the church, the body of Christ. Following Jesus Christ for us today entails living as human beings and as the church for the whole Earth community. The church has a key role to play in motivating followers of Jesus to love Earth and all of its inhabitants so deeply that they are moved to take up their ecological cross and adopt a sacrificial way of life on Earth. The church is called to proclaim with clarity that Jesus lived his life for Earth and all of its inhabitants, that he died on

21. Leopold, *Sand County Almanac*, 26.

the cross for the suffering Earth as well as for sinful human beings, and that God raised him from the dead to affirm that the way he lived is God's way on Earth.

To fulfill this role with integrity the church must be willing to acknowledge its own contributions to the degradation of Earth, to confess its ecological sins of commission and omission. We in the church must be willing to take the ecological log out of our own eyes so that we can see clearly to help other individuals and groups take the ecological logs out of their eyes. Our proclamation is to be in word and deed. Our ecological witness will lack integrity if we do not practice what we preach.

A story has been told about a mother who came to Mahatma Gandhi and asked him to tell her son to stop eating sugar. "I ask that you come back next week," he responded, "and make the request again." The mother was puzzled, but she left and came back the next week. Once again she asked Gandhi to talk to her son about the dangers of eating sugar. Gandhi simply said, "Please, come back and see me in a week." Though disappointed, the mother left and returned the next week. This time Gandhi agreed to talk to with her son. She was grateful but asked him why he could not have talked to him two weeks ago. He replied, "Because first I had to see if I could go without sugar before I asked someone else to do so."[22]

If we are to have integrity in calling people to engage in ecological reforms that provide for the well-being of the whole Earth community, we need to take up our ecological cross now and make the sacrifices that put those reforms into practice in our personal lives and in our communal life as the church. We need to discern what it means in concrete terms to take up our ecological cross.

It is also crucial to be aware that we do not have to be of one mind with other communities of faith and organizations on all core beliefs and values in order to work with them in caring for Earth and its inhabitants. Within the Christian community we have significant differences on what are considered core beliefs and values, yet we dare not allow our differences to keep us from the task of caring for Earth. In the same way we must not let differences prevent us from allying ourselves with other traditions for the good of all. Islamic scholar Ingrid Mattson can be a model for us; she counsels her fellow Muslims to work with "those who share many of our core

---

22. A version of this story about Gandhi is found in White, *Stories for the Journey*, 96–97. Al Gore also includes a version in *Earth in the Balance*, 14. Some have questioned whether this story has its source in an actual encounter with Gandhi. In any case the point it makes is relevant in encouraging people to engage in ecological reform.

beliefs and values, and we can work with them as long as they are respectful of our faith and practices."[23] Given the urgency of the ecological crisis, we need to be open to working with anyone who shares a basic concern for the well-being of Earth. We will work together for the well-being of the whole Earth community, or we will perish together along with the rest of life on Earth. Taking up our ecological cross will involve sacrificing some things we hold very dear.

The Cost of Ecological Reformation

During World War II American soldiers made major sacrifices on the battlefield in the fight against Nazi Germany and the other Axis powers. The American people on the home front also made significant sacrifices. The whole economy was geared up to support the war effort. My dad has shared stories about his life during World War II as a young boy on a poor family farm in rural Wisconsin. They always had food on the table, but gas and many other products were rationed. Tom Brokaw coined the term "the Greatest Generation"[24] to describe those who weathered the Depression, fought World War II, and built up our country into a superpower after the war. Addressing the ecological crisis in this century will require an even greater effort. David Rhoads explains that at a national and global level we need "a transformation to renewable energy, transition to eating local foods, massive reforestation projects, replanting of native species everywhere, cultivation of resources to develop and share new technologies, limits to the use of pesticides and herbicides, prohibition of the clearing of forests and the stripping of land, rationing of energy and water, protection for wetlands and wilderness, among many others things." That is a daunting agenda for ecological reform. Whether or not governments and corporations rise to the occasion, individuals and communities need to take up these reform tasks "*now* on a voluntary and unilateral basis."[25]

In *A Climate for Change* Katherine Hayhoe and Andrew Farley state that global warming "may very well be the most serious problem of the twenty-first century." They ask the question, "Will we stand up to the

23. Mattson, "Road Back to Paradise," 164.

24. Brokaw, *The Greatest Generation*. This book is also available as a documentary film.

25. Rhoads, "Reflections on a Lutheran Theology of Creation," 3.

challenge, or will we turn our faces to the wall?"[26] They are especially concerned that just when we have the opportunity to move forward decisively with alternative forms of sustainable energy, we as a nation are investing enormous resources to preserve our way of life with traditional energy resources. Hayhoe, a scientist, and Farley, a pastor, are both part of the Evangelical Christian tradition. Their book was inspired in part by questions from fellow Christians who wanted to know the "truth" about climate change. They begin the introduction with a quotation from "Climate Change: An Evangelical Call to Action," a statement signed by more than two hundred evangelical leaders: "For most of us, until recently this has not been treated as a pressing issue or major priority. Indeed, many of us have required considerable convincing before becoming persuaded that climate change is a real problem and that it ought to matter to us as Christians."[27] One hopes that the Evangelical spirit that inspired the involvement of Christians in the struggle against slavery may also inspire Christians from across the spectrum to make necessary sacrifices to address the ecological crisis.

In our household we have been dabbling in ecological reform for a number of years. We are intentional in practicing the three r's: reducing, reusing, and recycling. We have an "Earth Machine" for composting. We drive one hybrid and one electric car. I occasionally bike to work. We have fifteen blueberry bushes and a small garden that fill up most of our small backyard. Recently, we had thirty-one solar panels installed on our roof. I do not want to diminish such small-scale efforts. Our small actions can help change our attitude and the attitudes of those who witness our actions. Recycling, composting, growing food in the backyard, bicycling or walking or taking mass transit to work, and putting solar panels on the roof are ways of participating in God's efforts to renew our Earth home. But the truth is that in our household we have not had to make any major sacrifices. We are still living a way of life that is not sustainable in the long term, especially if the rest of the world continues to adopt it. We may drive a hybrid and an electric car, each an improvement on traditional fossil fuel vehicles, but we are still a two-car family, and the hybrid still burns fossil fuels. Furthermore, it takes an enormous amount of energy to build the vehicles themselves. I remember working for the summer of 1985 at the Crown Zellerbach Paper Mill in Port Angeles, Washington. This mill produced large rolls of white

26. Hayhoe and Farley, *Climate for Change*, 155.

27. Quoted in ibid., xiii.

and yellow paper that publishers used to print phone books. I was amazed by the amount of energy needed simply to provide us with phone books.[28] Producing the materials necessary to build automobiles requires significantly more.

Dabbling in ecological reform could be used to justify holding on to a way of life that is dear to us. Our dabbling will serve a purpose if it prepares us for the major sacrifices to come. My oldest son, Isaac, worked for many summers as a wildland firefighter. One of their worst fears was getting caught in a blowup, in which a number of small fires "blow up" into a larger, uncontrolled fire. An ecological reform blowup could be a positive development, in which many small ecological reform actions blow up into the major ecological reform needed to move us decisively toward a sustainable way of life that leads to human well-being and the well-being of Earth and all of its inhabitants.

Martin-Schramm counsels us to "resist the temptation of despair" in addressing the issue of climate change. Taking a hint from Bonhoeffer's distinction between "costly grace" and "cheap grace,"[29] he warns against "cheap despair," a moral paralysis that can preserve the status of the rich and the powerful. According to Martin-Schramm, the task of Christians, empowered by costly grace, is "to work tirelessly with others as individuals, within church denominations, and as global citizens to live in harmony with the energy resources God has so abundantly provided."[30] At the same time Martin-Schramm adopts a realistic perspective to climate change, rejecting overly optimistic or pessimistic views of what human beings can do to address the current climate crisis. His realistic perspective leads him to take an incremental and gradualist approach. In most arenas of life, I tend to share this perspective and approach to change. The problem is that we may not have time for an incremental approach to climate change. We cannot afford to go past the tipping point on global warming and trigger a runaway greenhouse effect—what James Hansen refers to as the Venus syndrome.[31] The result would be catastrophic.

---

28. Energy for the Crown Zellerbach Mill was produced by two dams on the Elwha River. Those dams were recently removed. Within a year salmon were spawning in water opened up on the Elwha and its tributaries. For more on this dam removal, see Nijhuis, "World's Largest Dam Removal Unleashes U.S. River."

29. See Bonhoeffer, *Discipleship* (DBWE 4), 43–56.

30. Martin-Schramm, *Climate Justice*, 5.

31. See earlier reference to the Venus syndrome on pages 25–26.

At the Convocation of Teaching Theologians of the Evangelical Lutheran Church in America, held August 13–15, 2012, at Trinity Seminary in Columbus, Ohio, Martin-Schramm raised the possibility that we may be entering into a *statis confessionis* or "stand of confession" on the issue of climate change.[32] *Statis confessionis* refers to articles of faith by which the church stands or falls in a given time and place. Martin-Schramm referenced the Barmen Declaration as an example of such a *statis confessionis*. The Barmen Declaration was issued in 1934 by Confessing Church leaders in Germany in resistance to the inroads of the Nazi government into the life of the church. Confessing Church leaders believed Hitler and the Nazis were usurping spiritual authority that belonged to God and the church. In the case of climate change it is not as clear how a *statis confessionis* would apply. Martin-Schramm acknowledged that he did not have all the details worked out. But presumably the church would take a definitive stand on resisting a way of life based on exploitation of Earth and advocate for a sustainable way of life based on care of Earth and all of its inhabitants. The faith of the church would come down decisively on the side of caring for the whole Earth community. A *statis confessionis* is generally associated with more radical change—not with an incremental and gradualist approach. Martin-Schramm's raising the possibility of a *statis confessionis* indicates that he himself recognizes the limitations of his incremental and gradualist approach in addressing the climate-change issue. He wants to show that "realism and bold decisive action are not mutually exclusive"[33] and that both will be needed in the effort to achieve climate justice.

Three Costly Sacrifices

Applying the principle of *statis confessionis* to the climate-change issue is provocative. Followers of Jesus are not being called to take a stand only on articles of faith. We are being called to take a stand on the side of Earth and all of its inhabitants. Human well-being and the well-being of life on Earth will stand or fall inasmuch as we are able to sacrifice our old, exploitive way of life and adopt a new, sustainable way of life. Preserving the status quo is not an option for followers of Jesus. Care of Earth is not something for us

32. Martin-Schramm's paper has been published as "Lutheran Theology and the Environment: Bonhoeffer, the Church, and the Climate Question," 55–68. On climate change and a "stand of confession," see especially 64–66.

33. Martin-Schramm, *Climate Justice*, xvi.

to dabble in. It is to be a way of life. It will entail significant sacrifices of key elements of our prevailing way of life. Three will be highlighted here: our indulgent consumption; our subjugation to chronological time; and our love affair with the automobile. We are not to sacrifice these elements to feel better about ourselves or alleviate guilt; rather, we are called to sacrifice so that we might have life and have it in abundance. Sacrificing our old way of life to take up a new sustainable way of life is intended to move us toward our own well-being and the well-being of the whole Earth community. Thus, such sacrificing will be liberating.

Sacrificing Our Indulgent Consumption

Our first significant sacrifice is to leave behind our indulgent, consumptive way of life. In chapter 2 we focused on "acute affluenza" as a diagnosis for our consumptive ways. One limitation of this diagnosis is that it associates something we find unpleasant, an illness, with something we find alluring, namely, our indulgent way of life. My generation, the baby boomer generation, has been on a continuous spending spree or buying binge for decades. Recession or unemployment or some other life crisis may slow us down, but the basic pattern of consumption has continued virtually unabated in my lifetime. We enjoy shopping and consuming what we buy. Our indulgent consumption feeds into an economics of endless growth. Our survival and the survival of life on Earth depend on the willingness of human beings to move toward an "economics of ecological sustainability."[34] Such an economics would entail a willingness to accept limits on consumption and to accept limits on population growth.

When it comes to consumption, we resist having too many limits placed upon us. We like being able to buy what we want, precisely when we want to buy it. Stores stay open long hours, most of them seven days a week, so that we can satisfy our consumptive urges at any time. In this country our spending frenzy reaches a climax on Black Friday, the day after Thanksgiving. Some major stores open as early as midnight to give shoppers the maximum amount of time to fulfill their spending desires.

Juliet Schor laments that we have gotten caught up in an "insidious cycle of 'work-and-spend.' Employers ask for long hours. The pay creates a high level of consumption. People buy houses and go into debt; luxuries

34. See Denis Edward's discussion of John Cobb's "economics of ecological sustainability" in *Jesus the Wisdom of God*, 163–66.

become necessities; Smiths keep up with Joneses. Each year, 'progress,' in the form of annual productivity increases, is doled out by employers as extra income rather than as time off. Work-and-spend has become a powerful dynamic keeping us from a more relaxed and leisured way of life."[35] This last sentence is a sad commentary on our consumptive way of life. It has such a powerful grip on us that we are sacrificing a "more relaxed and leisured way of life," which would provide for our well-being and help us tread more lightly on the Earth community.

In *Affluenza* the authors ponder whether we have become a nation so caught up in our consumptive ways that we are "too distracted to care" about the consequences of the way we live. They compare us to medium-size fish that eat small fish: "We consume franchise products in the privacy of our homes, then watch helplessly as the big-fish franchise companies bite huge chunks out of our public places, swallowing jobs, traditions, and open space. We assume that someone else is taking care of things—we pay them to take care of things so we can concentrate on working and spending. But to our horror, we discover that many of the service providers, merchandise retailers, and caretakers are not really taking care of us anymore. It might be more appropriate to say they're *consuming* us."[36] Yet we go right on spending, oblivious to the consequences to ourselves, other human beings, and the rest of the Earth community.

Al Gore makes the striking claim that our civilization is "addicted to the consumption of the earth itself." Gore expresses concern that we have become numb to the "pain of what we have lost: a direct experience of connection to the vividness, vibrancy, and aliveness of the rest of the natural world."[37] We may be numb, or we may just be mindless in our consumption: naïve about where our products come from, how the workers are treated, what resources are extracted, who reaps the benefits, the impacts on the natural world, and so on. What we need to sacrifice is *mindless* consumption for *mindful* consumption that takes into account our interconnectedness with other human beings and other creatures. We need to sacrifice the thrill of buying whatever we want for intentional spending on what we need.

Sacrificing mindless, impulsive consumption is the least we can do for the well-being of Earth and all of its inhabitants. That does not mean it will

35. Schor, "Excerpt from *The Overworked American*," 34.
36. De Graaf et al., *Affluenza*, 71.
37. Gore, *Earth in the Balance*, 220.

be an easy sacrifice to make in a culture so geared toward consumption. After 9/11 the president and a number of our political leaders even gave Americans the impression that it was our patriotic duty for the sake of the economy to consume more. For followers of Jesus, sacrificing impulsive consumption is basic to the way of life we are called to by Jesus. It is a first step in taking up and bearing our ecological cross. The more urgent the ecological crisis becomes, the more our consumer choices will cease to be choices; they will be necessary sacrifices.

Another common-sense way to reduce the impact of consumption caught my attention in *Affluenza*. This one applies to the supplier of goods. Corporations would be required to "take full responsibility for the entire life cycle of their products." This idea is gaining wide acceptance in Europe. The effect is that "companies would no longer sell us products but lease them. Then, when the products reach the end of their useful lives, the same companies would take them back to reuse and recycle them, saving precious resources."[38] Consumers would have to sacrifice their sense of ownership—which does not seem too much to ask for the sake of "saving precious resources." We would be functioning more as stewards of the products than as consumers. One could envision a company not leasing to someone who is not a responsible steward of the product. This would be a direct way to hold consumers accountable for mindless, impulsive consumption.

Giving Up Our Subjugation to Chronological Time

A second sacrifice we are called to make is to give up our subjugation to chronological time, the time measured by our clocks and calendars. We drive ourselves to live at a feverish pace and in the process compromise the well-being of ourselves, of other human beings, and of the Earth community as a whole. As Henri Nouwen explains, our sense of being constantly hurried, of not having enough time, is the "experience of time as chronology, a randomly collected series of incidents and accidents over which we have no control and which gives us a sense of fatalism."[39] We feel caught on a treadmill that we cannot get off.

God does not want us to live a hurried and harried life. The biblical tradition offers us a concept of time distinctly different from time as *chronos*: namely, time as *kairos*. Kairos is the right time, the fitting time, God's

38. De Graaf et al., *Affluenza*, 230.

39. Nouwen, "Contemplation and Ministry," 53–54.

time to take action. When we are in touch with God's time, we have time to savor what we are doing. Sacrificing a life governed by chronological time liberates us to live the abundant life governed by kairotic time, which then leads to human well-being and the well-being of the whole Earth community.

In our stress on chronological time, asserts Larry Rasmussen, we have superimposed the "o'clock world" on the real world. We need to pay more attention to nature's rhythms and the seasons of life.[40] Native Americans tend to be more aware of these rhythms and seasons and tend to be less governed by the clock. Randy Woodley is a Keetoowah Cherokee and a distinguished professor of faith and culture and director of indigenous and intercultural studies at George Fox Evangelical Seminary in Portland, Oregon. He draws a distinction between "Indian time" and the Euro-western concept of time.[41] Whereas Native Americans are more place-oriented and land-based—they view themselves as bound to place—Euro-westerners are more time-oriented and concerned about events happening on time. As Woodley explains, "While it may seem like a good use of time to people from western cultures to mark the hours and even the minutes, Native Americans lean more toward valuing the organic interactions of place and people."[42] Euro-westerners operate as if "they have a clock inside their head."[43] Native Americans tend to prefer a less rigid, more relaxed time schedule.

This approach to time helps explain why many Native Americans have a greater sense of connectedness and kinship with Earth and all its creatures. Woodley does not explicitly compare "Indian time" to kairotic time. But neither concept of time is regulated by a clock. Woodley stresses that "Indian time is regulated by place, relationship, and the experience of the now."[44] In Mark 1:14–15 Jesus proclaims the good news of God, saying, "The time [*kairos*] is fulfilled, and the kingdom of God has come near; repent, and believe in the good news." Place, relationship, and the urgency of the now shape what it means for the kairos to be fulfilled.

40. Rasmussen, *Earth Community, Earth Ethics*, 35.

41. See Woodley, *Shalom and the Community of Creation*, esp. 112–20 and 135–37.

42. Ibid., 116.

43. Ibid., 115.

44. Ibid., 118.

Coming from the Buddhist tradition, Thích Nhất Hạnh laments that "under the pressure of time" (chronological time) we have become slaves and victims of a system we cannot control:

> For most of us who want to have a house, a car, a refrigerator, a television, and so on, we must sacrifice our time and our lives in exchange. We are constantly under the pressure of time. In former times, we could afford three hours to drink one cup of tea, enjoying the company of our friends in a serene and spiritual atmosphere. We could organize a party to celebrate the blossoming of one orchid in our garden. But today we can no longer afford these things. We say that time is money. We have created a society in which the rich become richer and the poor become poorer, and in which we are so caught up in our own immediate problems that we cannot afford to be aware of what is going on with the rest of the human family or our planet Earth.[45]

In order to respond in a faithful, fitting way to the ecological crisis we need to be aware of what is going on with our human family and our planet Earth. If our approach to time hinders our ability to gain such awareness, then that approach is to be sacrificed. Too much is at stake to let ourselves be swept up in a harried, frenzied way of life. Thích Nhất Hạhn warns us that the "bells of mindfulness are calling out to us, trying to wake us up, reminding us to look deeply at our impact on the planet."[46] How sad if we do not hear those bells ringing because we are caught up in feverish activity. Contuition—learning to see Earth and all its inhabitants as God sees them—takes time, unhurried time. Pondering and becoming mindful of what is going on with the rest of the creation takes time, unhurried time.

Cecile Andrews also stresses living mindfully in our daily lives. Living mindfully is a challenge for us because we can be so anxious about time. As with money, we never seem to have enough. Andrews observes, "That little voice always creeps in, You'd better hurry, you've got a lot to do, you're not getting enough done, time is running out." He laments that we spend so much of our time "in ways that kill our spirit, our capacity to enjoy the moment, to experience the depth of the moment."[47] Inspired by Thoreau, Andrews conceives of mindfulness as being fully alive and "living fully in the present." We so easily become distracted. We need to slow down and pay

45. Nhất Hạhn, "Bells of Mindfulness," 26.
46. Ibid., 25.
47. Andrews, "Spirituality of Everyday Life," 39.

attention to what is happening in us and around us in the present moment. Living mindfully means to "become deeply absorbed in what we are doing, appreciating the people we are with, being conscious of the wind on our face. It means paying attention to what you are doing, and not doing ten things at once. Taking the time to notice, slowing down, sitting peacefully, and just being."[48] How will we engage in ecological reform and in making peace on Earth and with the Earth community unless we are slowing down and focusing our attention on what is happening in us and around us?

In modern society it has been a common assumption that advances in technology lead to more leisure time—time for slowing down—and less working time, but we have actually gone in the other direction. According to the authors of *Affluenza*, we are suffering from a "time famine": "We have computers, fax machines, cell phones, e-mail, robots, express mail, freeways, jetliners, microwaves, fast food, one-hour photos, digital cameras, pop tarts, frozen waffles, instant this and instant that. But we have *less* free time than we did thirty years ago."[49] Increased technology has also increased expectations of the amount of work to be done in the time available. Swedish economist Staffan Linder warned in 1970 that we would become a "harried leisure class."[50] He has proven to be a prophet.

Time famine limits the time we have to savor what is happening in our lives. "In the trance of overwork," Wayne Muller sadly acknowledges, "we take everything for granted. We consume things, people, and information. We do not have time to savor this life, nor to care deeply and gently for ourselves, our loved ones, or our world; rather, with increasingly dizzying haste, we use them all up, and throw them away."[51] More time savoring life and less time working will enhance our capacity to care.

Time famine limits our ability to participate in worthwhile causes such as Earth care. We may wish to take up such causes; but as the authors of *Affluenza* state, "We're just too busy, too uncertain where to start, or too tired."[52] We may still dabble in a worthwhile cause but be hesitant to invest too deeply in it.

Time famine also limits our time to connect with nature. Louv stresses that "*time in nature is not leisure time; it's an essential investment in our*

48. Ibid., 38.

49. De Graaf et al., *Affluenza*, 39–41.

50. Quoted in ibid., 41.

51. Muller, *Sabbath*, 4, quoted in Hamilton-Poore, *Earth Gospel*, 129.

52. De Graaf et al., *Affluenza*, 208.

children's health." While Louv's point is well taken, given our busy way of life the case can be made that leisure time would likewise be an essential investment in our children's health. Children need relaxed time to play outdoors and to explore natural settings. To illustrate this point, Louv tells the story of a PTA officer in Shawnee Mission, Kansas, who confessed to him that her family had fallen into a time-consuming high-achievement trap:

> Our son was overstressed. We were overstressed. This realization came to us on one of those nights when all of our voices had raised an octave and all our eyes were opened just a little wider than normal and we all were just . . . it was just too much. We peaked out. Suddenly we realized we were giving our son the message that he had to achieve to be lovable. My husband and I were doing it, too: he was working long hours to be lovable and I was doing all these extracurricular activities to be lovable in the community, and it was just crazy. We were getting less lovable.[53]

The family finally decided to get out of the trap they were in. They compiled a list of what they loved to do and what they hated to do. They found out their son did not like soccer. They all liked being outside, camping or walking. The parents cut back on work, and they started going on walks or hikes. It helped them re-establish a connection with nature.

For years when Matthew Sleeth would give a talk at a church and someone would ask what he or she could do to be a better steward of the earth, his standard answer was, "Go home and replace all your light bulbs with efficient ones." Being a Christian, Sleeth liked the "symbolism of beginning a change with light." Changing light bulbs was something that could be done immediately and after an initial outlay of expense would save money on energy costs as well as help the environment. But more recently he has emphasized that one of the first and greatest things we can do for a "dying planet" is to obey the commandment to observe the Sabbath. The message of that commandment is to "STOP." We need to set aside a day to cease from our feverish activity. Sleeth cites Psalm 46:10: "Be still, and know that I am God!" He also highlights Jesus's invitation in Matthew 11:28: "Come to me, all you that are weary and are carrying heavy burdens, and I will give you rest."[54] Often our weariness is physical, but it can also be mental, emotional, or spiritual.[55] God set an example for us by resting on

53. Louv, *Last Child in the Woods*, 176.

54. Sleeth, *Gospel according to the Earth*, 80.

55. Cf. Maathai, *Replenishing the Earth*, 153–55.

the seventh day of creation. The first thing God does after completing God's creative work is to set aside time to rest and savor the creation. Even God sets aside time to rest in order to enhance God's capacity to care.

The people of Israel understood that the land also needed rest. Every seventh year was to "be a year of complete rest for the land" (Lev 25:5). Calvin DeWitt clarifies that the Sabbath year protects the land from "relentless exploitation," rejuvenates it, and gives it time to rest and be restored.[56] Our whole weary Earth home is desperately in need of Sabbath rest. A year of complete rest for the land is not possible if life is to continue on Earth. But if human beings were to slow down and develop a sustainable way of life—to cease from relentless exploitation—it would do wonders for the well-being of the land and our Earth home.

Ending Our Love Affair with the Automobile

A third significant sacrifice we must undertake is to end our love affair with the automobile. In the same way that the salmon has been identified as the iconic symbol of the Pacific Northwest, the automobile could be considered the iconic symbol of our American way of life. Purchasing a new automobile can be a consumptive rush. We love the freedom of being able to go wherever and whenever we want to go without having to spend forever getting there. As long as we have an automobile, we can live almost anywhere and still have access to work, shopping, family and friends, church, and leisure activities.

H. Paul Santmire describes the relationship of Americans to their automobiles as idolatrous:

> The automobile in America has become a kind of god, which millions adore with virtually unquestioned devotion. But not only does this god pollute mercilessly, it has become a default planning agent, whose pervasive use has mindlessly driven the reorganization of our national life, and in the process destroyed the vitality of countless urban neighborhoods and adversely affected whole bioregions, via freeways and suburban sprawl. Many think they cannot live without the automobile. Probably it is closer to the truth to say that, unless radical social, economic, and environmental changes are made, we cannot live with it.[57]

56. DeWitt, "Reading the Bible through a Green Lens," I-30.
57. Santmire, *Nature Reborn*, 125.

Santmire questions whether the Christian community has the courage to take a stand on the issue of something Americans hold so dear.

Fossil fuels are still essential in order to power most automobiles. In November 2012 Bill McKibben and 350.org went on a nationwide "Do the Math" tour to issue a call for educational and religious institutions, city and state governments, and other institutions that serve the public good to divest from fossil fuels. Less than a year later six colleges and universities, eighteen cities, two counties, thirteen religious institutions, three foundations, and four other institutions had made some kind of commitment to divest from fossil fuels. Hundreds more were considering the possibility. In order for this fossil fuel divestment movement to have maximum integrity, it may be a good idea to provide an ongoing accounting of how many in the movement have divested from their automobiles that run on fossil fuels. As mentioned earlier in this chapter, Gandhi refused to tell a young man not to eat sugar until he had proved to himself that he could go without it. Unless we are willing to give up our own automobiles, our stand against fossil fuels and the automobile will lack integrity. The first step in taking a stand is to see whether we can live without our automobiles or at least dramatically reduce our usage of them. Riding a bike or walking to work occasionally does not constitute a dramatic reduction in automobile usage. That counts as good exercise, but not as a major sacrifice.

Divesting from our automobiles in a suburban context would require sacrificing our expectations for what can be accomplished in a given amount of time. In the long run that would contribute to a slowing down of our pace of life. But in the short term there would be challenging adjustments and sacrifices to be made. My family and I live in Beaverton, Oregon, a classic American suburb with a Pacific Northwest flavor to it. These past ten years our three youngest children could not have been as involved in school, church, athletic, and other community activities unless my wife and I both had a car. No other form of transportation would have made it possible for them to participate in these activities, all of which were intrinsically wholesome. If neither my wife nor I had a car, the simple act of getting groceries would become much more cumbersome. Our whole suburban way of life has been built around the automobile.

If I were to divest from my automobile, the congregation I serve would need to accept that I am not going to be able to attend as many meetings and make as many visits as I have traditionally done. For example, if I were making hospital visits on a given afternoon, I could get to any hospital in the Portland metro area by alternative forms of transportation. However, I could probably only make a visit or two at one hospital instead of a number of visits at different hospitals; and I could not make a visit, rush back for a meeting at the church, and then make another visit. Without an automobile I probably would not come home for dinner if I had an evening meeting. If I rode my bicycle to work and had an evening meeting, then much of the year I would be riding home in the dark; even with streetlights, and lights on my bicycle, bicycling home would not be as safe as driving home in a car, especially in rainy Oregon weather.

My point is that divesting from automobiles is not a simple proposition. Many other people are involved. Giving up our automobiles will also impact our ability to consume and our use of time. It cuts right to the heart of our American way of life. Neither the ecologically enlightened nor the ecologically unenlightened will be eager to give up the way of life we have enjoyed, which is, of course, so dependent on fossil fuels and our automobiles. Although in the last several years the number of young people and others giving up on having cars has increased slightly,[58] my hunch is that most of us will explore every possible alternative to keep our automobiles running before we accept any restrictions in our use of time or freedom to travel. I would love to be wrong on this hunch.

Sacrificing our indulgent consumption, our subjugation to chronological time, and our love affair with the automobile goes beyond dabbling in ecological reform—such sacrifices are costly. But there are other costly sacrifices to be made. Each of us must discern specifically what taking up our ecological cross and following Jesus means for us today. And yet, we should not make major sacrifices impulsively or mindlessly without counting the cost. Jesus, to instruct his followers on the cost of discipleship, tells them this parable in Luke 14:28–30: "For which of you, intending to build a tower, does not first sit down and estimate the cost, to see whether he has enough to complete it? Otherwise, when he has laid a foundation and is not able to finish, all who see it will begin to ridicule him, saying, 'This fellow began to build and was not able to finish.'"

In Bonhoeffer's letter to Ruth Roberta Stahlberg of March 23, 1940, he asserts that when pastors speak, their words carry weight when they come not "from some semantic reflection or observation" but "from daily personal intimacy with the crucified Jesus Christ." Only then will we be able to speak from a position of composure. It is not easy, as Bonhoeffer

58. Maynard, "4 Big Reasons Why People Are Giving Up Cars."

acknowledges, to gain such composure.[59] We need time to ponder, to pray, to rest. Our harried, impulsive, indulgent way of life mitigates against cultivating such composure. As followers of Jesus in a time of ecological crisis, we must persist in daily personal intimacy with both the incarnate, crucified, and risen Jesus and with Earth and all of its inhabitants. Any decision to make a major ecological sacrifice needs to be made from a position of composure. Our motivation needs to be deeply rooted in our faith, in our relationships to God, our fellow human beings, and our fellow creatures. Given the urgency of the ecological crisis, we do not want to tarry or put off decisions to make needed sacrifices; and yet at the same time we do not want to rush and risk causing greater damage. Our decisions are to be faithful and thoughtful. Recognizing our limitations as human beings, we want to seek to see things as best we can as God sees them. Our decisions are to embody our core values: love of God, love of neighbor, love of creation, and love of self. We need to count the cost of our decisions to all with whom we are interconnected. Finally, we need to decide and act, trusting that God will use our action in some way to move the community of God, human beings, and all creatures toward *shalom*.

Into the Streets

In *Storms of My Grandchildren* James Hansen uses the term "greenwash" to refer to the tendency of governments to express "concern about global warming and the environment" without taking action "to actually stabilize climate or preserve the environment."[60] Hansen exhorts us to put pressure on our governments to take at least two essential actions to respond to the threat of climate change: "first, a significant and continually rising price on carbon emission, as the underpinning for a transformation to eventual carbon-free global energy systems, with collected revenues returned to the public so they have the resources to change their lifestyle accordingly"; second, "a strategic approach that leaves most fossil carbon in the ground."[61] The first action is the most critical for moving beyond fossil fuels to a clean energy future. The second action must entail a rapid phaseout of coal use. He also expresses particular concern about "unconventional," horrendously polluting fossil fuels such as tar sands and oil shale. In a May

59. Bonhoeffer, *Conspiracy and Imprisonment: 1940–1945* (DBWE 16), 41.

60. Hansen, *Storms of My Grandchildren*, ix–x.

61. Ibid., 269.

9, 2012, opinion piece in the *New York Times* Hansen asserts that if Canada proceeds with its plans to exploit its tar sands reserves, and we do nothing to stop it, "it will be game over for the climate." He laments that President Obama talks of a "planet in peril" but has not provided the decisive leadership needed to move the world in a new direction on climate change.

In President Obama's final term in office he has been more decisive in addressing the climate-change issue. The White House has published a plan to fight climate change. This plan consists of two key steps: first, "in June 2014, the Environmental Protection Agency (EPA) proposed the Clean Power Plan—the first-ever carbon pollution standards for existing power plants that will protect the health of our children and put our nation on the path toward a 30 percent reduction in carbon pollution from the power sector by 2030"; and second, "in November 2014, in a historic joint announcement with China, President Obama laid out an ambitious but achievable target to reduce greenhouse gas emissions in the United States in the range of 26 to 28 percent below 2005 levels by 2025, while China announced its intent to peak carbon emissions around 2030 and to double its share of zero-carbon energy to 20 percent."[62] On February 24, 2015, the President vetoed a bill approving the Keystone XL pipeline, which would transport oil from the tar sands of Canada. It was his first veto in five years.[63] This veto is precisely the kind of decisive leadership James Hansen has been calling for. President Obama has also included a $500 million request in the FY2016 federal budget for the recently created Green Climate Fund. That is one-sixth of the $3 billion the U.S. has pledged to this fund. The Green Climate Fund is a project of the parties to the U.N. Framework Convention on Climate Change. It aims to cultivate sustainable development by promoting a "paradigm shift towards low-emission and climate-resilient development pathways by providing support to developing countries to limit or reduce their greenhouse gas emissions and to adapt to the impacts of climate change, taking into account the needs of those developing countries particularly vulnerable to the adverse effects of climate change."[64] In these efforts to address climate change President Obama continues to face significant resistance from Congress. It is ironic that some of the stiffest

62. "Climate Change and President Obama's Action Plan," https://www.whitehouse.gov/climate-change.

63. Liptak, "Obama Rejects Keystone XL Bill."

64. Green Climate Fund, "Behind the Fund," http://www.gcfund.org/about/the-fund.html.

resistance comes from more conservative members of Congress, who one might think by definition would take the lead in seeking to *conserve* our Earth home.[65]

Taking a cue from Bonhoeffer, when the government fails to fulfill its responsibility to provide leadership in addressing the threat of catastrophic climate, the first thing the church is called to do is to name the sin—name the irresponsible behavior. The second action Bonhoeffer identifies is to aid the victims of government action or in this case inaction. At the pace we seem to be going, the number of victims will be overwhelming. If the government refuses to heed the critique of its irresponsible actions and to pay attention to the victims of government action or inaction, then a third alternative becomes necessary: direct political action. One form direct political action can take is the writing of letters to our elected leaders. For example, Bread for the World is "a collective Christian voice urging our nation's decision makers to end hunger at home and abroad."[66] One key strategy Bread for the World employs is to sponsor an annual "offering of letters." Members of churches are invited to write letters to their senators and representatives urging them to support specific legislation that will benefit the hungry. Bread for the World has had some amazing successes along the way with this approach.

James Hansen supports similar efforts in response to the climate-change issue. He first testified before Congress on the issue of climate change in the 1980s. He has produced many scientific papers, given many talks, and written many editorials. As far as he can tell, these efforts do not seem to have had much effect. The problem is "there are thousands of oil, gas, and coal lobbyists in Washington. These lobbyists are very well paid. It is no wonder that government energy policies are so hospitable to the fossil fuel industry."[67] So powerful are the fossil fuel interests that citizens need to "take to the streets" to demand action on climate change.[68] Hansen acknowledges that there are some local initiatives that have had an impact in the right direction. But we are faced with a global climate catastrophe. Decisive urgent global action is needed. Incremental local steps in themselves

---

65. My father considers himself a moderate to conservative Republican and a green Republican. Green Republicans are a minority group that we can hope, for the sake of our Earth home, will grow in the coming years.

66. "About Bread for the World," http://www.bread.org/about.

67. Hansen, *Storms of My Grandchildren*, 224.

68. Ibid., 277.

are not likely to be enough to set us on a sustainable course. The time has come to "force the present government to do its job."[69] "Civil resistance," proposes Hansen, "may be our best hope."[70] To give our civil resistance more teeth, Hansen also advocates filing suit against the government for failing to provide for our grandchildren and other young people who will inherit the disastrous ecological consequences of our irresponsible behavior. He also favors filing suit against the fossil fuel industry for using the "atmosphere as an open sewer without charge."[71] Hansen looks to religious communities not for scientific expertise but for leadership in advocating for preserving the planet for future generations. Peter Sawtell has observed how challenging it can be to "mobilize the politically diverse constituencies of congregations for advocacy and action."[72] But when Earth and major groups of its inhabitants are being ruthlessly exploited, the church has every reason to be in the streets, demanding mercy and justice for the exploited.

In the last chapter I mentioned how disillusioned Bonhoeffer was by the church's relative silence about the plight of the Jews in Nazi Germany. He was especially disturbed by the church's failure to make any public statement in the wake of *Kristallnacht*, the "Night of Broken Glass," November 9, 1938, when Nazi forces and German civilians targeted Jews and their synagogues, businesses, and institutions all over Germany.[73] This silence was a significant factor in pushing him toward involvement in the conspiracy.[74] In the face of global ecological exploitation and degradation, silence is not an option for those called to take up their ecological cross. The followers of Jesus are called to add our voices and our actions to the emerging coalition of people who care deeply for the well-being of Earth and all of its inhabitants. Just because it is hard to mobilize the church to resist issues such as ecological exploitation does not relieve us of the responsibility to do so.

69. Ibid., 292.

70. Ibid., 277.

71. Ibid., 294.

72. Sawtell, "Shalom Principle," 209.

73. "In two days, over 250 synagogues were burned, over 7,000 Jewish businesses were trashed and looted, dozens of Jewish people were killed, and Jewish cemeteries, hospitals, schools, and homes were looted while police and fire brigades stood by." "The 'Night of Broken Glass,'" United States Holocaust Memorial Museum, https://www.ushmm.org/outreach/en/article.php?ModuleId=10007697.

74. Bonhoeffer's involvement in the conspiracy against Hitler went beyond direct political action—it was an act of treason.

In the public struggle for climate justice a broad coalition of people and groups who care about our Earth home is needed. Hansen encourages his readers to support Bill McKibben and 350.org. McKibben, an active participant in the United Methodist Church and a scholar in residence at Middlebury College in Vermont, was instrumental in the formation of 350. org, a climate-change awareness campaign that in October 2009 coordinated what CNN called "the most widespread day of political action in the planet's history."[75] Three hundred fifty parts per million (ppm) of carbon dioxide has been proposed as a safe limit in the atmosphere. We have reached four hundred ppm and are still climbing. On 10/10/10 350.org was the catalyst for the largest global work party in history. In more than 7,400 sites in 188 countries around the globe people engaged in hands-on projects to address the ecological crisis. At my home congregation, St. Andrew Lutheran Church in Beaverton, Oregon, a team of people worked on restoring our wetland. About half of them were members, and half were volunteers from the community. What united us was a desire to do something tangible to care for our Earth home.

350.org has been a catalyst for a number of other national and global Earth-care action events. In late August and early September 2011 McKibben and more than twelve hundred others were arrested while protesting in front of the White House against the Keystone XL Pipeline project. Moving Planet, September 24, 2011, was a day to move beyond fossil fuels and use alternative forms of transportation such as walking, biking, and mass transit. People in more than 175 countries participated. As I mentioned earlier in this chapter, the "Do the Math" tour in November 2012 kicked off the move to encourage educational, religious, governmental, and other organizations to divest from their investments in fossil fuels. On September 21, 2013, organizations across the globe were encouraged to "Draw the Line" on the Keystone XL Pipeline.[76] 350.org was one of many sponsoring organizations for the People's Climate March on September 21, 2014. Well over three hundred thousand people from all over the country and the world took the call to address climate change to the streets of New York City. It was the largest demonstration on behalf of the planet in history.[77] More than 2,600 solidarity events in 160-plus countries were held on that

75. McKibben, *eaarth*, 211.

76. For information on these and other events see the 350.org website: http://350. org/.

77. Foderaro, "Taking a Call for Climate Change to the Streets."

day.[78] A number of us from St. Andrew Lutheran Church in Beaverton participated in a smaller march of five thousand people along the waterfront in Portland.

The jury is still out on whether we will be able to carve out a sustainable way of life on the tough new planet McKibben calls "eaarth." Reading the first part of his book *eaarth* one could easily give in to despair, hopelessness, and cynicism. McKibben acknowledges that "it's true that by some measures we have started too late"[79] to confront the ecological disasters we face; and he shares his fear that the reality described in his book, "and increasingly evident in the world around us, will be an excuse to give up."[80] In the end McKibben vows to keep on fighting, hoping to limit the damage of the destructive forces we have unleashed. We must be willing to take the fight into the streets as McKibben, a diverse coalition of participants in 350. org, and other organizations concerned about our Earth home have done. At the same time we must learn, asserts McKibben, to live "lightly, carefully, gracefully."[81]

One of the most creative and pragmatic responses to ecological degradation has been that of the late Wangari Maathai and the Green Belt Movement. Maathai had a deep appreciation for the power of a tree. As she explains, the tree has not simply been "a source of food, medicine, and building material but a place of healing, consolation, and connection—with other human beings and with the divine."[82] Because of their spiritual significance trees have been natural places for a community to gather together to address difficult issues. Maathai's faith and the power of a tree inspired the Green Belt Movement. Maathai recognized that "behind the everyday hardships of the poor—environmental degradation, deforestation, and food insecurity—were deeper issues of disempowerment, disenfranchisement, and a loss of the traditional values."[83] Government in Kenya had not addressed any of these issues adequately; it had not done its job.

78 "People's Climate March: To Change Everything, We Need Everyone, Everywhere." See http://peoplesclimate.org/.

79 McKibben, *eaarth*, 211.

80. Ibid., xv.

81. Ibid., 212.

82. Maathai, *Replenishing the Earth*, 83–84.

83. Green Belt Movement, "Our History," http://www.greenbeltmovement.org/who-we-are/our-history. Maathai gives a more complete account of the inspiring story of this movement in *The Green Belt Movement*.

Bonhoeffer's three options for responding to an irresponsible government can help us analyze the development of the Green Belt Movement. In its inception Maathai and this movement focused on aiding the victims of government inaction. Their work expanded as the movement matured. They realized they could not wait for the government to do its job, nor could they simply expect God to take care of the difficult issues for them. The Green Belt Movement became involved in all three of the options Bonhoeffer identified: naming the sin, aiding the victims, and engaging in direct political action. A series of questions by Maathai reflects the scope of their work: "Can we honestly ask God to intervene, or do we write letters to the relevant ministers of government? Do we demonstrate in the streets to register our disappointment with poor governance of natural resources or do we ask the angels in Heaven to do something about it? Do we make the connection between environmental degradation and the problems which communities face every day?"[84] For Maathai, God motivates us and guides us to engage in whatever form of action will address the real issues people and the whole Earth community face.

Maathai took action as part of a movement. But a movement of only one person engaged in an act of resistance can also bring about profound change. Sometimes we cannot wait for a movement to form. A matter may be so pressing it compels us to act here and now. This was true for Julia Butterfly Hill, who in December 1997, at the age of twenty-three, decided she was not going to sit idly by and watch an ancient redwood she called Luna be chopped down. She climbed Luna and set up a tent on a tiny platform high in the tree. She stayed for two years, much longer than she anticipated. While in the tree, she developed a close relationship with it. Her protest generated national and international interest concerning the protection of old-growth forests in California and around the world. Finally the lumber company relented and decided not to cut down Luna. A number of other redwoods were saved along with Luna. Julia's protest exemplified the power of one. An act of timely resistance by one person can result in radical change for the better.[85]

As we face the ecological crisis and seek to discern what action to take, Maathai offers this practical advice: "Look at the problem in front of you and try to solve it. Don't peer too far down the road and ask, 'What can I do

84. Quoted in Hamilton-Poore, *Earth Gospel*, 159.

85. For a brief account of Hill's protest, see Maathai, *Replenishing the Earth*, 99–101. Hill tells the full story in her book *The Legacy of Luna*.

then?' For you risk being overwhelmed."[86] For followers of Jesus the question is, what am I being called to do today? Julia Butterfly demonstrated that one person can trigger tremendous change. At the same time, Maathai counsels that we need to be aware of our limits. She has caught herself thinking, "If only I had fifty more years, I could do so much, because now I know what to do—and there are so many more problems to be solved! But life isn't like that. Sometimes you don't have enough time, and too much needs to be done. I have come to accept that you cannot do everything, and no one should expect you to—including yourself." She highlights one piece of advice for young people: "It's important not to waste time—particularly because you think there are many years ahead. Don't fret about looking around to find the absolutely right vocation."[87] As followers of Jesus, we are called to act today. What does it mean to be a human being for Earth and all of its inhabitants today?

86. Ibid., 190.
87. Ibid., 191.

7

Coming Home to Earth

The Parable of the Prodigal Species

In the parable of the Prodigal Son (Luke 15:11–32) the youngest son asked for his share of the family inheritance, gathered all his belongings, and left home. He traveled to a distant land; and free to do whatever he wanted with what he had, he squandered his inheritance in dissolute living. When a severe famine set in, he began to experience hunger. In desperation he hired himself out as a field hand to feed pigs. Since the Jews considered pigs to be unclean, working with pigs represented a real fall—it was as low as he could go. He was so hungry himself that he would have gladly eaten the pods he was feeding the pigs. Finally, he came to his senses and realized his father's field hands were living better than he was. He knew he had no right to live as his father's son. But he resolved to confess the error of his ways and ask his father to hire him as a field hand. As the story goes, his father saw him coming while he was still a long way off. Filled with compassion, the father ran and threw his arms around him and kissed him. Even as the son tried to confess his sins, the father began planning a party to celebrate the return of his beloved boy. He exclaimed, "This son of mine was dead and is alive again; he was lost and is found!"

Like the Prodigal Son, we humans have been given our share of the family inheritance—that is, a portion of our Earth home. And like the Prodigal Son, we have imposed our exile on ourselves and engaged in extravagant, wasteful living. In fact, our prodigality has surpassed that of the indulgent son: we have squandered more than our fair share of our Earth home, and other creatures have had to pay the price. As was the father in the parable, God is eagerly waiting for us to come home. Will we, the prodigal species, come to our senses before it is too late? Will we come home and care for our Earth community in such a way that all humankind and otherkind can thrive?

Whether we impose exile on ourselves or have it imposed on us, it is one of the most painful human experiences. When Jerusalem fell to the Babylonians in 587 BCE, the people of God were exiled to Babylon. It would be fifty long years before the exiled people of God were allowed to return home. In exile they wondered if God still cared about them. In Isaiah chapters 34–35 and 40–55 the prophet shares with the exiles reassuring words from the Lord that the Lord still cares and is still Lord of creation and history.

In our own time, without leaving our Earth home, it is as if we have gone into ecological exile. We have this growing sense that life is ecologically out of balance. The rapid increase in species extinction, the steady loss of fertile topsoil, the diminishment of clean water, the contamination (and engineering) of foods, cruelty to animals, air pollution, the spread of invasive species, and climate change are evidence of this imbalance. Our consumptive way of life is destroying our homeland.

Wendell Berry once said that "no sane creature befouls its own nest."[1] Given the ways we have misused and abused our Earth home, we could question our sanity as human beings. Or it could be more a matter of losing our sense of Earth as our home. Sadly, asserts Berry, "we no longer know the earth we come from, have no respect for it, keep no responsibilities to it." The modern household contributes to our disconnect from the sources of our bodily life. In fact, "the modern home is a veritable factory of waste and destruction." Berry wrote these words in the 1970s; but even today in most of our homes, our various gadgets and machines are "all powered by energies that are destructive of land or air or water, and connected to work, market, school, recreation, etc., by gasoline engines." The energy efficiency has improved in many of our appliances, but we have added more appliances and electronic gadgets such as computers. The typical modern household may be viewed as the mainstay of the economy, but it is an

---

1. Berry, *Unsettling of America*, 51.

ecological catastrophe that "takes in the world's goods and converts them into garbage, sewage, and noxious fumes."[2]

Dramatic changes in our way of life are needed to restore ecological balance and our sense of being at home on Earth. We have squandered our bountiful inheritance with extravagant, wasteful living. My generation, the baby boomers, may be remembered in the history books as the most wasteful generation in the history of Earth. It is time to come home to Earth. We have been in ecological exile for far too long. To come home to Earth is to come to our senses and realize that the ecological destruction of Earth and all of its inhabitants also negatively impacts human beings. The good news is that the reverse is also true. In promoting healing for the whole Earth community, we promote our own well-being. Thus, as Maathai clarifies, "we can love ourselves by loving the earth; feel grateful for who we are, even as we are grateful for the earth's bounty; better ourselves, even as we use that self-empowerment to improve the earth; offer service to ourselves, even as we practice volunteerism for the earth."[3]

No Place Like Our Earth Home

In December 1968 the Apollo 8 crew left our Earth home behind to embark on the first manned mission to the moon. On Christmas Eve they entered lunar orbit. Astronauts Frank Borman, Jim Lovell, and William Anders broadcast live from space and showed pictures of Earth and the moon. The most famous of these photos was "Earthrise." Lovell commented, "The vast loneliness is awe-inspiring and it makes you realize just what you have back on Earth."[4] Toward the end of the broadcast they read the first ten verses of the creation story in Genesis 1. Then Borman finished with this blessing, "And from the crew of Apollo 8, we close with good night, good luck, a Merry Christmas, and God bless all of you—all of you on the good Earth."[5]

What the Apollo 8 crew realized in those awe-inspiring moments is that they had a home back on the good Earth. Carl Sagan was thrilled when a picture of Earth "from the outskirts of the solar system" was finally able to be taken before his death in 1996. Earth, explained Sagan, "was a pale blue dot. No continents, no national boundaries, no beings, no humans, just a

2. Ibid., 52.

3. Maathai, *Replenishing the Earth*, 16–17.

4. NASA, "Apollo 8: Earthrise."

5. NASA, "Apollo 8: Christmas at the Moon."

dot. That's us. That's where we live. That's where everyone we know, everyone we love, everyone we ever heard of, every human being who ever lived has lived: on that pale blue dot." For Sagan that pale blue dot underscored how fragile and vulnerable Earth is. He then asserted that "our central responsibility is to cherish and care for the environment on the only home we have ever known and the only home for all those other beings with whom we are so profoundly connected."[6] Even if we have never left Earth, we need to rediscover it as home.

No Escape from Our Earth Home

As I mentioned in chapter 1, in the Christian tradition I grew up in, the earth was viewed as a temporary home. We were taught to hope that after death we would go to heaven, our eternal home, to be with Jesus. This otherworldly emphasis was not unique to my Norwegian Lutheran tradition. As Dietrich Bonhoeffer asserts in "Thy Kingdom Come," Christians have been otherworldly in our orientation "ever since we discovered the devious trick of being religious, indeed 'Christian,' at the expense of the Earth." Otherworldliness is a form of "religious escapism."[7] It can be difficult, especially in the face of suffering and evil, not to succumb to the temptation of leaving Earth behind and looking forward to a better world, an eternal home, on the other side.

The better world we hope for is not some eternal heavenly home for those fortunate enough to have escaped the cruel, suffering world in which we live. We envision a new heaven and a new earth. Earth is not left behind. It is resurrected—transformed. Earth is a vital part of any eternal home with God. As Revelation 21:3 affirms, "See, the home of God is among mortals." We have no promised eternal home apart from our Earth home.

Christians could be tempted to escape to a better world on the other side of ecological doom. Such a vision of a better world may be comforting to those feeling overwhelmed by the ecological crises we face. But we have no escape from our Earth home. Larry Rasmussen clarifies that this primordial community known as Earth is the place where we belong: "We are at home here. Our lives, their excitement, and their fulfillment are here. We are most ourselves when we are most intimate with the rivers, mountains, forests, meadows, sun, moon, stars, air, soil, rocks, otherkind, and

6. Quoted in Hamilton-Poore, *Earth Gospel*, 116.
7. Bonhoeffer, "Thy Kingdom Come," in *Berlin: 1932–1933* (DBWE 12), 286.

humankind. This and no other is our own primordial community. This primordial community is a home without an exit."[8] We have no eternal escape to a heavenly home with God apart from Earth.

The Home We Share

Growing up primarily in Wisconsin and Oregon, I had never seen our national bird, the bald eagle, which had become an endangered species in the Lower 48, in large part due to the chemical pollution Rachel Carson exposed in *Silent Spring*. In August 1983 my wife, Donna, our young children, Isaac and Rachel, and I traveled to Juneau, Alaska, where I served for a year as the Intern Pastor of Resurrection Lutheran Church. The only way to get in to Juneau is by ferry or airplane—the farthest one can travel by car outside of Juneau is about forty miles. Over the years, building a road along the southeast Alaska coastline to connect Juneau, the state capital, with the rest of Alaska had been discussed but never acted upon. The construction costs were enormous, and there were laws prohibiting building a road within a certain distance of an eagle's nest. There was an eagle's nest about every half-mile along the southeast Alaska coastline. One of the highlights of my year in Juneau was traveling along this coastline by boat and seeing eagle after eagle perched in the trees above me. Since our time in Juneau, the bald eagle population has recovered in the Lower 48—one of the great success stories of the Endangered Species Act. Bald eagles were removed from the endangered species list in August 2007. In May 2015 I hiked with a friend up Table Mountain on the Washington side of the Columbia River, near Bonneville Dam. From the top we had breathtaking views of the Columbia Gorge. But nothing could compare with the bald eagle that soared in front of us as we were eating lunch. I felt like reaching out and blessing it.

Now bald eagles are threatened once again, but they are not alone. All species are endangered by the threat of ecological catastrophe in the form of climate change. The rate of species extinction is accelerating. The whole Earth community is under assault. That is why John Chryssavgis makes the striking statement that the "most endangered species is not the whale or the forest; it is the earth that we share. The earth is our home . . . ; it is where all of us—whales, trees, and people alike—live and die."[9] Denis Edwards defines "the ecology" as "the home we share." More precisely, ecology is

8. Rasmussen, *Earth Community, Earth Ethics*, 325–26.
9. Chryssavgis, "Cry of the Earth," 94.

the study of the home we share. In studying the home we share, it becomes clear that "if our home is polluted, exploited and denuded, the poor of the Earth suffer and die along with fauna and flora." That is why ecological issues and human justice issues are "radically interrelated." Edwards calls for an ethics that includes an "intelligent and enduring commitment to the homeless and the hungry and to the ecological integrity of the Earth."[10]

Coming home to Earth entails fulfilling this commitment to ecological integrity and justice. We do not come home to Earth or fulfill this commitment in general. We do so in a particular place—our home place. In a global warming unit taught by Brady Bennon at Madison High School in Portland, Oregon, when Bennon asked why places affect people so profoundly, a student named Alex responded, "Places are important because they can make us feel like we belong. We all need a home."[11] We are far more likely to take care of a place that feels like home, like we belong.

In Peter Bakken's sermon "Landscape of Grace" he asserts that our home place or region can "open a window into understanding and learning how to care for the wider world."[12] The vast scale of the ecological problems on Earth can seem overwhelming, and it can be difficult to know where to start. Bakken suggests that a good place to begin is with our home place or region. At St. Andrew Lutheran Church in Beaverton, we began by focusing on restoring our wetland and are now helping initiate efforts to restore our local watershed. The focus for our spring 2015 Earth Care Forum was on "Watershed Discipleship." In the Pacific Northwest, the 2000 Catholic Bishops' Letter on the Columbia River Watershed was a significant contribution in teaching us to think of watersheds as our primary geographic reality, as our home.[13] In April 2013 theologian and activist Ched Myers led an Earth care workshop at St. Andrew. The highlight of the day for him appeared to be a tour of our wetland and Sanctuary of the Firs, an outdoor sanctuary in the midst of majestic Douglas Fir trees. He was especially encouraged by the interest of the Earth Care Team in pursuing the restoration of not just our upland/wetland but also our local watershed. Myers has issued a

---

10. Edwards, *Jesus the Wisdom of God*, 4

11. Bennon, "Paradise Lost," 55.

12. Bakken, "Landscape of Grace," 17.

13. "The Columbia River Watershed: Caring for Creation and the Common Good," an international pastoral letter by the Catholic Bishops of the Watershed Region, signed on Feast of the Baptism of the Lord, June 8, 2001.

call for a "watershed discipleship alliance."[14] Watershed discipleship entails a commitment by followers of Jesus to healing our world by restoring the health of our respective watersheds. This requires watershed literacy. To paraphrase Baba Dioum, a Senegalese environmentalist, "We won't save places we don't love. We can't love places we don't know. And we don't know places we haven't learned."[15] For followers of Jesus, watershed discipleship offers a way of coming to learn, know, and love our home place.

Wendell Berry identifies the first American revolution and the one with the greatest impact as the "coming of people who did *not* look upon the land as a homeland."[16] They had lost their sense of a home place. They focused on getting what they could out of the land and moved on to greener pastures when the land did not produce enough. Native Americans moved around at times, but they retained a deep sense of the land as their home. Randy Woodley highlights this deep sense by using the image of being "married" to the land. Indigenous people, explains Woodley, "understand themselves as inseparable from the land." They "know their land . . . every hill, spring, and tree."[17] The idea of owning the land was anathema to most Native American traditions. In this same vein, Berry is willing to accept the idea of ownership, but only if as many people as possible share in the ownership of the land and work the land. They would be bound to the land "by economic interest, by the investment of love and work, by family loyalty, by memory and tradition."[18]

Berry refers to this idea of shared ownership of the land as "settlement" or "domestic permanence." He observes that many of his family's stories and their meanings survived because his family remained connected to their home place. His grandfather and father grew up on and served as caretakers of the family farm in Henry County, Kentucky. Berry's brother resides on and cares for what they affectionately refer to as the "home place." As mentioned earlier, Berry and his wife, Tanya, have lived on their farm in their home neighborhood since 1965. Berry is quite sure that "if we, like most of our generation, had moved away, the place with its memories

---

14. "Toward a Watershed Discipleship Alliance."

15. Quoted in Myers, "A Reflection on Isaiah 5." For more on watershed discipleship, see also Myers, "Watershed Moment," 20–24.

16. Berry, *Unsettling of America*, 4.

17. Woodley, *Shalom and the Community of Creation*, 120.

18. Berry, *Unsettling of America*, 13.

would have been lost to us and we to it."[19] He highlights the virtues of set-
tling down and practicing domestic permanence. But his main point is not
that we have to live in the same place all our lives. The key is to have a deep
affection for the places we live and a deep connection to the land. The land
is not something we simply use. It is not simply a resource. It is our home.
"Indeed, once our homeland, our source, is regarded as a resource," warns
Berry, "we are all sliding downward toward the ash heap or the dump."[20]

A sense of our Earth as our home place reflects where we are in our
relationship to God. How can we love God whom we have not seen if we
do not love our home place which we have seen? How can we long for an
eternal home with God if we do not appreciate our Earth home God has
given us? Heaven is as close as the ground on which we walk.

The Sunriver Story

I would never have thought that a five-star destination resort could have
been a home place for me and my family, but ever since Donna and I were
married in 1977, Sunriver, in the high desert of central Oregon, has been
just that. Sunriver is a small community about ten miles south of Bend.
During a typical summer week, some twenty thousand people will stay
there, but fewer than two thousand are permanent residents. Since my dad
retired in 1995, my parents have lived there in the modest vacation home
they built in the late 1970s. Soon after its founding in 1968, Sunriver was
discovered by people with significant financial means, and they built some
amazing high-end homes.

We have never lived in Sunriver, and I have never been a strong fan
of destination resorts, but it has always felt like home. My wife and I and
all our children enjoy spending time there. During married life together
Donna and I have moved thirteen times, so Sunriver has been a constant
home away from home. It has given us a sense of place; we feel we belong
there. Part of the reason has been my parents' presence there. But this sense
of place also stems from the way Sunriver was designed and built up in its
natural setting.

When Don and Mary McCallum were invited by Lee Evans to visit
the old ranch that would become Sunriver, they were drawn to the natural
beauty of the place. As Dave Ghormley writes, "They wandered beside the

19. Berry, *It All Turns on Affection*," 12.
20. Berry, *Home Economics*, 136.

river and had a picnic under a big ponderosa tree and looked at Bachelor Butte looming up beyond the little pasture, framed by the river and a beautiful grove of trees. They fell in love with it all." Enthused by their visit, they arranged with Evans to become part owners. John Gray, who had developed Salishan Lodge on the Oregon coast, was also introduced to the property and became a part owner.[21]

The original plan for Sunriver was to construct a series of small villages connected by winding paths. The developers contemplated limiting transportation to bikes and golf carts. "Each village," explains Ghormley, "would be unique and isolated, enveloped in the woods and the fields and ponds, close to Nature's animals and bird life. A touch of heaven safely tucked away in the piney woods."[22] Over the years the developers and owners gradually gave up on the idea of villages being distinctive and self-contained. Nonetheless, vestiges of the village concept remain to this day; and wherever one is in Sunriver, one senses a close connection to nature's animals, birdlife, and trees and plants. It is also true that it is often easier to walk or bike the pathways within or between villages than to drive a car. The speed limit in Sunriver is twenty-five miles per hour. Even without a speed limit traffic would go slower than usual due to the series of ten roundabouts, twisting streets, and relaxed feel of Sunriver.

From early on Sunriver developers and owners were committed to preserving the natural beauty of the place. It is not clear what was the origin of this concern for the environment at Sunriver. In any case that concern was incorporated into the Sunriver Plan, a document that has guided development there to the present. One way a commitment to the environment was implemented from the outset was the creation of the position of Resident Naturalist. The Resident Naturalist was responsible for the "protection of the land and waters and all flora and fauna. The naturalist was also in charge of the Nature Center (originally called the Ecologium) which is used as a center for education. His most important function, however, was as the final arbiter of any controversy regarding the environment."[23] According to the Sunriver Plan, cherished older trees were to "be carefully preserved during construction of the homes, roads, paved bicycle paths, golf courses, swimming pools, tennis courts, playgrounds, quaint shops,

21. Ghormley, "Beginnings," 14–15.
22. Ibid., 15.
23. Redding, *Suddenly Settlers*, 7.

airport, observatory, restaurants, and lodge."[24] When trees were displaced, new trees were to be planted. The lead article of the January 1971 issue of *American Home* highlighted the positive attitude of Sunriver homeowners toward ecology and nature. They "planted native trees and shrubs and left the ground cover in more or less a natural and unprotected state, often planting wild flowers and spacing boulders and logs to create natural beauty."[25]

In 1978 a Design Review Committee was established to monitor this process of removing and planting trees. The committee recognized that every house and structure had a "sphere of influence" and that it was necessary to "firmly defend the integrity of the forest environment." They stipulated the planting of five, ten, or more Ponderosa pines to re-establish the forest. The planting of these trees was considered the "strongest and most effective way to mitigate and soften the presence of a house or other structure."[26] The Design Review Committee is also responsible for regulation of architecture. The basic principle is that "Sunriver is the kind of place where the natural surroundings are at least as important as the houses and we would rather have the houses blend in than stand out."[27]

Sunriver is a testimony to how development can work with nature, and the word got out early on about this well-planned development. Paul and Pat Redding had read about it in the *San Francisco Chronicle*. In July 1970, while touring the Northwest, they stopped at a motel in Bend. When they asked the motel owner about Sunriver, he said, "There are some pretty awful real estate developments going on around here, but Sunriver is great. All the growth in the county should be as well planned." The Reddings toured this new development and bought a lot. Paul Redding commented, "As we toured Sunriver we became more and more impressed with the amenities, in a setting for the gods and complete with the purest air and water we had encountered anywhere."[28]

When my family visits Sunriver, I join my parents on their morning walk and enjoy breathing in the pure air that impressed the Reddings. My parents do not just walk; they pick up litter and collect refundable cans and bottles along the way. Whoever walks with them is expected to do the same.

24. Bending, "Design and Planning of Sunriver," 55.
25. Article referred to in Redding, *Suddenly Settlers*, 15.
26. Bending, "The Design and Planning of Sunriver," 55.
27. Redding, *Suddenly Settlers*, 15.
28. Ibid., 2.

They turn in these cans and bottles at the Sunriver Marketplace and use the refund money to pay for their morning coffee. They have been following this routine since they retired to Sunriver more than twenty years ago. Not long after they became permanent residents, they decided to invite others to pick up litter and trash. A number of people joined them, and the LT (Litter and Trash) Rangers came into existence. Each person or couple has an assigned area along the roads and bike paths to keep clean. The LT Rangers number among their ranks retired business executives, physicians, and lawyers as well as a variety of others. It is endearing and encouraging to see these high-powered, well-off people picking up trash and litter rather than just hiring someone else to do it. It is a sign that they love their home place. Governor Tom McCall would have been proud. Picking up litter and trash at Sunriver is not going to solve the major ecological crises we face. But learning to care for our Earth home enough to clean it up will be essential to avoiding ecological catastrophe and providing for the well-being of the whole Earth community. Even a destination resort can be a home place if our connection to our Earth home is taken into account.

The Beaverton Story

Sunriver has influenced not only the development of other destination resorts in central Oregon and around the Northwest but also recent development in established communities such as nearby Bend. A couple of years ago we drove through the westside of Bend on our way to a day hike. The combination of roundabouts, bike paths separated from the streets, and open spaces had a Sunriver feel to it.

Established communities, like our home community of Beaverton, seldom have the luxury of pursuing Earth-friendly development in a pristine natural setting, as the Sunriver community had. Beaverton is working hard to build a system of bike paths. But it is difficult and expensive to do in an established suburb built up around the automobile as its primary means of transportation. So many of our bike paths are simply narrow lanes along a busy street. One of my worst fears as a driver is turning right into the pathway of a bike. As a biker, I appreciate the efforts to provide bike paths; but whenever possible, I try to avoid bike paths along busy streets. My favorite bike path in Beaverton is the Fanno Creek Trail, which is for the most part separated from the streets. It is the closest thing we have to a Sunriver bike path.

To its credit, the City of Beaverton has gained national attention for its efforts to use green or renewable power. It is the only city that purchases all of its power from Portland General Electric's renewable power program. It has achieved PGE's Platinum Clean Wind ranking, the highest ranking available. In 2012, the City of Beaverton was given the Green Power Community of the Year Leadership Award by the Environmental Protection Agency. Beaverton's commitment to sustainability has also been recognized nationally. The U.S. Conference of Mayors awarded the City of Beaverton its 2012 Mayors' Climate Protection Award. Beaverton has also encouraged residents and businesses to purchase green power.[29]

Recycling is also a major emphasis of the City of Beaverton. For the majority of residents recycling has become a way of life. The roll carts for recyclable material and yard debris are larger than the roll carts for garbage. In the summer of 2014 the City of Beaverton published "Every Day is a Recycling Day" and distributed it to the residents and businesses. This eight-page color brochure details where all the stuff goes that the garbage hauler picks up, what can go into home and workplace recycling, what can be done with stuff that cannot go into home or workplace recycling but does have recyclable value, and what do with products that may be especially harmful to the environment, such as old computers, other electronic equipment, and unused paint. It also provides tips on home composting and junk mail reduction. It made me proud to live in Beaverton and enhanced my sense of Beaverton being our home place. It would make me even prouder if our culture as a whole would learn to produce less stuff that needs to be hauled away. Coming home to Earth begins with caring for the local communities and places in which we live.

For the Love of Earth?

Earth care is one of our five core care values at St. Andrew Lutheran Church in Beaverton, Oregon. Not everyone in the congregation is fully committed to this core value, however, nor is everyone convinced that climate change is an unfolding ecological catastrophe, at least not one for which human beings are primarily responsible. When I discuss this issue with climate-change skeptics, I make the point that if there is even a 10 percent chance of climate change leading to ecological catastrophe, would we not want to do whatever it takes to minimize that 10 percent chance?

29. "Green Power in Beaverton," 10.

Hayhoe and Farley address *A Climate for Change* to the Evangelical Christian faith community, in particular, a community with a significant number of climate-change skeptics. They encourage these skeptics to take the same approach to climate change that they take with auto or home insurance. If we took a similar approach, they assert, "we'd probably be doing something about climate change right now. And we'd probably invest in that security even if we thought there wasn't much chance that something bad would actually happen. The actual risk involved with global climate change is higher than many of us are normally willing to accept in our personal lives."[30] As misguided as climate-change skeptics may be, or as cynical as political leaders or fossil-fuel company executives may be who use climate-change skepticism for personal gain, these skeptics are not the major obstacle standing in the way of addressing the impending ecological catastrophe before us. The major obstacle is ourselves. Are we willing to sacrifice an unsustainable way of life that we hold dear (or at least aspire to)?

In the course of this project I have come across numerous approaches or strategies for motivating people to address climate change. The first is to scare the hell out of people with frightening ecological facts and to make them feel guilty for contributing to the ecological mess we face. This is the ecological version of "hellfire and brimstone" preaching. We are doomed if we do not do something soon. Such an approach serves to get people's attention, and it may motivate them to take action for a time. But it is questionable whether such a gloom-and-doom approach will lead to a sustainable way of life. Theodore Roszak indicts environmentalists for investing so deeply in "scaring and shaming people." He questions whether environmentalists "can go on doing that indefinitely . . . [pushing] that same fear-guilt button over and over again. As psychologists will tell you, when a client comes in with an addiction, they are already ashamed. You don't shame them further."[31] The confrontational tactics of organizations such as Greenpeace, Sea Shepherd, and Earth First! at their best compel us to reflect more deeply on the profound change needed in our way of thinking and our way of life. But these tactics, if repeated continually, risk pushing the fear-guilt button over and over again.

The gloom-and-doom approach also runs the risk of encouraging people to give up and give in to passivity in the face of an overwhelming

---

30. Hayhoe and Farley, *Climate for Change*, 24.

31. Quoted in Louv, *Last Child in the Woods*, 147.

situation. Christians who long for an eternal home in heaven apart from Earth may be especially prone to falling into what Maathai refers to as a disheartening passivity. They forsake "all belief in their own ability to bring about the change they would like to see in their lives. Instead of, for example, taking strength from their faith to empower themselves, they are leaving all the power—all the agency—in God's hands." The Green Belt Movement, founded by Maathai, encourages us "not to wait for divine intervention." It is not enough for people of faith to pray that God will provide. God expects us "to take action and rise up and walk!"[32]

A second approach is to appeal to human self-interest. The ecological threat to ourselves is serious enough that self-interest ought to motivate humans to care for Earth and all of its creatures. We are discovering that our own well-being is intimately connected with the well-being of other creatures. Eco-psychologist Terrance O'Connor affirms that enlightened self-interest is the key to motivating people to change their way of life and to exercise ecological responsibility: "If this is not my planet, whose is it? I am the cause, and I am the cure. When I act out of this realization, I act not out of guilt but out of self-love. I break through my denial and see that humankind is facing an absolutely unprecedented crisis. I act not out of obligation or idealism, but because I live in a straw house and I smell smoke."[33]

People of faith may have a tendency to dismiss this appeal to self-interest too quickly, insisting on purer motives. But love of nature/earth/creation may not be enough to motivate people locked in on pursuing the good life for themselves. Given the urgency of the ecological crisis, it may be a mistake to insist on pure motives. We may need to start right where people are, with a variety of motives. With those preoccupied with themselves, the place to begin may be with love of self. The second greatest commandment is "You shall love your neighbor as yourself." Love of self is essential to love of neighbor. It is also essential to love of Earth. What we have discovered is that our way of life needs to change for our own ecological well-being. Even if we are simply concerned for ourselves, we need to make major changes in our way of life. Love of self to the exclusion of all others is sin. But love of self may need to be the starting point in motivating many people. And after all, the self is created and loved by God, so it is valued by God.

---

32. Maathai, *Replenishing the Earth*, 143.
33. Quoted in De Graaf et al, *Affluenza*, 205.

Having said all this, love of self in itself is not an adequate motive for embracing a sustainable way of life. Love of self often goes hand in hand with short-term thinking. When it appears to be to our advantage, we can be quick to sacrifice other plants and animals. Other creatures have their own value in God's eyes. They have their own biotic rights. For people of faith an appeal to all four of our core values—love of God, love of neighbor, love of creation, and love of self—will motivate the most firm embrace possible of a sustainable way of life.

A third approach is ecological enlightenment or consciousness-raising. It is an appeal for humankind to fully employ our capabilities for scientific inquiry, moral reasoning, and ethical decision-making for the well-being of the whole human family and the whole Earth community. A shining example of this approach is the Earth Charter Initiative. The Earth Charter, "a product of a decade-long, worldwide, cross-cultural dialogue on common goals and shared values," was adopted on June 29, 2000. More than six thousand international organizations have endorsed it. The Earth Charter Initiative website describes it as "a declaration of fundamental ethical principles for building a just, sustainable, and peaceful global society in the 21st century. It seeks to inspire in all people a new sense of global interdependence and shared responsibility for the well-being of the whole human family, the greater community of life, and future generations. It is a vision of hope and a call to action." The Earth Charter seeks to promote the "transition to sustainable ways of living and sustainable human development." It stresses the importance of ecological integrity, but at the same time "recognizes that the goals of ecological protection, the eradication of poverty, equitable economic development, respect for human rights, democracy, and peace are interdependent and indivisible."[34] In addressing the ecological crisis we need a comprehensive vision of the well-being of humankind and the well-being of the whole Earth community, and we need the best possible science to inform us, the best possible ethical principles to guide us, and the best possible political process to shape our decision-making in seeking to fulfill that vision.

The Earth Charter is an enlightened and noble document. It represents a vital step forward in addressing the ecological crisis and in pursuing a sustainable way of life for humankind and the whole Earth community. But enlightenment or consciousness-raising in itself is not able to move

34. Earth Charter Initiative, "What Is the Earth Charter?," http://earthcharter.org/discover/what-is-the-earth-charter/.

people to action. The Earth Charter itself affirms that the way forward "requires a change of mind and heart."

Thomas Berry offers a fourth approach: to appeal to the emerging story of the universe. He believes this story can provide the vision and energies "for bringing ourselves and the entire planet into a new order of survival."[35] In his estimation the "religions are too pious, the corporations too plundering, the government too subservient" to accomplish the Great Work.[36] He turns to the universities for the insight and freedom to guide the community in the needed direction. They should also have the critical capacity to influence other organizations. The story of the universe can provide needed perspective in addressing the ecological crisis, but is it enough to motivate us to make radical changes in our way of life? Universities have a vital ecological role to play, but in crisis situations throughout history universities have proven to be as subject to human foible and folly as other human institutions. A notorious example in recent history is the complicity of many universities and university professors with the Nazis.

A fifth motivational approach is to urge people to take future generations into account. In the Preamble to the Constitution is the phrase "to ourselves and our Posterity." The implication is that we have a responsibility to act in the best interest of future generations as well as our own. As we explored previously, we need to engage in what has been called "seventh-generation thinking" in Native American traditions.[37] A better understanding of the climate crisis, especially of its likely impacts on our children and grandchildren, will lead the public to do what needs to be done to reverse the effects of human-made climate change. Presumably that was a key motivation for Hansen in writing *Storms of My Grandchildren*. His book is a gift to our generation as well as future generations. According to a 1995 MIT report, "For those who have children, the anchoring of environmental ethics in responsibility to descendents gives environmental values a concrete and emotional grounding stronger than that of abstract principle."[38] Martin-Schramm observes that we are in a position to bless or curse future generations by our action or inaction in reducing carbon emissions. If we

35. T. Berry, *Great Work*, 71.

36. Ibid., 79. Berry names the Great Work as "the task of moving industrial civilization from its present devastating influence on the Earth to a more benign mode of presence" (ibid., 7).

37. See pages 21, 127–28.

38. Cited in Louv, *Last Child in the Woods*, 304.

fail to reduce carbon emissions aggressively now, we are condemning "future generations to a rate and degree of warming unprecedented in human civilization." Inspired by Proverbs 29:18 in the King James Version—"Where there is no vision, the people perish"—Martin-Schramm maintains that "the only way change can come and justice will be done is if we envision a different future and then act on it."[39]

As compelling and necessary as this appeal to concern for future generations may be, the jury is still out on whether clearing our minds on climate change and envisioning a different future will be enough to instigate the radical change in behavior needed to reverse the devastating ecological consequences that lie ahead. An unprecedented radical change of heart is needed—a massive ecological conversion of humankind. In the brief article "Why We Don't Care about Saving Our Grandchildren," Bryan Walsh identifies time as the biggest obstacle to dealing with climate change. Effective climate policy asks the present generation to sacrifice for future generations. That, asserts Walsh, is "like saving for a retirement you know you'll never live to see." He cites a new study that "shows human beings are too selfish to endure present pain to avert future climate change."[40]

A sixth approach is to rediscover the joy and wonder of nature. This approach is at the heart of Louv's efforts to reconnect children and adults with the natural world and save human beings from "nature-deficit disorder." Louv envisions "letting our children lead us to their own special places" where "we can rediscover the joy and wonder of nature. By exploring those places we enter our children's world and we give these patches of nature a powerful blessing for our children. By expressing interest or even awe at the march of ants across these elfin forests, we send our children a message that will last for decades to come, perhaps even extend generation to generation. By returning to these simple but enchanted places, we see, with our child, how the seasons move and the world turns and how critter kingdoms rise and fall."[41] The more disconnected we and our children become from nature the less likely we are to have a passionate concern for the well-being of our backyard, our watershed, or our Earth home as a whole. For Louv this passionate concern is the "long-distance fuel" in the struggle to save our natural heritage. He stresses that "passion does not arrive on videotape or CD; passion is personal. Passion is lifted from the earth itself

---

39. Martin-Schramm, *Climate Justice*, 158.

40. For more on this study, see Walsh, "Why We Don't Care," paras. 4–6.

41. Louv, *Last Child in the Woods*, 172.

by the muddy hands of the young; it travels along grass-stained sleeves to the heart."[42]

This approach—rediscovering wonder and joy in nature—is close to my heart. In Oregon we are blessed with a rich array of places in nature that cultivate wonder and joy. How I appreciate opportunities to hike along the Oregon coast or on a trail through majestic Douglas Fir trees or up one of Oregon's numerous peaks. David James Duncan, who was born and raised in Oregon, has said that "wonder is my second favorite condition to be in, after love, and I sometimes wonder whether there's a difference; maybe love is just wonder aimed at a beloved."[43] My experiences in nature have increased my love of Oregon and of our Earth home. Wonder and joy in nature are crucial to overcoming our deep alienation from the natural world and seeking healing for our Earth home. Rediscovering our connection to the natural world will be an essential aspect of any strategy to motivate humankind to respond to the ecological crisis. Louv's insights into the restorative power of nature are profound. Rabbi Abraham Joshua Heschel stressed that life is to be lived in amazement.[44] Nothing in life should be taken for granted, including the natural world. For people of faith, praise and thanksgiving are at the heart of our relationship to God. Rediscovering wonder and joy in nature is a wonderful way to cultivate such praise and thanksgiving, so that we can join together with everything that breathes to praise the Lord (Ps 150:6)!

As powerful as wonder and joy can be, they too will not be enough in themselves to cultivate the deep love of our Earth home that will move humankind to make the radical change needed in our way of life. We are dealing with more than a "nature-deficit disorder"—as astute as Richard Louv's diagnosis may be. All the other approaches mentioned above have something to contribute to motivating human beings to change our ecological ways. We do not have to discount any of them. But none of them are sufficient in themselves.

Sittler asserts that the radical change needed will require "something vastly more than a combination of frightening facts and moral concern." Human beings, observes Sittler, "are quite capable of marching steadily into disaster fully equipped with the facts"—or with moral concern or with wonder and joy in nature. Sittler first published *Essays on Nature and*

42. Ibid., 159.

43. Duncan, *My Story as Told by Water*, 88.

44. Louv, *Last Child in the Woods*, 291–92.

Grace in 1972. At that time he noted that "pride, comfort, and an idolatrous and brutal hardness of heart have for several generations permitted
the American nation to stare straight into the face of poverty, injustice,
and the calcified privilege of the powerful—and leave national priorities
unchallenged."[45] It is not hard to make the case that a similar "hardness of
heart" continues to dominate the American psyche. We are quite capable
of marching steadily—even precipitously deeper—into ecological disaster,
fully equipped with the facts and unwilling to change our priorities.

Humankind will conquer and destroy our Earth home unless we
come to love it deeply. In our Judeo-Christian tradition we are commanded
to love God with heart, soul, mind, and strength—that is, with the whole
self. In loving our neighbor as our self we are to also love with our whole
self. We need to cultivate a love of our Earth home and all of its inhabitants
that involves us entirely—heart, soul, mind, and strength.

In our faith tradition we do not believe that human beings can simply
conjure up this love. David James Duncan compares wonder to grace, "in
that it's not a condition we grasp; it grasps us."[46] Grace is God's unconditional love for us and for all God has created. Grace is God's deep love for
human beings and the whole Earth community. We need to be grasped by
God's unconditional love. Our love for our Earth needs to be deeply rooted
in God's love for Earth. Earth is God's home as well as our home. Indeed,
our four core values—love of God, love of neighbor, love of self, and love
of Earth—are deeply rooted in God's love. Confident that we and our Earth
home are dearly loved by God, we are free to live by grace, embodying our
four core values in daily life in our home places. God's love is manifested
in delight over all God has created, in grief for the suffering human beings
have caused the Earth community, in Jesus's sacrifice to reconcile all things
to God, and in the Spirit's tireless pursuit of well-being (*shalom*) for Earth
and all of its creatures. We participate in God's love by sharing in God's delight, grieving with God, sacrificing ourselves for our fellow human beings
and creatures, and pursuing the well-being of the whole Earth community.
This one-of-a-kind planet is our home. It is God's home. God is not going
to give us some other home. This is the home we have been given by God to
love. God has not promised some other eternal home apart from Earth. Recalling Brian McLaren's prayer petition cited in chapter 5, he gives thanks
that Jesus "taught us to see every creature as beloved by you" and "called us

45. Sittler, *Essays on Nature and Grace*, in *Evocations of Grace*, 186.
46. Duncan, *My Story as Told by Water*, 88.

to live with your love pulsing in our hearts." Then he petitions God to "let us learn to see and love this good Earth as Jesus did, and to care for it and enjoy it and rejoice in it."[47] Without God's love pulsing through our whole selves, as it did through Jesus, we will not have the motivation necessary to make radical changes in our way of life and to come home to Earth.

The Church's Primary Ecological Responsibility

In responding to a state or government not fulfilling its ecological responsibilities, a church that cares for our Earth home will be fearless in naming ecological sin, aiding the victims of ecological degradation, and engaging in direct political action on behalf of the whole Earth community.[48] If necessary, the church will venture "into the streets." It will partner with a variety of people and organizations to fulfill these ecological responsibilities.

But in fulfilling these responsibilities, the church does not want to lose focus on its primary ecological task: to proclaim in word and deed God's deep love for our Earth home and all of its inhabitants. This proclamation is at the core of the gospel. We need a proclamation of the gospel of Jesus Christ powerful enough and cosmic enough and motivating enough to radically change our way of life. This gospel must be proclaimed in word and deed. The hope is that this gospel proclamation will cultivate in human beings a deep love for our Earth home and fellow creatures. Most important, for the sake of our suffering Earth and all of its inhabitants, this gospel must be enacted. The church's main ecological agenda is to convert people to love of our Earth home. The church's primary contribution will be on the motivational side of the ecological movement, not on the enlightenment side. The church as church has no special scientific, political, economic, or agricultural expertise. People in our churches may be experts in these fields, and part of the church's task is to encourage them to make full use of their expertise. But the church's primary ecological task is to proclaim God's deep love for Earth and thereby cultivate a deep love of Earth in humankind.

The core ministry initiatives of the church from the beginning have been worship and Christian education. Worship and Christian education are the primary ways the church incorporates core values into the way of

---

47. See petition in chapter 4, page 74, quoted from McLaren, "This Good Earth," 168.

48. See my discussion of Bonhoeffer's three possible ways for the church to respond to a state or government not fulfilling its responsibilities (chapter 5, page 105).

life of followers of Jesus. The ecological crisis before us does not compel us to change our core ministry initiatives. What is needed is a clear, unambiguous, strong emphasis in worship and Christian education on the depth of God's love for Earth and on the core value of love of Earth. The ecological stakes are so high at this point in history that we may need to lift up love of creation as a third great commandment. We are trying to overcome not only centuries of appalling silence on ecological concerns but also centuries of abuse of our Earth home—abuse in which our faith tradition has been complicit. To be silent or passive on caring for our Earth home in our day and age is irresponsible and unfaithful. The message we proclaim and the lessons we teach will need to be matched by the way we live if our message is to have credibility. It is especially important for followers of Jesus to live and breathe our core value of love of Earth in a time characterized by a loss of love for Earth and its creatures.[49]

Many leading scientists, to their credit, recognize the need for religious communities to step up and focus on motivating people to care for our Earth home. In 1990, in a statement titled "Preserving and Cherishing the Earth," thirty-two Nobel laureates and other scientists as well as 271 well-known spiritual leaders from eighty-three countries issued this urgent appeal: "Problems of such magnitude, and solutions demanding so broad a perspective, must be recognized from the outset as having a religious as well as a scientific dimension. Mindful of our common responsibility, we scientists, many of us long engaged in combating the environmental crisis, urgently appeal to the world religious community to commit, in *word and deed*, and as boldly as is required, to preserve the environment of the Earth."[50] In *The Creation*, a book written in the form of a letter to a Southern Baptist pastor, biologist E. O. Wilson identifies religion and science as "the two most powerful forces in the world today." While acknowledging the differences in point of view between him and the pastor, he asserts that "if there is any moral precept shared by people of all beliefs, it is that we owe ourselves and future generations a beautiful, rich, and healthful

---

49. Laura Ruth Yordy has issued a call for a "green witness." In *Green Witness* her primary goal is not to encourage the church's participation in the environmental movement but to motivate the church to bear witness to Christ's transformation of creation distorted by sin and corruption. The task of the church is to embody this green witness in word and deed. Green witness takes shape both in worship and in a way of life, which Yordy describes as "eco-discipleship."

50. "Preserving and Cherishing the Earth," para. 3.

environment."[51] Wilson observes that a number of evangelical Christians have awakened to the God-given call to care for creation. They have shown a willingness to work with scientists in caring for creation, even if they do not agree on all matters of faith. In December 2007 Wilson and a group of scientists and evangelical leaders met for a consultation in Georgia. They agreed to use the word "creation" and to "work in concert to care for creation."[52]

Followers of Jesus need to remember that God did not send Jesus first and foremost to turn people into Christians. God sent Jesus to cultivate in human beings a deep love of God, neighbor, self, and creation. Earth is our home place in creation. We share this Earth home with people of a variety of faith traditions or no faith tradition at all. As Fr. Richard Rohr observes, "We all breathe the same air and drink the same water. There are no Jewish, Christian, or Muslim versions of these universal elements"[53]—or, we might add, no Hindu, Buddhist, agnostic, or atheist versions. Followers of Jesus are to be courageous enough to call to account anyone degrading our Earth home and open enough to partner with anyone intent on caring for our Earth home. In responding to the ecological crisis we do not have to seek out great tasks. We can focus on whatever tasks God presents to us in our given time and place—in our home place. Whatever the task, we need to bring a passionate love for the whole Earth community to it.[54] That passionate love is essential in coming home to Earth.

A Final Appeal

As human beings we have been a prodigal species. We have squandered our Earth home inheritance. We have imposed ecological exile upon ourselves, and we and the whole Earth community are paying the price. But like the Father in the parable of the Prodigal Son, God is eager to welcome us home. God grieves what we have done to degrade our Earth home; nonetheless, God has not stopped loving us and our Earth home. It is time to come to our senses. However, it will not be enough simply to come to our senses; our whole selves need to be converted so that we can come home to Earth. In the process of coming home bold decisive action will need to be taken.

51. Wilson, *Creation*, 5.

52. DeWitt, "Science, Scripture, and Con-serving Creation," 75.

53. Rohr, "Creation as the Body of God," 240.

54. Maathai, *Replenishing the Earth*, 152–53.

We may make some mistakes along the way. God has given us the freedom to act without fear of making mistakes. Without this freedom, we could be too cautious, afraid to make radical changes in our way of life. It would be easy to succumb to a disheartening passivity or hopeless cynicism. Followers of Jesus, filled with the hope of the resurrection, will not give up on our Earth home. They will not yield to cynicism. They will not walk by on the other side of suffering Earth.

In chapter 3 we explored one of the key themes in Bonhoeffer's *Letters and Papers from Prison*: sharing in the suffering of God. In his letter to his dear friend Eberhard Bethge written on the day after the failed July 20, 1944, assassination attempt on Hitler, Bonhoeffer reaffirms the importance of sharing in the suffering of God in the world.[55] Bonhoeffer stresses that the suffering of God embraces the whole of human suffering. To share in the suffering of God is to share in the suffering of our fellow human beings. Today we need to stress that the suffering of God also embraces the suffering Earth community. To share in the suffering of God includes sharing in the suffering of Earth and all of its creatures. God loves Earth too deeply to give up on it. God does not need cynics. God needs resolute people of faith who care so much for our Earth home that even when hope is dead, they will not write it off; instead, they will hope by faith and continue to invest themselves deeply in the well-being of the Earth community.[56] Like the salmon they will expend every last ounce of energy they can muster for the purpose for which God created them. They will not rest until their journey home to Earth is complete. God needs these resolute people of faith now.

---

55. Bonhoeffer, *Letters and Papers from Prison* (DBWE 8), 486.
56. This sentence inspired by Reinhold Niebuhr, *Nature and Destiny of Man*, 2:285–86.

Acknowledgments

I have been blessed with so many who have been a part of my journey home to Earth and have inspired my passion for and influenced my thinking on Earth care. I am grateful for all of them. A number of people were especially involved in bringing *Coming Home to Earth* to fruition, and I want to give special thanks to them.

Thank you to the people of St. Andrew for providing a sabbatical for me to do intensive work on *Coming Home to Earth* and for supporting me in bringing this project to completion. I am proud and privileged to serve in a congregation in which Earth care is a core value in our life and ministry. It is a special blessing to serve with my pastoral colleague Robyn Hartwig, who shares a deep commitment to caring for our Earth home. Terry Moe served as Sabbatical Interim Lead Pastor at St. Andrew; and he, Pastor Hartwig, and the whole staff did a fine job during my time away.

Thank you to Pacific Lutheran University and Marilyn Knutson for the invitation to deliver the Fifth Annual David and Marilyn Knutson Lecture, "No Salvation Apart from the Earth." As chapter 1 clarifies, that lecture was the catalyst for *Coming Home to Earth*. I only wish my professor David Knutson were still alive so that he could see how his teaching bore fruit in this project.

Thank you to my doctoral advisers at the University of Chicago Divinity School, Robin Lovin and William Schweiker, who guided me through the process of writing my dissertation on Bonhoeffer's ethics of responsibility. I especially appreciated their concern for rigorous and responsible scholarship.

Thank you to the Louisville Institute for a Pastoral Study Project Grant to work on turning the Knutson Lecture into a book. I am grateful to my Mutual Ministry Committee—LuAnn Staul, Steve Christiansen, Ralph Riley, and Gary Grafwallner—for helping me prepare the application for the grant and promoting my sabbatical with our congregation. David Rhoads and Robyn Hartwig wrote thoughtful letters of recommendation. Following my sabbatical, I attended the Winter Seminar at the Institute. I so appreciated the insightful feedback from my cohort group led by Assistant Director Don Richter. Members of the cohort group were: Jared Boyd, Sherry Cothran, Tim Hartman, Cynthia Jarvis, Caleb Maskell, Sheila McCarthy, Amy Schacht, Shiveley Smith, Josef Sorett, and Beth Waltemath.

Thank you to the Sabbatical Colleague Group who met with me for a series of lunch conversations in preparation for my time of study and writing. Their incisive comments and questions focused my thinking on Earth care and salvation and their encouragement motivated me as I headed into the sabbatical. Participants included Brian Brandt, Colin Brown, Gary Grafwallner, Dick Harmon, Robyn Hartwig, Stuart Holland, Katherine Jesch, Lloyd Meyer, Ross Miller, Terry Moe, Solveig Nilsen-Goodin, and Ray Venghaus. Carol Hogan, our St. Andrew Housekeeper, prepared healthy, Earth-friendly lunches.

Thank you to all who provided a place for me to study and write while on sabbatical. For the first six weeks the people of St. Matthew Lutheran Church freed up space in their library office for me. Ben and Lisa Flesher gave me a nook on the lower level of their Key Peninsula home overlooking Puget Sound. John and Christine Core offered me their cabin near one of my favorite Oregon rivers, the McKenzie. They also let me use their cabin for a couple of weeks the following summer. I spent a week writing a draft of chapter 6 in the Bay Room of Pacific Lutheran Theological Seminary in Berkeley. I am also grateful to Trinity Lutheran Church in Riverside, California, who, on the final Sunday of my sabbatical, invited me to preach on the theme "Because God Delights"—the first formal presentation of the fruits of this project.

Thank you to Megan Webber for reading through the first drafts of my manuscript and bluntly telling me that it "was not a compelling read for a lay person." She encouraged me to write something my grandchildren might actually want to read someday. I trust this book is at least more compelling than it would have been without her honest advice.

Thank you to my daughter and former student, Pastor Rachel Brocker Langford, for her excellent editorial comments in the last stages of preparing the manuscript. She spent hours making detailed suggestions for each chapter, almost all of which I incorporated. I was so impressed with her knowledge of what I was trying to say and her sensitivity to how the readers would hear it. I, of course, take responsibility for any shortcomings that still remain.

Thank you to my editor Charlie Collier, my copy editor Jacob Martin, and the staff of Wipf and Stock Publishers for guiding me through the process of preparing *Coming Home to Earth* for publication. As a Lutheran pastor and scholar living in Oregon in the shadow of the Cascade Mountains, I am thrilled to have a publisher in my home state with a Cascade Books imprint.

Thanks to my parents, Frank and Ruth (1937–74), for instilling faith and sowing the seeds of creation care in me and for moving us to Oregon. I also appreciate how my dad and Barb have encouraged me in my work and have helped us feel so at home whenever we visit Sunriver.

Special thanks to my wife, Donna, for her love and support. What a blessing it has been to be married to a partner who shares a deep commitment to faith, family, and Earth care! And special thanks to our whole family who have been a part of this journey with us: Isaac and Jenny and our grandchildren Avari, Dean, and Amity; Rachel and Andrew; Matia and Daniel and grandchild Penelope; Hailey; Luke; and Mary. All our children are glad to be part of a family in which Earth care is a priority, and they are committed to instilling care of our Earth home in the next generation.

Workshop-Evolution-Creation

(Presented by Frank Brocker, early 1970s)

I. Talk about change in procedure because of talk
    A. With Paul Holte
    B. Letter received

II. Use letter to kick off comments on Bible as Who—Why—not how
—Jonah—

III. Creation Theology
    A. Exclusionist—Gen. 1:27
        1. Nature set apart from man
        2. Natural world is a challenge to be controlled
        3. Have control over earth—subdue or conquer it
        4. Logical results are obvious—take what is wanted or needed—
           Alaska Pipeline Dave & Paul & snowmobiles
    B. Inclusionist—Gen. 1
        1. All things created good
        2. Man in total rel. to rest of creation
        3. Brother Sun/Sister Moon (St. Francis)
        4. Chief Seattle's comments when asked to sell land—
        5. Mention book *I Heard the Owl Call My Name*
    C. Church position—
        1. Strongly exclusionist
        2. Not unappreciative of whole of creation
        3. Definitely placed nature second to saving souls
           a) Probably one good reason the church is often irrel.
           b) Spawned really from Greek concept of soul/body sep.
              All matter is ult. bad

        c) Strong emphasis on hereafter rather than now
          "If Heaven's Not My Home"
        d) EXAMPLE: Camp staff
    D. There is a real need to return to creation theology
      1. Affirms God as creator of all
      2. Emph. on first and third articles as well as second
      3. Man is integral part of whole creation
      4. READ from Sigurd Olson

Bibliography

Andrews, Cecile. "The Spirituality of Everyday Life." In *Simpler Living, Compassionate Life*, edited and compiled by Michael Schut, 37–40. Denver: Living the Good News, 2002.

Bahnson, Fred, and Norman Wirzba. *Making Peace with the Land: God's Call to Reconcile with Creation*. Downers Grove, IL: InterVarsity, 2012.

Bakken, Peter. "Landscape of Grace: Home, Commons, Sanctuary." In *Earth and Word: Classic Sermons on Saving the Planet*, edited by David Rhoads, 15–24. New York: Continuum, 2007.

Bartholomew I, Ecumenical Patriarch of Constantinople. *Cosmic Grace, Humble Prayer: The Ecological Vision of the Green Patriarch Bartholomew I*. Edited by John Chryssavgis. Grand Rapids: Eerdmans, 2003.

———. "The Orthodox Church and the Environmental Crisis." In *Holy Ground*, edited by Lyndsay Moseley and the staff of Sierra Club Books, 33–41. San Francisco: Sierra Club, 2008.

Bending, Glen. "The Design and Planning of Sunriver." In *Sunriver Lite*, a collection compiled by The Writers Group of The Sunriver Arts Association, 55–56. 1998.

Bennon, Brady. "Paradise Lost: Introducing Students to Climate Change through Story." *Rethinking Schools* 27 (2013) 54–60.

Berry, Thomas. *The Christian Future and the Fate of the Earth*. Edited by Mary Evelyn Tucker and John Grim. Maryknoll, NY: Orbis, 2009.

———. *The Dream of the Earth*. San Francisco: Sierra Club, 1988.

———. *The Great Work: Our Way into the Future*. New York: Three Rivers, 1999.

Berry, Wendell. *Another Turn of the Crank*. Washington, DC: Counterpoint, 1995.

———. *The Art of the Commonplace: The Agrarian Essays of Wendell Berry*. Edited by Norman Wirzba. Washington, DC: Shoemaker & Hoard, 2002.

———. *Home Economics*. Berkeley: Counterpoint, 1987.

———. *It All Turns on Affection: The Jefferson Lecture & Other Essays*. Berkeley: Counterpoint, 2012.

———. "A Limitless Reality." In *Holy Ground*, edited by Lyndsay Moseley and the staff of Sierra Club Books, 47–56. San Francisco: Sierra Club, 2008.

———. *The Unsettling of America: Culture & Agriculture*. New York: Avon, 1977.

Bethge, Eberhard. *Dietrich Bonhoeffer: A Biography*. Translated by Eric Mosbacher et al. Edited by Victoria J. Barnett. Rev. ed. Minneapolis: Fortress, 2000.

Billman, Kathleen, and Daniel Migliore. *Rachel's Cry: Prayer of Lament and Rebirth of Hope*. 1999. Reprint, Eugene, OR: Wipf & Stock, 2006.

Boff, Leonardo. *Cry of the Earth, Cry of the Poor*. Translated by Philip Berryman. Ecology and Justice. Maryknoll, NY: Orbis, 1997.

Bohmbach, Karla G., and Shauna K. Hannan, eds. *Eco-Lutheranism: Lutheran Perspectives on Ecology*. Minneapolis: Lutheran University Press, 2013.

Bonhoeffer, Dietrich. *Berlin: 1932–33*. Edited by Larry L. Rasmussen. Translated by Isabel Best and David Higgins. Dietrich Bonhoeffer Works 12. Minneapolis: Fortress, 2009.

———. *Conspiracy and Imprisonment: 1940–1945*. Edited by Mark S. Brocker. Translated by Lisa E. Dahill. Dietrich Bonhoeffer Works 16. Minneapolis: Fortress, 2006.

———. *Discipleship*. Edited by Geffrey B. Kelly and John D. Godsey. Translated by Barbara Green and Reinhard Krauss. Dietrich Bonhoeffer Works 4. Minneapolis: Fortress, 1996.

———. *Ethics*. Edited by Clifford J. Green. Translated by Reinhard Krauss et al. Dietrich Bonhoeffer Works 6. Minneapolis: Fortress, 2005.

———. *Letters and Papers from Prison*. Edited by Eberhard Bethge. Enlarged ed. New York: Simon & Schuster, 1997.

———. *Letters and Papers from Prison*. Edited by John W. de Gruchy. Translated by Isabel Best et al. Dietrich Bonhoeffer Works 8. Minneapolis: Fortress, 2010.

———. *Sanctorum Communio*. Edited by Clifford J. Green. Translated by Reinhard Krauss and Nancy Lukens. Dietrich Bonhoeffer Works 1. Minneapolis: Fortress, 1998.

Bouma-Prediger, Steven. *For the Beauty of the Earth: A Christian Vision for Creation Care*. 2nd ed. Grand Rapids: Baker Academic, 2010.

Brock, Rita Nakashima, and Rebecca Ann Parker. *Saving Paradise: How Christianity Traded Love of This World for Crucifixion and Empire*. Boston: Beacon, 2008.

Brokaw, Tom. *The Greatest Generation*. New York: Random House, 1998.

Brown, William P. *The Seven Pillars of Creation: The Bible, Science, and the Ecology of Wonder*. New York: Oxford University Press, 2010.

Brueggemann, Walter. *Peace*. St. Louis: Chalice, 2001.

Brunner, Daniel L., et al. *Introducing Evangelical Ecotheology: Foundations in Scripture, Theology, History, and Praxis*. Grand Rapids: Baker, 2014.

Bryant, Bunyan, ed. *Environmental Justice: Issues, Policies, and Solutions*. Washington, DC: Island Press, 1995.

Byrne, Brendan. "Creation Groaning: An Earth Bible Reading of Romans 8.8–12." In *Readings from the Perspective of Earth*, edited by Norman C. Habel, 193–203. Sheffield: Sheffield Academic, 2000.

Carson, Rachel. *The Sea Around Us*. Illustrated commemorative ed. New York: Oxford University Press, 2003.

———. *Silent Spring*. 40th anniversary ed. New York: Houghton Mifflin, 2002.

———. *Under the Sea Wind*. New York: Penguin, 2007.

Chryssavgis, John. "The Cry of the Earth—the Cry of the Heart." In *Earth and Word: Classic Sermons on Saving the Planet*, edited by David Rhoads, 88–94. New York: Continuum, 2007.

Clarkson, Linda, et al. *Our Responsibility to the Seventh Generation: Indigenous Peoples and Sustainable Development*. International Institute for Sustainable Development, Winnipeg, MB, 1992. https://www.iisd.org/pdf/seventh_gen.pdf.

"The Columbia River Watershed: Caring for Creation and the Common Good." An international pastoral letter by the Catholic bishops of the Columbia River Watershed, signed on Feast of the Baptism of the Lord, June 8, 2001. http://www.thewscc.org/images/stories/Resources/Statements/crplp.pdf.

Colwell, Matthew. *Sabbath Economics: Household Practices.* Published by Tell the Word, a project of The Church of the Saviour, Washington, DC, 1999.

Cone, James. "Whose Earth Is It, Anyway?" In *Earth Habitat: Eco-Injustice and the Church's Response,* edited by Dieter Hessel and Larry Rasmussen, 23–32. Minneapolis: Fortress, 2001.

De Graaf, John, et al. *Affluenza: The All-Consuming Epidemic.* 2nd ed. San Francisco: Berrett-Koehler, 2005.

Delio, Ilia. *Simply Bonaventure: An Introduction to His Life, Thought, and Writings.* 2nd ed. Hyde Park, NY: New City Press of the Focolare, 2013.

DeWitt, Calvin. *Earthwise: A Guide to Hopeful Creation Care.* 3rd ed. Grand Rapids: Faith Alive Christian Resources, 2011.

———. "Reading the Bible through a Green Lens." In *The Green Bible,* I-25–34. San Francisco: HarperCollins, 2008.

———. "Science, Scripture, and Con-serving Creation." In *Holy Ground,* edited by Lyndsay Moseley and the staff of Sierra Club Books, 74–88. San Francisco: Sierra Club, 2008.

Diamond, Jared. *Collapse: How Societies Choose to Fail or Succeed.* New York: Penguin, 2005.

Duncan, David James. "A Prayer for the Second Coming of the Salmon." In *My Story as Told by Water,* 181–214. San Francisco: Sierra Club, 2001.

———. "Song of Salmon." In *Holy Ground,* edited by Lyndsay Moseley and the staff of Sierra Club Books, 89–94. San Francisco: Sierra Club, 2008.

Earth System Research Laboratory: Global Monitoring Division. "Trends in Atmospheric Carbon Dioxide: Mauna Loa, Hawaii." http://www.esrl.noaa.gov/gmd/ccgg/trends/index.html.

EcoFaith Recovery. "River's Lament Ritual Walk." http://www.ecofaithrecovery.org/events-2/the-rivers-lament/.

Edwards, Denis. *Jesus the Wisdom of God: An Ecological Theology.* 1995. Reprint, Eugene, OR: Wipf & Stock, 2005.

Finch, Robert. "Introduction: The Delights and Dilemmas of *A Sand County Almanac.*" In *A Sand County Almanac,* by Aldo Leopold, xv–xxviii. New York: Oxford University Press, 1989.

Fischer, Kathleen. *Loving Creation: Christian Spirituality, Earth-Centered and Just.* Mahwah, NJ: Paulist, 2009.

Foderaro, Lisa W. "Taking a Call for Climate Change to the Streets." *New York Times,* September 21, 2014. http://www.nytimes.com/2014/09/22/nyregion/new-york-city-climate-change-march.html?_r=0.

Fox, Matthew. *Original Blessing: A Primer in Creation Spirituality.* Santa Fe, NM: Bear, 1983.

Francis, Pope. *On Care for Our Common Home: The Encyclical Letter Laudato Si'.* Mahwah, NJ: Paulist, 2015.

Fretheim, Terence E. *Creation Untamed: The Bible, God, and Natural Disasters.* Grand Rapids: Baker Academic, 2010.

———. *God and World in the Old Testament: A Relational Theology of Creation.* Nashville: Abingdon, 2005.

Friedman, Thomas L. *Hot, Flat, and Crowded: Why We Need a Green Revolution—and How It Can Renew America.* New York: Farrar, Straus, and Giroux, 2008.

Gebara, Ivone. *Longing for Running Water: Ecofeminism and Liberation.* Translated by David Molineaux. Minneapolis: Fortress, 1999.

Ghormley, Dave. "Beginnings." In *Sunriver Lite,* a collection compiled by The Writers Group of The Sunriver Arts Association, 4–16. 1998.

Gifford, Terry. "Introduction." In *John Muir: The Eight Wilderness Discovery Books,* 13–20. Seattle: Mountaineers, 1992.

Gore, Albert. *Earth in the Balance: Ecology and the Human Spirit.* Paperback ed. New York: Rodale, 2006.

Gottlieb, Roger S. *A Greener Faith: Religious Environmentalism and Our Planet's Future.* New York: Oxford University Press, 2006.

The Green Bible. NRSV. Michael G. Maudlin and Marlene Baer, project editors. San Francisco: HarperCollins, 2008.

"Green Power in Beaverton." *Beaverton, Oregon: The Best of Oregon, Your City,* March/April 2014, 10. http://www.beavertonoregon.gov/ArchiveCenter/ViewFile/Item/3230.

Gustafson, James M. *A Sense of the Divine: The Natural Environment from a Theocentric Perspective.* Cleveland: Pilgrim, 1994.

Habel, Norman C., ed. *Readings from the Perspective of Earth.* The Earth Bible 1. Cleveland: Pilgrim, 2000.

Habel, Norman C., and Peter Trudinger, eds. *Exploring Ecological Hermeneutics.* Society of Biblical Literature Symposium Series 46. Atlanta: Society of Biblical Literature, 2008.

Hamilton-Poore, Sam. *Earth Gospel: A Guide to Prayer for God's Creation.* Nashville: Upper Room, 2008.

Hansen, James. *Storms of My Grandchildren: The Truth about the Coming Climate Catastrophe and Our Last Chance to Save Humanity.* New York: Bloomsbury, 2009.

Hart, John. *Sacramental Commons: Christian Ecological Ethics.* Lanham, MD: Rowman & Littlefield, 2006.

Hawken, Paul. *Blessed Unrest: How the Largest Social Movement in History Is Restoring Grace, Justice, and Beauty to the World.* New York: Penguin, 2007.

Hayhoe, Katharine, and Andrew Farley. *A Climate for Change: Global Warming Facts for Faith-Based Decisions.* New York: Faith Words, 2009.

Hessel, Dieter, ed. *After Nature's Revolt: Eco-justice and Theology.* Minneapolis: Fortress, 1992.

———. "The Church Ecologically Reformed." In *Earth Habitat: Eco-Injustice and the Church's Response,* edited by Dieter Hessel and Larry Rasmussen, 185–206. Minneapolis: Fortress, 2001.

Hessel, Dieter, and Larry Rasmussen, eds. *Earth Habitat: Eco-Injustice and the Church's Response.* Minneapolis: Fortress, 2001.

Hill, Julia Butterfly. *The Legacy of Luna: The Story of a Tree, a Woman, and the Struggle to Save the Redwoods.* San Francisco: HarperSanFrancisco, 2000.

Holy Ground: A Gathering of Voices on Caring for Creation. Edited by Lyndsay Moseley and the staff of Sierra Club Books. San Francisco: Sierra Club, 2008.

Intergovernmental Panel on Climate Change, 2007. "Summary for Policymakers." In *Climate Change 2007: The Physical Science Basis; Contribution of Working Group I to the Fourth Assessment Report of the Intergovernmental Panel on Climate Change,* edited by S. Solomon et al. Cambridge: Cambridge University Press, 2007. https://www.ipcc.ch/pdf/assessment-report/ar4/wg1/ar4-wg1-spm.pdf.

Intergovernmental Panel on Climate Change, 2013. "Summary for Policymakers." In *Climate Change 2013: The Physical Science Basis; Contribution of Working Group I to the Fifth Assessment Report of the Intergovernmental Panel on Climate Change*, edited by T. F. Stocker et al. Cambridge: Cambridge University Press, 2013. https://www.ipcc.ch/pdf/assessment-report/ar5/wg1/WG1AR5_SPM_FINAL.pdf.

Jenkins, Willis. *Ecologies of Grace: Environmental Ethics and Christian Theology.* New York: Oxford University Press, 2008.

Jensen, Derrick. *Endgame.* 2 vols. New York: Seven Stories, 2006.

John Paul II, Pope. "Peace with God the Creator, Peace with All of Creation." Message for the World Day of Peace, January 1, 1990. http://www.vatican.va/holy_father/john_paul_ii/messages/peace/documents/hf_jp-ii_mes_19891208_xxiii-world-day-for-peace_en.html.

Julian of Norwich. *Showings.* In *Love's Trinity: A Companion to Julian of Norwich*, translated by John-Julian, with commentary by Frederick S. Roden. Collegeville, MN: Liturgical Press, 2009.

Kline, Benjamin. *First Along the River: A Brief History of the U.S. Environmental Movement.* 4th ed. Lanham, MD: Rowman & Littlefield, 2011.

Lasher, Connie. "The Religious Humanism of Rachel Carson: On the 50th Anniversary of the Publication of *Silent Spring.*" *Journal of Oriental Studies* 22 (2012) 193–205. http://www.iop.or.jp/Documents/1222/193-205.pdf.

Lear, Linda. *Rachel Carson: Witness for Nature.* Boston: Mariner, 2009.

Leopold, Aldo. *A Sand County Almanac, and Sketches Here and There.* Special commemorative ed. New York: Oxford University Press, 1989.

Liptak, Kevin. "Obama Rejects Keystone XL Bill." *CNN Politics*, February 25, 2015. http://www.cnn.com/2015/02/24/politics/obama-keystone-veto/.

Louv, Richard. *Last Child in the Woods: Saving Our Children from Nature-Deficit Disorder.* Updated and expanded ed. Chapel Hill, NC: Algonquin, 2008.

Loya, Melissa Tubbs. "'Therefore the Earth Mourns': The Grievance of Earth in Hosea 4:1–3." In *Exploring Ecological Hermeneutics*, edited by Norman C. Habel and Peter Trudinger, 53–62. Atlanta: Society of Biblical Literature, 2008.

Lundeberg, Steve. "Sanctuary in the Firs: Oregon Congregation Tends Land on which It Was Planted." *The Lutheran*, June 2010.

Maathai, Wangari. *The Green Belt Movement.* Rev. ed. New York: Lantern, 2004.

————. *Replenishing the Earth: Spiritual Values for Healing Ourselves and the World.* New York: Doubleday, 2010.

————. *Unbowed: A Memoir.* New York: Anchor, 2007.

Martin-Schramm, James B. *Climate Justice: Ethics, Energy, and Public Policy.* Minneapolis: Fortress, 2010.

————. "Lutheran Theology and the Environment: Bonhoeffer, the Church, and the Climate Question." In *Eco-Lutheranism: Lutheran Perspectives on Ecology*, edited by Karla G. Bohmbach and Shauna K. Hannan, 55–68. Minneapolis: Lutheran University Press, 2013.

Martin-Schramm, James B., and Robert L. Stivers. *Christian Environmental Ethics: A Case Method Approach.* Maryknoll, NY: Orbis, 2003.

Mattson, Ingrid. "The Road Back to Paradise." In *Holy Ground*, edited by Lyndsay Moseley and the staff of Sierra Club Books, 158–65. San Francisco: Sierra Club, 2008.

May, Gerald. "Entering the Emptiness." In *Simpler Living, Compassionate Life*, edited and compiled by Michael Schut, 41–51. Denver: Living the Good News, 2002.

Maynard, Micheline. "4 Big Reasons Why People Are Giving Up Cars." *Forbes*, October 8, 2013. http://www.forbes.com/sites/michelinemaynard/2013/10/08/4-big-reasons-why-people-are-giving-up-cars/.

McCall, Tom. "Inaugural Message, 1967." http://arcweb.sos.state.or.us/pages/records/governors/guides/state/mccall/inaugural1967.html.

———. "Legislative Message, 1973." http://arcweb.sos.state.or.us/pages/records/governors/guides/state/mccall/legis1973.html.

McFague, Sallie. *The Body of God: An Ecological Theology*. Minneapolis: Fortress, 1993.

———. *Life Abundant: Rethinking Theology and Economy for a Planet in Peril*. Minneapolis: Fortress, 2000.

———. *A New Climate for Theology: God, the World, and Global Warming*. Minneapolis: Fortress, 2008.

McGaa, Ed, Eagle Man. *Nature's Way: Native Wisdom for Living in Balance with the Earth*. San Francisco: HarperSanFrancisco, 2005.

McKibben, Bill. *Eaarth: Making a Life on a Tough New Planet*. New York: Henry Holt, 2010.

———. *The End of Nature*. New York: Random House, 2006.

McLaren, Brian. "The Good Earth." In *Holy Ground*, edited by Lyndsay Moseley and the staff of Sierra Club Books, 166–68. San Francisco: Sierra Club, 2008.

Meadows, Donella, et al. *The Limits to Growth: A Report for the Club of Rome's Project on the Predicament of Mankind*. New York: Signet, 1972.

———. *Limits to Growth: The 30-Year Update*. White River Junction, VT: Chelsea Green, 2004.

Meine, Curt. *Aldo Leopold: His Life and Work*. Madison: University of Wisconsin Press, 2010.

Middleton, Richard J. *A New Heaven and a New Earth: Reclaiming Biblical Eschatology*. Grand Rapids: Baker, 2014.

Moe-Lobeda, Cynthia D. *Resisting Structural Evil: Love as Ecological and Economic Transformation*. Minneapolis: Fortress, 2013.

Moltmann, Jürgen. *God in Creation: A New Theology of Creation and the Spirit of God*. Translated by Margaret Kohl. San Francisco: Harper & Row, 1985.

Muir, John. *John Muir: Spiritual Writings*. Selected by Tim Flinders. Maryknoll, NY: Orbis, 2013.

———. *My First Summer in the Sierra*. In *John Muir: The Eight Wilderness Discovery Books*, 185–287. Seattle: Mountaineers, 1992.

———. *Our National Parks*. In *John Muir: The Eight Wilderness Discovery Books*, 453–605. Seattle: Mountaineers, 1992.

———. *A Thousand Mile Walk to the Gulf*. In *John Muir: The Eight Wilderness Discovery Books*, 113–83. Seattle: Mountaineers, 1992.

———. *The Yosemite*. In *John Muir: The Eight Wilderness Discovery Books*, 607–716. Seattle: Mountaineers, 1992.

Myers, Ched. "A Reflection on Isaiah 5, Ecological Solipsism, and 'Watershed Discipleship.'" July 2010. http://www.chedmyers.org/node/322.

———. "A Watershed Moment." *Sojourners*, May 2014, 20–24.

NASA. "Apollo 8: Christmas at the Moon." https://www.nasa.gov/topics/history/features/apollo_8.html.

———. "Apollo 8: Earthrise." http://www.nasa.gov/multimedia/imagegallery/image_feature_1249.html.

Nash, James A. *Loving Nature: Ecological Integrity and Christian Responsibility.* Nashville: Abingdon, 1991.

Newell, J. Philip. *The Book of Creation: An Introduction to Celtic Spirituality.* New York: Paulist, 1999.

———. *Christ of the Celts: The Healing of Creation.* San Francisco: Jossey-Bass, 2008.

Nhất Hạnh, Thích. "The Bells of Mindfulness." In *Spiritual Ecology: The Cry of the Earth,* edited by Llewellyn Vaughan-Lee, 25–28. Point Reyes, CA: Golden Sufi Center, 2013.

Niebuhr, Reinhold. *The Nature and Destiny of Man.* Vol. 2, *Human Destiny.* New York: Scribner's, 1964.

Nijhuis, Michelle. "World's Largest Dam Removal Unleashes U.S. River after Century of Electric Production." *National Geographic,* August 27, 2014. http://news.nationalgeographic.com/news/2014/08/140826-elwha-river-dam-removal-salmon-science-olympic/.

Nothwehr, Dawn M. *Ecological Footprints: An Essential Franciscan Guide for Faith and Sustainable Living.* Collegeville, MN: Liturgical, 2012.

Nouwen, Henri. "Contemplation and Ministry." In *Simpler Living, Compassionate Life,* edited and compiled by Michael Schut, 52–57. Denver: Living the Good News, 2002.

O'Brien, Kevin J. *An Ethics of Biodiversity: Christianity, Ecology, and the Variety of Life.* Washington, DC: Georgetown University Press, 2010.

———. "*La Causa* and Environmental Justice: César Chávez as a Resource for Christian Ecological Ethics." *Journal of the Society of Christian Ethics* 32 (2012) 151–68.

Oregon Department of Land Conservation and Development. "40th Anniversary of Senate Bill 100." http://www.oregon.gov/lcd/pages/SB100_40th_Anniversary.aspx.

"People Who Made a Difference: John Muir (1838–1914)." Supplement to *The National Parks: America's Best Idea,* a film by Ken Burns. Public Broadcasting Service. http://www.pbs.org/nationalparks/people/historical/muir/.

"Preserving and Cherishing the Earth: An Appeal for Joint Commitment in Science and Religion." Presented in January 1990 to the Global Forum of Spiritual and Parliamentary Leaders Conference, Moscow, Russia. http://fore.yale.edu/publications/statements/preserve/.

Quinn, James W. *Sunriver: The First 20 Years.* 1990. With a reprinting of Paul Redding, *Suddenly Settlers,* 1981.

Quinn, Pat. "Seeing the Kingdom: Reflection on Today's Gospel." Franciscan Friars, Third Order Regular, Province of the Immaculate Conception. Tuesday, October 26, 2010. http://franciscanfriarstor.blogspot.com/2010/10/seeing-kingdom-reflection-on-todays.html.

Radcliff, David. "Hippos Called My Name." In *Holy Ground,* edited by Lyndsay Moseley and the staff of Sierra Club Books, 175–81. San Francisco: Sierra Club, 2008.

Rasmussen, Larry L. "The Baptized Life." In *Holy Ground,* edited by Lyndsay Moseley and the staff of Sierra Club Books, 182–92. San Francisco: Sierra Club, 2008.

———. *Earth Community, Earth Ethics.* Maryknoll, NY: Orbis, 1996.

———. "An Earth-Honoring Faith." *Sojourners,* June 2010, 22–26.

———. *Earth-Honoring Faith: Religious Ethics in a New Key.* New York: Oxford University Press, 2013.

Redding, Paul. *Suddenly Settlers.* 1981. Reprinted in *Sunriver: The First 20 Years,* by James W. Quinn, 1–44. 1990.

Rhoads, David, ed. *Earth and Word: Classic Sermons on Saving the Planet.* New York: Continuum, 2007.

———. "Reflections on a Lutheran Theology of Creation: Foundations for a New Reformation." *Seminary Ridge Review* 15 (2012) 1–49.

Roberts, Elizabeth, and Elias Amidon, eds. *Earth Prayers from around the World: 365 Prayers, Poems, and Invocations Honoring the Earth.* San Francisco: HarperSanFrancisco, 1991.

Rockefeller, Steven C. "Global Interdependence, the Earth Charter, and Christian Faith." In *Earth Habitat: Eco-Injustice and the Church's Response*, edited by Dieter Hessel and Larry Rasmussen, 101–21. Minneapolis: Fortress, 2001.

Rohr, Richard. "Creation as the Body of God." In *Spiritual Ecology: The Cry of the Earth*, edited by Llewellyn Vaughan-Lee, 235–41. Point Reyes, CA: Golden Sufi Center, 2013.

Rossing, Barbara. *The Rapture Exposed: The Message of Hope in the Book of Revelation.* Boulder, CO: Westview, 2004.

Santmire, H. Paul. *Brother Earth: Nature, God, and Ecology in a Time of Crisis.* New York: Thomas Nelson, 1970.

———. *Nature Reborn: The Ecological and Cosmic Promise of Christian Theology.* Minneapolis: Fortress, 2000.

———. *The Travail of Nature: The Ambiguous Ecological Promise.* Philadelphia: Fortress, 1985.

Sawtell, Peter. "The Shalom Principle." In *Holy Ground*, edited by Lyndsay Moseley and the staff of Sierra Club Books, 205–13. San Francisco: Sierra Club, 2008.

Schor, Juliet. "Excerpt from *The Overworked American*." In *Simpler Living, Compassionate Life*, edited and compiled by Michael Schut, 33–36. Denver: Living the Good News, 2002.

Schut, Michael, ed. *Simpler Living, Compassionate Life.* Published in cooperation with Earth Ministry. Denver: Living the Good News, 2002.

Schweitzer, Albert. *Reverence for Life.* Translated by Reginald H. Fuller. New York: Harper & Row, 1969.

Seattle, Chief. *How Can One Sell the Air? Chief Seattle's Vision.* Edited by Eli Gifford et al. Rev. ed. Summertown, TN: Native Voices, 2005.

Shumskas, Jangela. "Haiti's Landscape: Tè a fatige." *Eu A-Mousoi: A Random Muttering of Thoughtful Things* (blog), January 16, 2010. http://pinxitluc.blogspot.com/2010/01/haitis-landscape-te-fatige.html.

Sinnott, Alice M. "An Earthling's Lament: Hell on Earth." In *Exploring Ecological Hermeneutics*, edited by Norman C. Habel and Peter Trudinger, 103–12. Atlanta: Society of Biblical Literature, 2008.

Sittler, Joseph. "The Care of the Earth." In *The Care of the Earth*, 49–62. Rev. ed. Facets. Minneapolis: Fortress, 2004.

———. *Evocations of Grace: Writings on Ecology, Theology, and Ethics.* Edited by Steven Bouma-Prediger and Peter Bakken. Grand Rapids: Eerdmans, 2000.

———. *The Structure of Christian Ethics.* Louisville: Westminster John Knox, 1998.

Sleeth, J. Matthew. *The Gospel According to the Earth: Why the Good Book Is a Green Book.* New York: HarperOne, 2010.

Solomon, Steven. *Water: The Epic Struggle for Wealth, Power, and Civilization.* New York: HarperCollins, 2010.

Speerstra, Karen, ed. *The Green Devotional: Active Prayers for a Healthy Planet.* San Francisco: Canari, 2010.

Sunriver Lite. A collection compiled by The Writers Group of The Sunriver Arts Association. 1998.

Swimme, Brian, and Thomas Berry. *The Universe Story: From the Primordial Flaring Forth to the Ecozoic Era—a Celebration of the Unfolding of the Cosmos.* San Francisco: HarperCollins, 1992.

Tinker, George. "Creation as Kin: An American Indian View." In *After Nature's Revolt,* edited by Dieter Hessel, 144–53. Minneapolis: Fortress, 1992.

Tonstad, Sigve. "Creation Groaning in Labor Pains." In *Exploring Ecological Hermeneutics,* edited by Norman C. Habel and Peter Trudinger, 141–49. Atlanta: Society of Biblical Literature, 2008.

"Toward a Watershed Discipleship Alliance." Watershed Discipleship: The Creation Waits… http://watersheddiscipleship.org/about/.

Vaughan-Lee, Llewellyn, ed. *Spiritual Ecology: The Cry of the Earth.* Point Reyes, CA: Golden Sufi Center, 2013.

Walsh, Bryan. "Why We Don't Care about Saving Our Grandchildren from Climate Change." *Time,* October 21, 2013. http://science.time.com/2013/10/21/why-we-dont-care-about-saving-our-grandchildren-from-climate-change/.

Walth, Brent. *Fire at Eden's Gate: Tom McCall and the Oregon Story.* Portland: Oregon Historical Society, 1994.

White, Lynn. "The Historical Roots of the Ecological Crisis." In *Ecology and Religion in History,* edited by David Spring and Eileen Spring, 15–31. New York: Harper & Row, 1974.

White, William. *Stories for the Journey: A Sourcebook for Christian Storytellers.* Minneapolis: Augsburg, 1988.

Wilson, Edward O. *The Creation: An Appeal to Save Life on Earth.* New York: Norton, 2006.

———. *The Future of Life.* New York: Random House, 2002.

Wilson, Jonathan R. *God's Good World: Reclaiming the Doctrine of Creation.* Grand Rapids: Baker Academic, 2013.

Wirzba, Norman. *Living the Sabbath: Discovering the Rhythms of Rest and Delight.* The Christian Practice of Everyday Life. Grand Rapids: Brazos, 2006.

———. *The Paradise of God: Renewing Religion in an Ecological Age.* New York: Oxford University Press, 2013.

———. "Reconciliation with the Land." In *Making Peace with the Land,* edited by Fred Bahnson and Norman Wirzba, 19–40. Downers Grove, IL: InterVarsity, 2012.

Woodley, Randy. *Shalom and the Community of Creation: An Indigenous Vision.* Grand Rapids: Eerdmans, 2012.

Yordy, Laura Ruth. *Green Witness: Ecology, Ethics, and the Kingdom of God.* Eugene, OR: Cascade, 2008.

Subject/Name Index

Scripture Index